IN SF MAC
MacFarlane, Todd.
Spawn

Todd McFarlane Productions & Image Comics present

S P A W N

BETRAYAL OF BLOOD

story
Todd McFarlane
Alan Moore

art
Greg Capullo
Todd McFarlane
Tony Daniel
Kevin Conrad

copy editor & lettering
Tom Orzechowski

color
Steve Oliff, Quinn Supplee, Olyoptics,
Todd Broeker, Roy Young

special thanks to
Kevin Conrad, Chance Wolf, Julia Simmons

cover pencils
Greg Capullo, Tony Daniel

cover inks
Todd McFarlane, Kevin Conrad

tpb cover illustration
Ashley Wood

president of entertainment Terry Fitzgerald

collected editions
editorial directors Ted Adams & Beau Smith

art director Brent Ashe

designer John Gallagher

editorial coordinator Melanie Simmons

**executive director
for image comics** Larry Marder

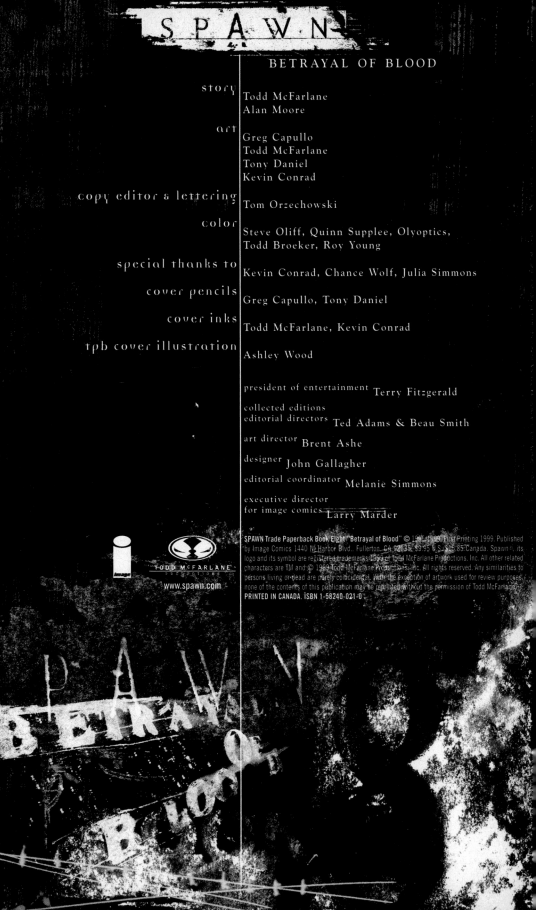

www.spawn.com

SPAWN Trade Paperback Book Eight "Betrayal of Blood" © 1996-1999. First Printing 1999. Published by Image Comics 1440 N. Harbor Blvd., Fullerton, CA 92635. $9.95 U.S./$16.85 Canada. Spawn, its logo and its symbol are registered trademarks 1999 of Todd McFarlane Productions, Inc. All other related characters are TM and © 1999 Todd McFarlane Productions, Inc. All rights reserved. Any similarities to persons living or dead are purely coincidental. With the exception of artwork used for review purposes, none of the contents of this publication may be reprinted without the permission of Todd McFarlane. PRINTED IN CANADA. ISBN 1-58240-021-0

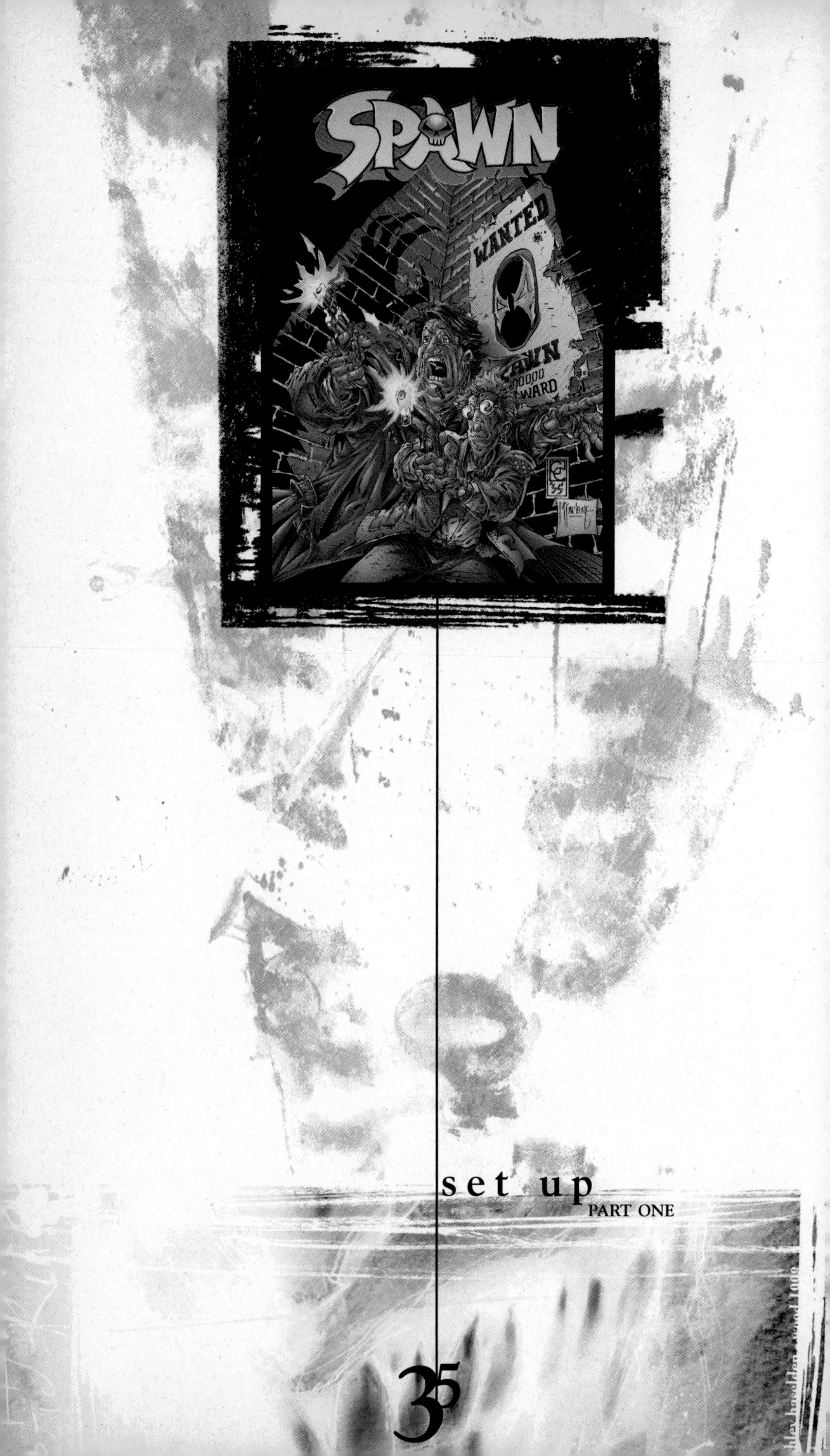
SPAWN
WANTED

set up
PART ONE

35

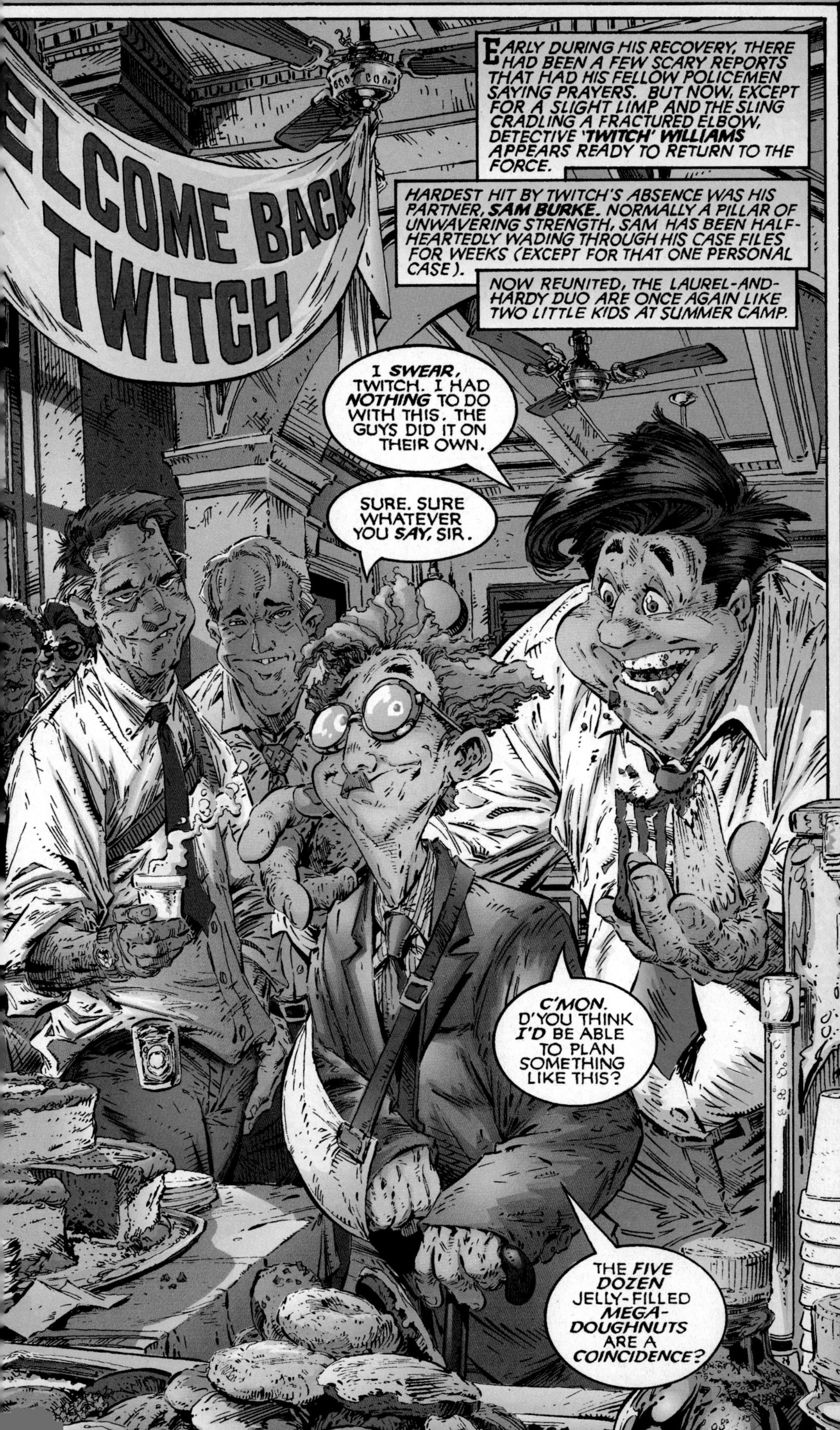

ELCOME BACK TWITCH
EARLY DURING HIS RECOVERY, THERE HAD BEEN A FEW SCARY REPORTS THAT HAD HIS FELLOW POLICEMEN SAYING PRAYERS. BUT NOW, EXCEPT FOR A SLIGHT LIMP AND THE SLING CRADLING A FRACTURED ELBOW, DETECTIVE 'TWITCH' WILLIAMS APPEARS READY TO RETURN TO THE FORCE.
HARDEST HIT BY TWITCH'S ABSENCE WAS HIS PARTNER, SAM BURKE. NORMALLY A PILLAR OF UNWAVERING STRENGTH, SAM HAS BEEN HALF-HEARTEDLY WADING THROUGH HIS CASE FILES FOR WEEKS (EXCEPT FOR THAT ONE PERSONAL CASE).
NOW REUNITED, THE LAUREL-AND-HARDY DUO ARE ONCE AGAIN LIKE TWO LITTLE KIDS AT SUMMER CAMP.
I SWEAR, TWITCH. I HAD NOTHING TO DO WITH THIS. THE GUYS DID IT ON THEIR OWN.
SURE. SURE WHATEVER YOU SAY, SIR.
C'MON. D'YOU THINK I'D BE ABLE TO PLAN SOMETHING LIKE THIS?
THE FIVE DOZEN JELLY-FILLED MEGA-DOUGHNUTS ARE A COINCIDENCE?

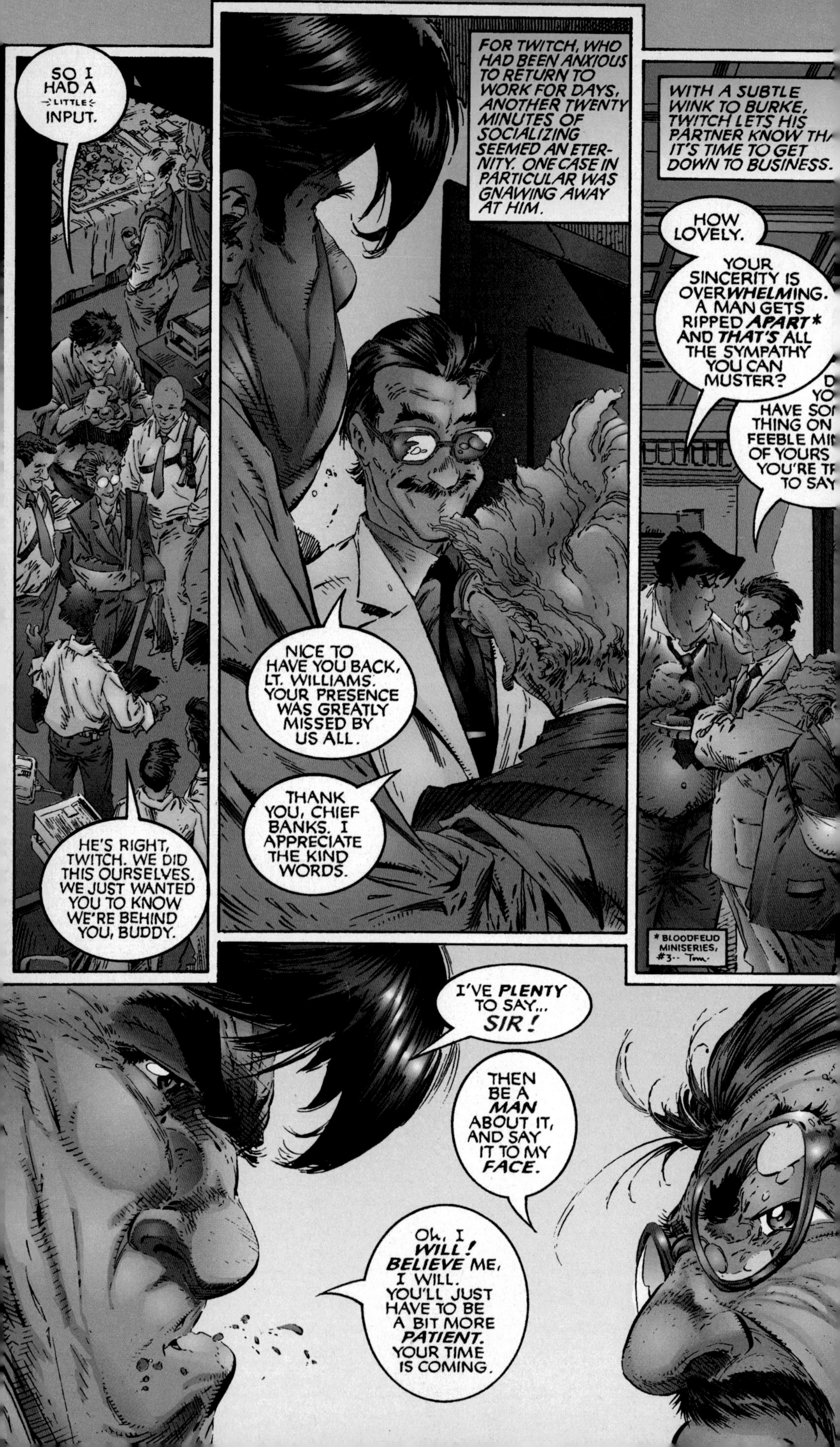
SO I HAD A LITTLE INPUT.
HE'S RIGHT, TWITCH. WE DID THIS OURSELVES. WE JUST WANTED YOU TO KNOW WE'RE BEHIND YOU, BUDDY.
FOR TWITCH, WHO HAD BEEN ANXIOUS TO RETURN TO WORK FOR DAYS, ANOTHER TWENTY MINUTES OF SOCIALIZING SEEMED AN ETERNITY. ONE CASE IN PARTICULAR WAS GNAWING AWAY AT HIM.
NICE TO HAVE YOU BACK, LT. WILLIAMS. YOUR PRESENCE WAS GREATLY MISSED BY US ALL.
THANK YOU, CHIEF BANKS. I APPRECIATE THE KIND WORDS.
WITH A SUBTLE WINK TO BURKE, TWITCH LETS HIS PARTNER KNOW TH IT'S TIME TO GET DOWN TO BUSINESS.
HOW LOVELY.
YOUR SINCERITY IS OVERWHELMING. A MAN GETS RIPPED APART* AND THAT'S ALL THE SYMPATHY YOU CAN MUSTER?
D YO HAVE SO THING ON FEEBLE MI OF YOURS YOU'RE T TO SAY
* BLOODFEUD MINISERIES, #3 -- Tom.
I'VE PLENTY TO SAY... SIR!
THEN BE A MAN ABOUT IT, AND SAY IT TO MY FACE.
Oh, I WILL! BELIEVE ME, I WILL. YOU'LL JUST HAVE TO BE A BIT MORE PATIENT. YOUR TIME IS COMING.

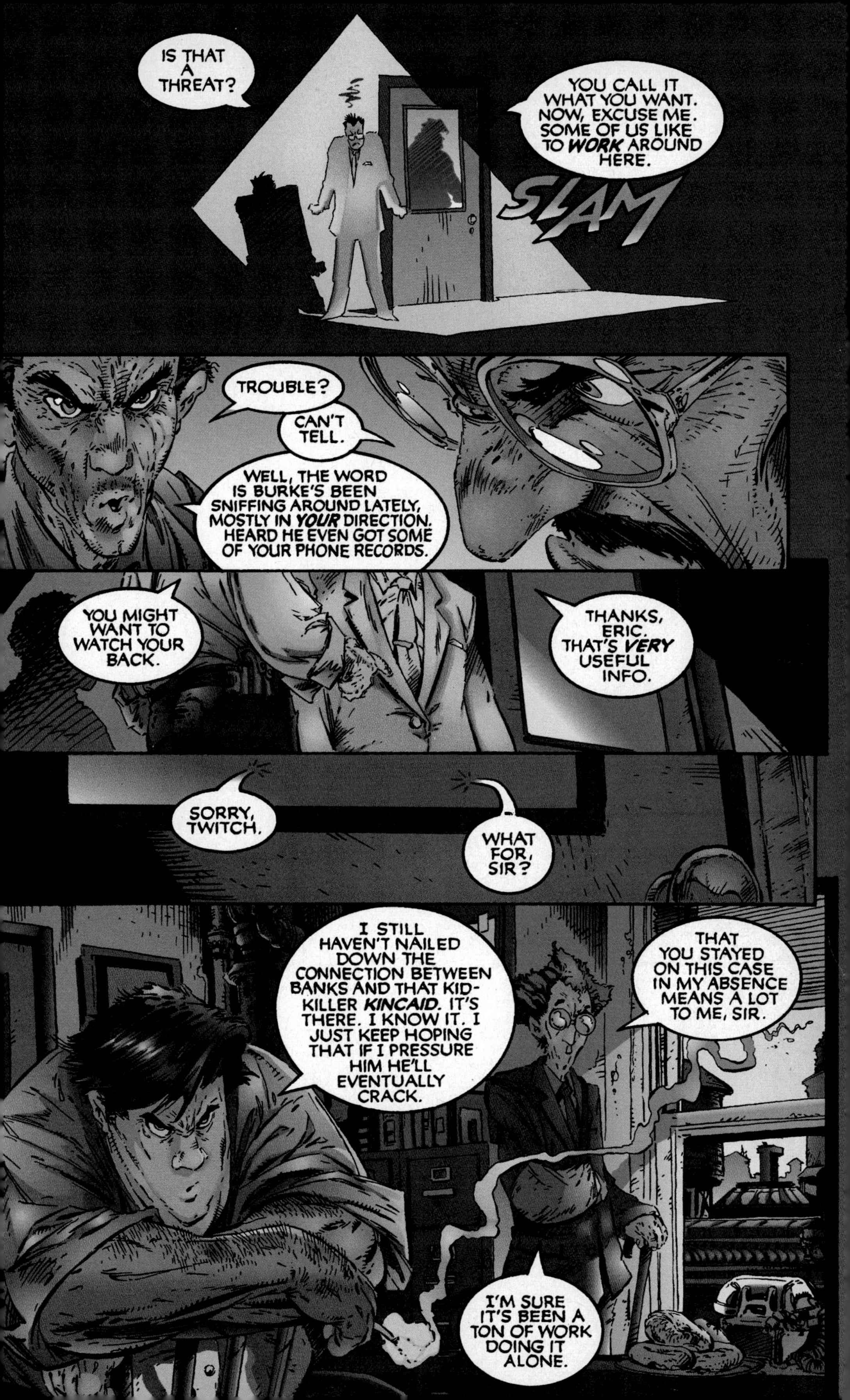
IS THAT A THREAT?
YOU CALL IT WHAT YOU WANT. NOW, EXCUSE ME. SOME OF US LIKE TO WORK AROUND HERE.
SLAM
TROUBLE?
CAN'T TELL.
WELL, THE WORD IS BURKE'S BEEN SNIFFING AROUND LATELY, MOSTLY IN YOUR DIRECTION. HEARD HE EVEN GOT SOME OF YOUR PHONE RECORDS.
YOU MIGHT WANT TO WATCH YOUR BACK.
THANKS, ERIC. THAT'S VERY USEFUL INFO.
SORRY, TWITCH.
WHAT FOR, SIR?
I STILL HAVEN'T NAILED DOWN THE CONNECTION BETWEEN BANKS AND THAT KID-KILLER KINCAID. IT'S THERE. I KNOW IT. I JUST KEEP HOPING THAT IF I PRESSURE HIM HE'LL EVENTUALLY CRACK.
THAT YOU STAYED ON THIS CASE IN MY ABSENCE MEANS A LOT TO ME, SIR.
I'M SURE IT'S BEEN A TON OF WORK DOING IT ALONE.

"--WHAT DO YOU MEAN, THEY'RE AFRAID? OF WHAT?"

"YOU...

"YOUR POTENTIAL, TO BE EXACT.

"THE TRADI-TION OF THE SPAWN IS A VERY SORDID STORY, AL.

"EACH OF THE SPAWN CAME THROUGH THEIR BAPTISM OF FIRE WITH VARYING DEGREES OF SUCCESS.

"SOME FOUGHT THEIR NEW STATUS. SOME ACCEPTED IT, *TOO* WILLINGLY. BUT NONE WERE EVER ABLE TO *REVERSE* THE SITUATION.

" I GUARANTEE THEY'LL NOT LET *YOU* BE THE FIRST. "

"YOU KNOW WHAT, COG. I DON'T GIVE A *CRAP* WHAT THEY HAD PLANNED FOR ME. *NO ONE'S* GOING TO DICTATE WHAT I DO

"UNFORTUNATELY, AL, THEY ALREADY *HAVE.* MEANWHILE, YOU'VE LEARNED HOW TO DEAL WITH THE *COST* OF USING YOUR POWERS...

"... HOW TO *KILL* MORE EFFICIENTLY...
AND HOW TO IGNORE THE *CONSEQUENCES*."

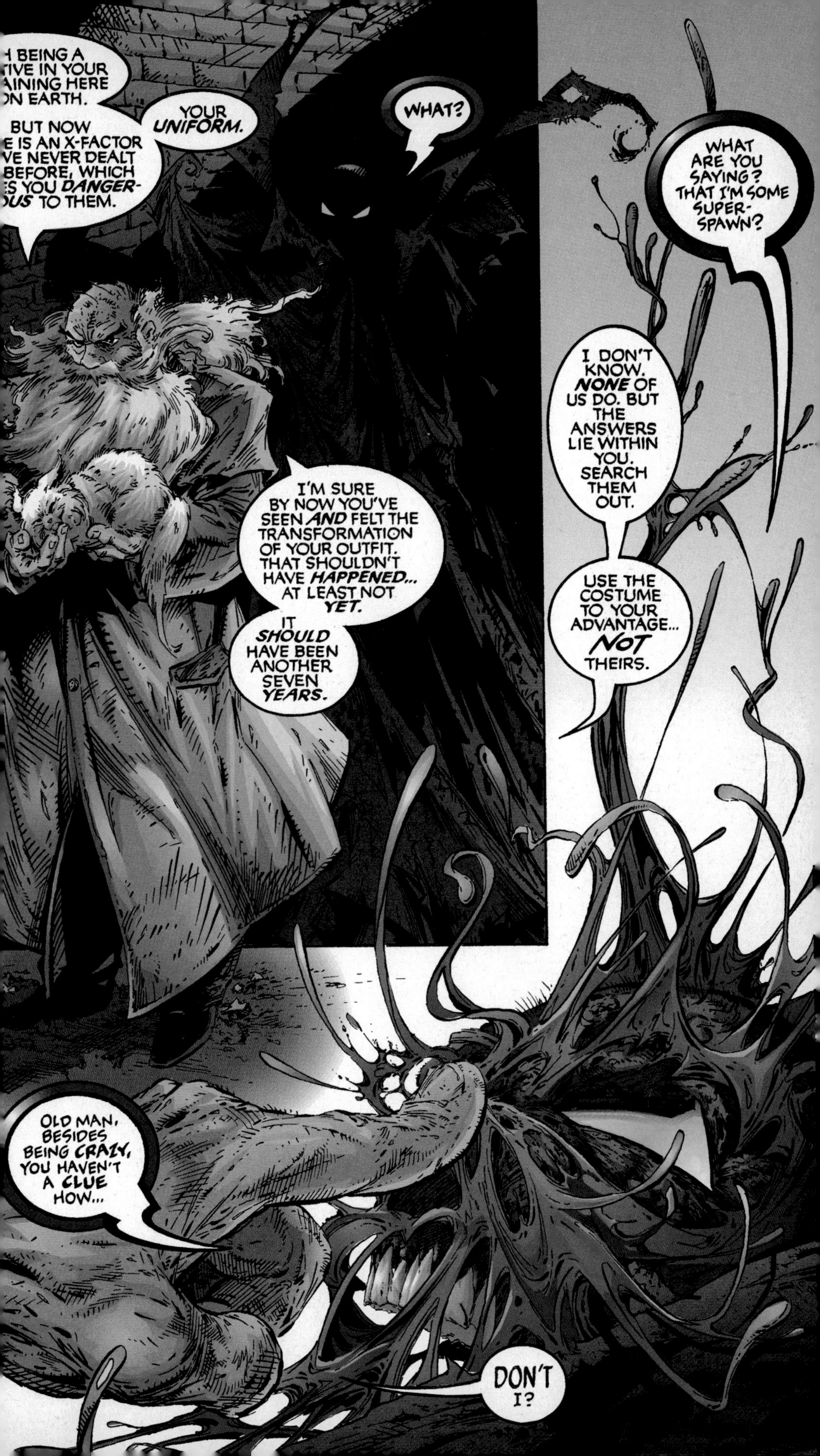
H BEING A
TIVE IN YOUR
AINING HERE
ON EARTH.
BUT NOW
E IS AN X-FACTOR
VE NEVER DEALT
BEFORE, WHICH
ES YOU DANGER-
OUS TO THEM.
YOUR UNIFORM.
WHAT?
WHAT ARE YOU SAYING? THAT I'M SOME SUPER-SPAWN?
I DON'T KNOW. NONE OF US DO. BUT THE ANSWERS LIE WITHIN YOU. SEARCH THEM OUT.
I'M SURE BY NOW YOU'VE SEEN AND FELT THE TRANSFORMATION OF YOUR OUTFIT. THAT SHOULDN'T HAVE HAPPENED... AT LEAST NOT YET.
IT SHOULD HAVE BEEN ANOTHER SEVEN YEARS.
USE THE COSTUME TO YOUR ADVANTAGE... NOT THEIRS.
OLD MAN, BESIDES BEING CRAZY, YOU HAVEN'T A CLUE HOW...
DON'T I?

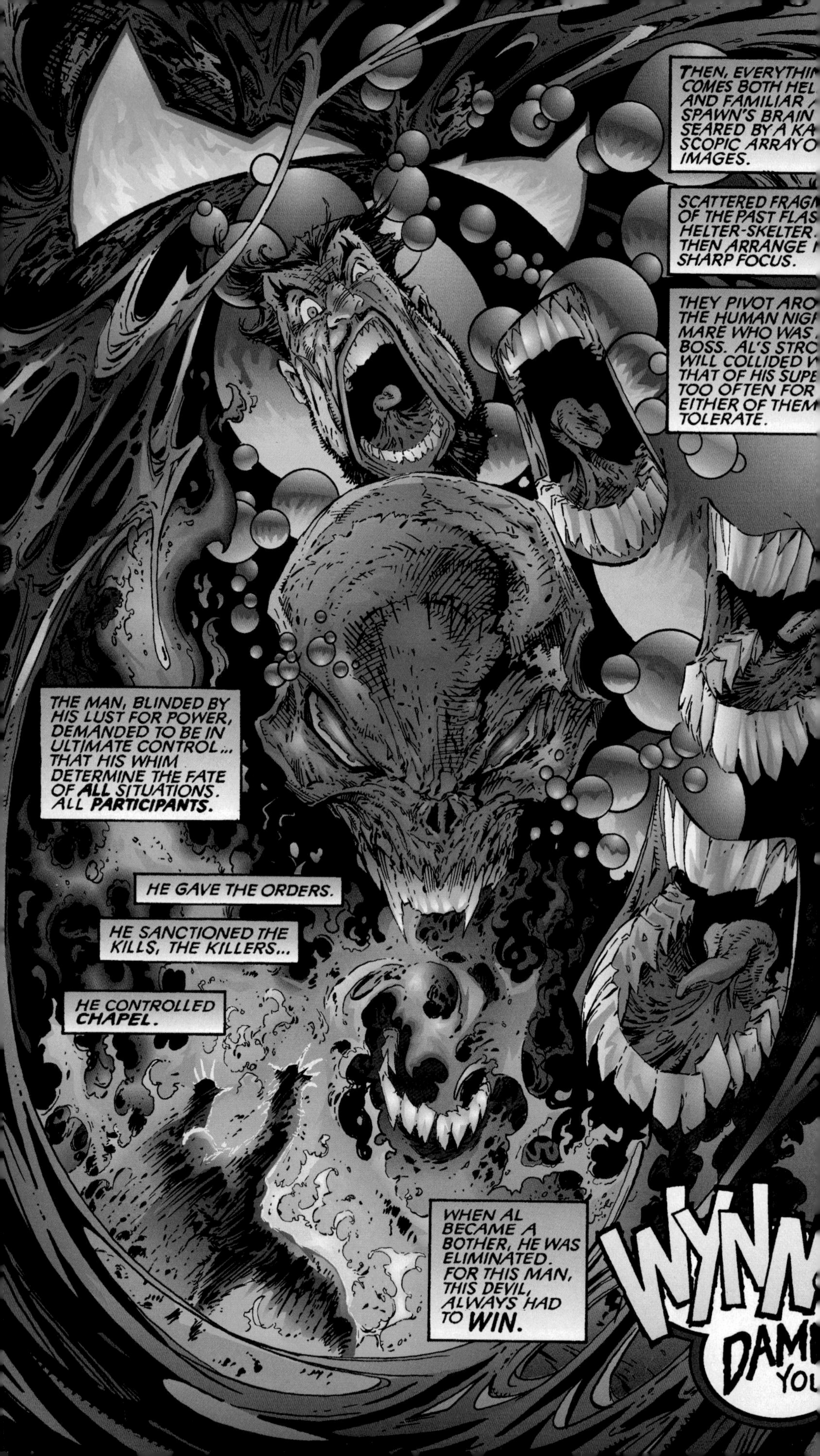
THEN, EVERYTHIN COMES BOTH HEL AND FAMILIAR SPAWN'S BRAIN SEARED BY A KA SCOPIC ARRAY O IMAGES.
SCATTERED FRAG OF THE PAST FLAS HELTER-SKELTER. THEN ARRANGE SHARP FOCUS.
THEY PIVOT ARO THE HUMAN NIGH MARE WHO WAS BOSS. AL'S STRO WILL COLLIDED W THAT OF HIS SUPE TOO OFTEN FOR EITHER OF THEM TOLERATE.
THE MAN, BLINDED BY HIS LUST FOR POWER, DEMANDED TO BE IN ULTIMATE CONTROL... THAT HIS WHIM DETERMINE THE FATE OF ALL SITUATIONS. ALL PARTICIPANTS.
HE GAVE THE ORDERS.
HE SANCTIONED THE KILLS, THE KILLERS...
HE CONTROLLED CHAPEL.
WHEN AL BECAME A BOTHER, HE WAS ELIMINATED. FOR THIS MAN, THIS DEVIL, ALWAYS HAD TO WIN.
WYNN
DAM YOU

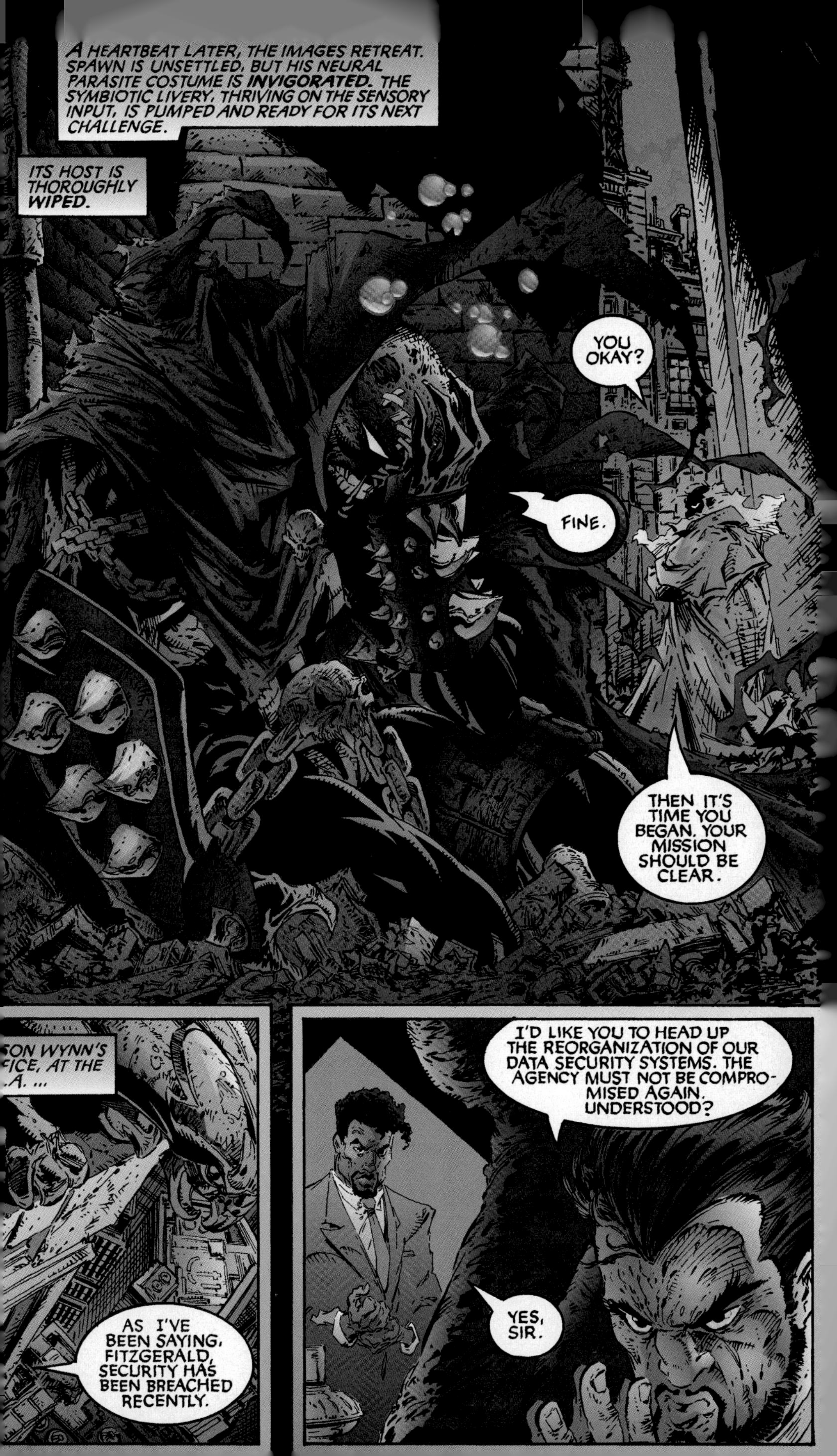
A HEARTBEAT LATER, THE IMAGES RETREAT. SPAWN IS UNSETTLED, BUT HIS NEURAL PARASITE COSTUME IS **INVIGORATED.** THE SYMBIOTIC LIVERY, THRIVING ON THE SENSORY INPUT, IS PUMPED AND READY FOR ITS NEXT CHALLENGE.
ITS HOST IS THOROUGHLY **WIPED.**
YOU OKAY?
FINE.
THEN IT'S TIME YOU BEGAN. YOUR MISSION SHOULD BE CLEAR.
SON WYNN'S FICE, AT THE .A. ...
AS I'VE BEEN SAYING, FITZGERALD, SECURITY HAS BEEN BREACHED RECENTLY.
I'D LIKE YOU TO HEAD UP THE REORGANIZATION OF OUR DATA SECURITY SYSTEMS. THE AGENCY MUST NOT BE COMPROMISED AGAIN. UNDERSTOOD?
YES, SIR.

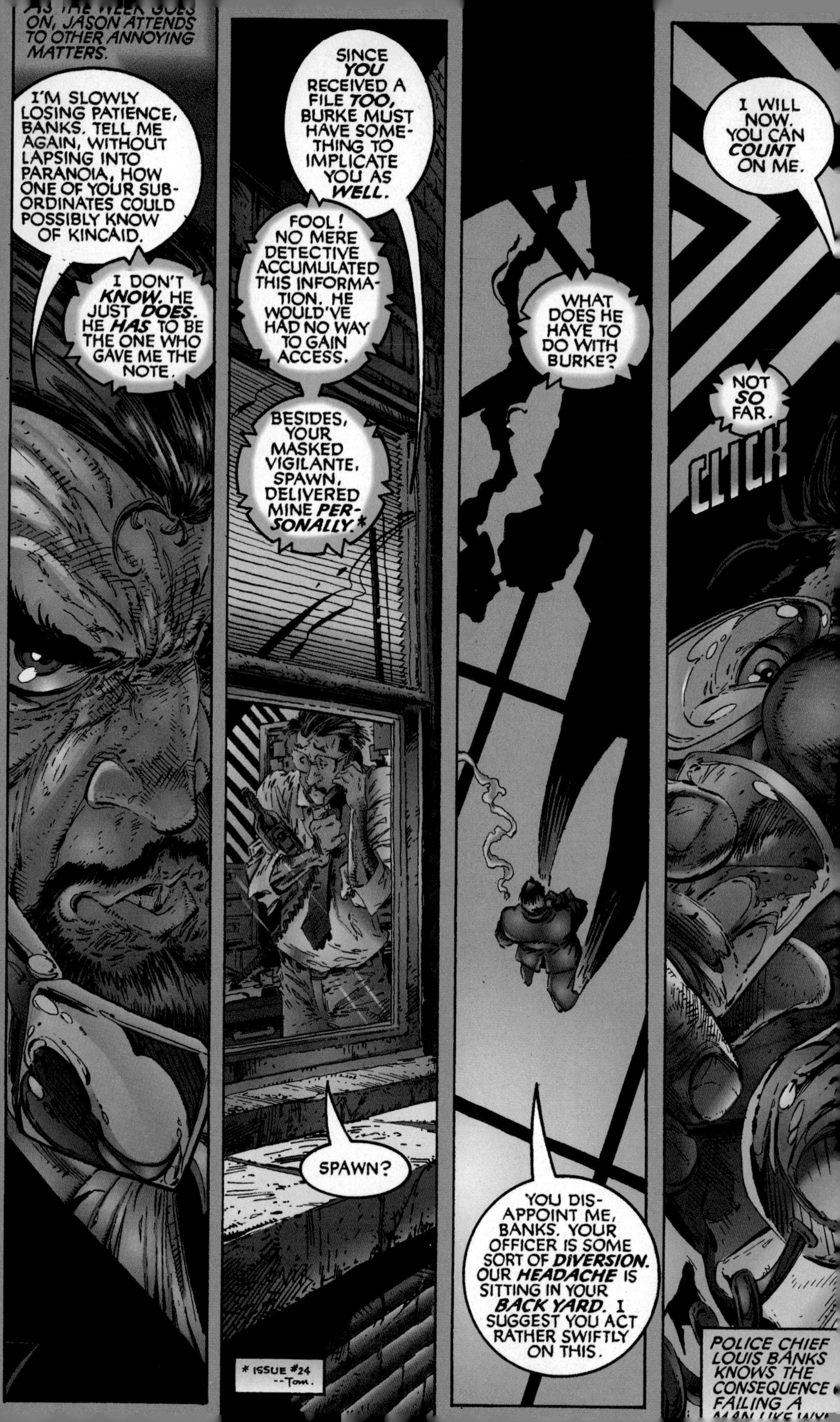
ON, JASON ATTENDS TO OTHER ANNOYING MATTERS.
I'M SLOWLY LOSING PATIENCE, BANKS. TELL ME AGAIN, WITHOUT LAPSING INTO PARANOIA, HOW ONE OF YOUR SUBORDINATES COULD POSSIBLY KNOW OF KINCAID.
I DON'T KNOW. HE JUST DOES. HE HAS TO BE THE ONE WHO GAVE ME THE NOTE.
SINCE YOU RECEIVED A FILE TOO, BURKE MUST HAVE SOMETHING TO IMPLICATE YOU AS WELL.
FOOL! NO MERE DETECTIVE ACCUMULATED THIS INFORMATION. HE WOULD'VE HAD NO WAY TO GAIN ACCESS.
BESIDES, YOUR MASKED VIGILANTE, SPAWN, DELIVERED MINE PERSONALLY.*
SPAWN?
* ISSUE #24 --Tom.
WHAT DOES HE HAVE TO DO WITH BURKE?
YOU DISAPPOINT ME, BANKS. YOUR OFFICER IS SOME SORT OF DIVERSION. OUR HEADACHE IS SITTING IN YOUR BACK YARD. I SUGGEST YOU ACT RATHER SWIFTLY ON THIS.
I WILL NOW. YOU CAN COUNT ON ME.
NOT SO FAR.
CLICK
POLICE CHIEF LOUIS BANKS KNOWS THE CONSEQUENCE FAILING A

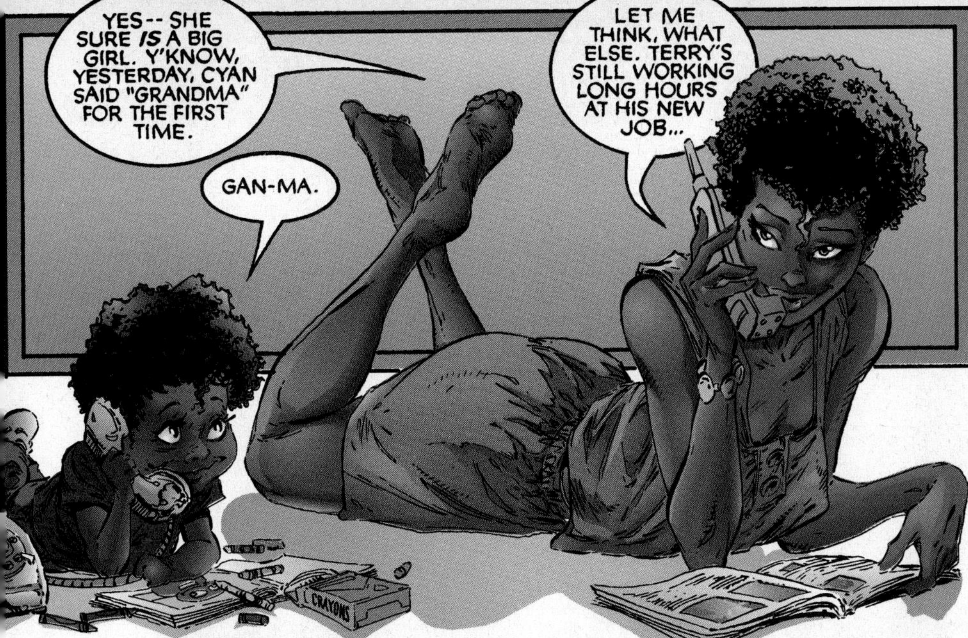
YES-- SHE SURE *IS* A BIG GIRL. Y'KNOW, YESTERDAY, CYAN SAID "GRANDMA" FOR THE FIRST TIME.
GAN-MA.
LET ME THINK, WHAT ELSE. TERRY'S STILL WORKING LONG HOURS AT HIS NEW JOB...
CRAYONS

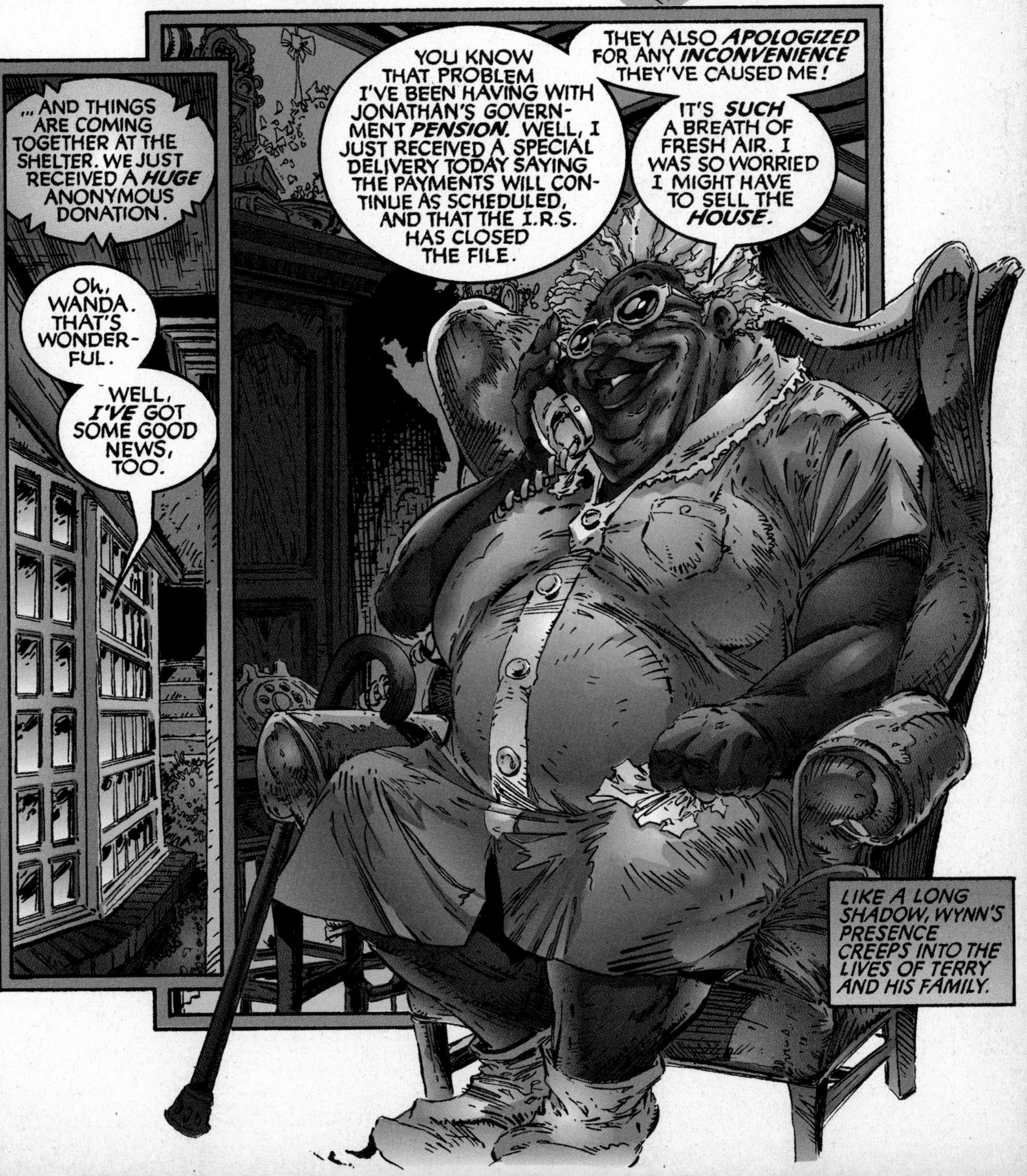
...AND THINGS ARE COMING TOGETHER AT THE SHELTER. WE JUST RECEIVED A *HUGE* ANONYMOUS DONATION.
Oh, WANDA. THAT'S WONDERFUL.
WELL, *I'VE* GOT SOME GOOD NEWS, TOO.
YOU KNOW THAT PROBLEM I'VE BEEN HAVING WITH JONATHAN'S GOVERNMENT *PENSION.* WELL, I JUST RECEIVED A SPECIAL DELIVERY TODAY SAYING THE PAYMENTS WILL CONTINUE AS SCHEDULED, AND THAT THE I.R.S. HAS CLOSED THE FILE.
THEY ALSO *APOLOGIZED* FOR ANY *INCONVENIENCE* THEY'VE CAUSED ME!
IT'S *SUCH* A BREATH OF FRESH AIR. I WAS SO WORRIED I MIGHT HAVE TO SELL THE *HOUSE.*
LIKE A LONG SHADOW, WYNN'S PRESENCE CREEPS INTO THE LIVES OF TERRY AND HIS FAMILY.

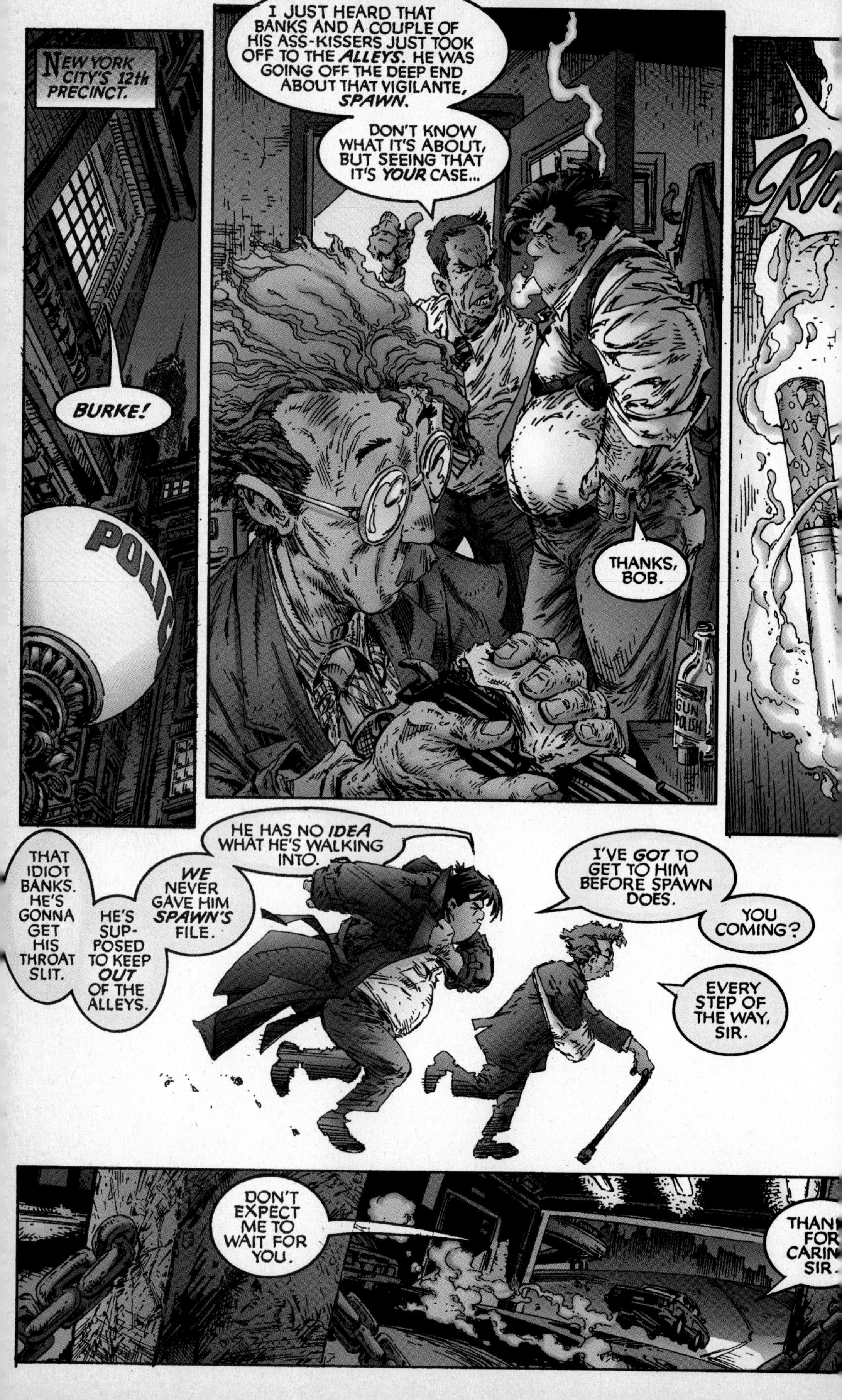

NEW YORK CITY'S 12th PRECINCT.
BURKE!
I JUST HEARD THAT BANKS AND A COUPLE OF HIS ASS-KISSERS JUST TOOK OFF TO THE ALLEYS. HE WAS GOING OFF THE DEEP END ABOUT THAT VIGILANTE, SPAWN.
DON'T KNOW WHAT IT'S ABOUT, BUT SEEING THAT IT'S YOUR CASE...
THANKS, BOB.
GUN POLISH
THAT IDIOT BANKS. HE'S GONNA GET HIS THROAT SLIT.
HE'S SUP-POSED TO KEEP OUT OF THE ALLEYS.
WE NEVER GAVE HIM SPAWN'S FILE.
HE HAS NO IDEA WHAT HE'S WALKING INTO.
I'VE GOT TO GET TO HIM BEFORE SPAWN DOES.
YOU COMING?
EVERY STEP OF THE WAY, SIR.
DON'T EXPECT ME TO WAIT FOR YOU.

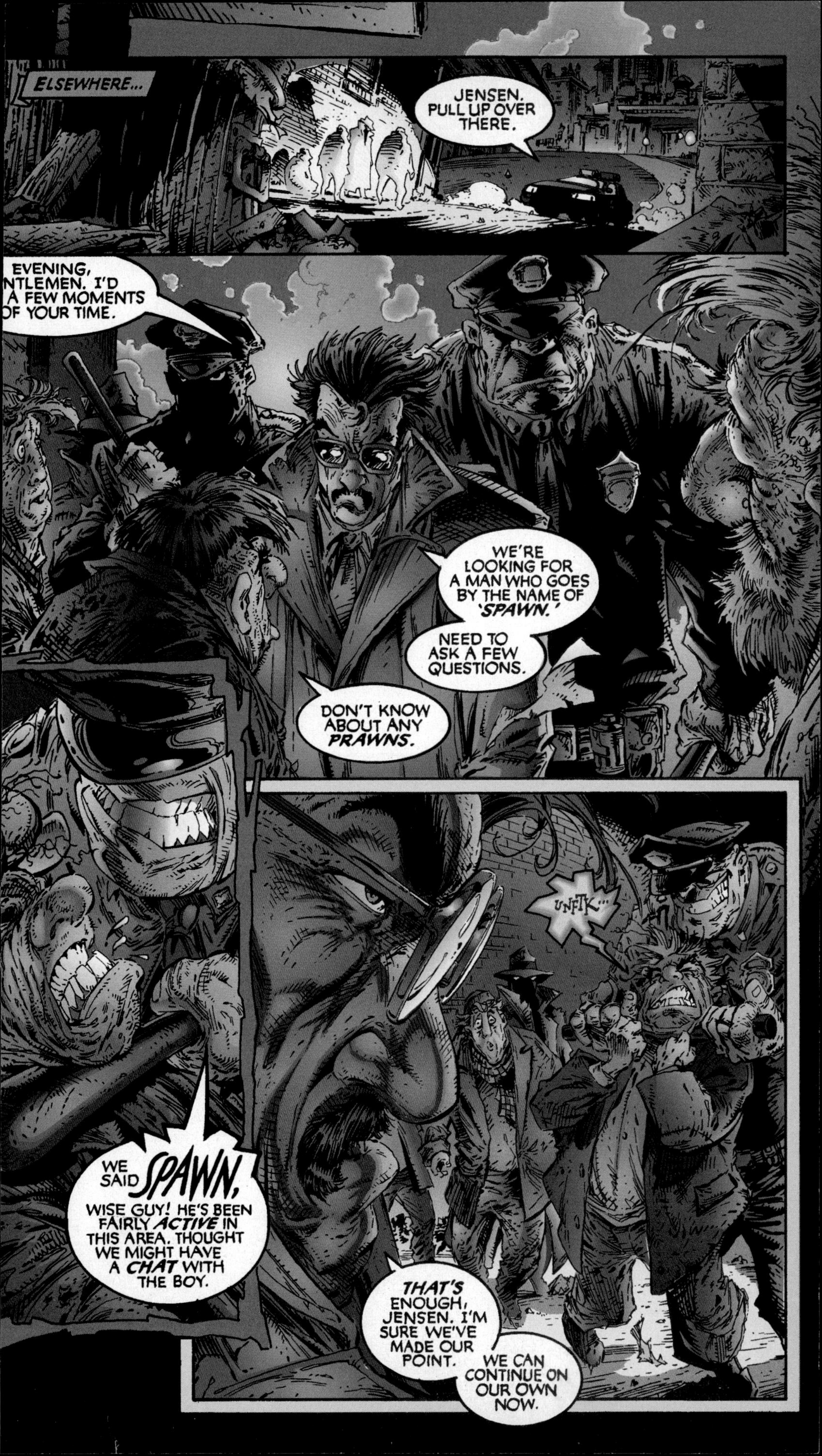
ELSEWHERE...
JENSEN. PULL UP OVER THERE.
EVENING, NTLEMEN. I'D A FEW MOMENTS OF YOUR TIME.
WE'RE LOOKING FOR A MAN WHO GOES BY THE NAME OF 'SPAWN.'
NEED TO ASK A FEW QUESTIONS.
DON'T KNOW ABOUT ANY PRAWNS.
WE SAID SPAWN, WISE GUY! HE'S BEEN FAIRLY ACTIVE IN THIS AREA. THOUGHT WE MIGHT HAVE A CHAT WITH THE BOY.
UNFTK...
THAT'S ENOUGH, JENSEN. I'M SURE WE'VE MADE OUR POINT.
WE CAN CONTINUE ON OUR OWN NOW.

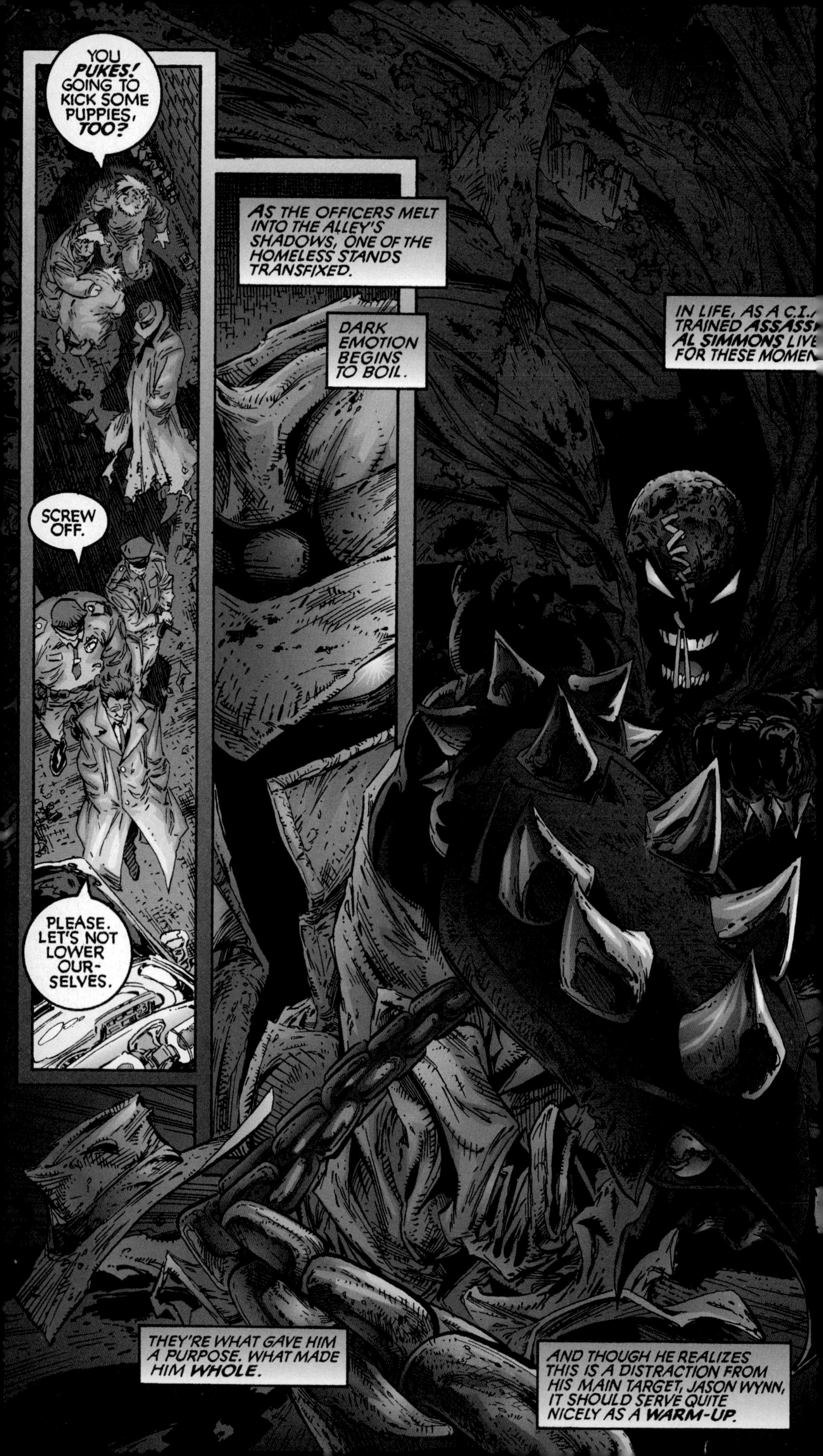
YOU PUKES! GOING TO KICK SOME PUPPIES, TOO?
AS THE OFFICERS MELT INTO THE ALLEY'S SHADOWS, ONE OF THE HOMELESS STANDS TRANSFIXED.
DARK EMOTION BEGINS TO BOIL.
IN LIFE, AS A C.I. TRAINED ASSASS AL SIMMONS LIVE FOR THESE MOMEN
SCREW OFF.
PLEASE. LET'S NOT LOWER OURSELVES.
THEY'RE WHAT GAVE HIM A PURPOSE. WHAT MADE HIM WHOLE.
AND THOUGH HE REALIZES THIS IS A DISTRACTION FROM HIS MAIN TARGET, JASON WYNN, IT SHOULD SERVE QUITE NICELY AS A WARM-UP.

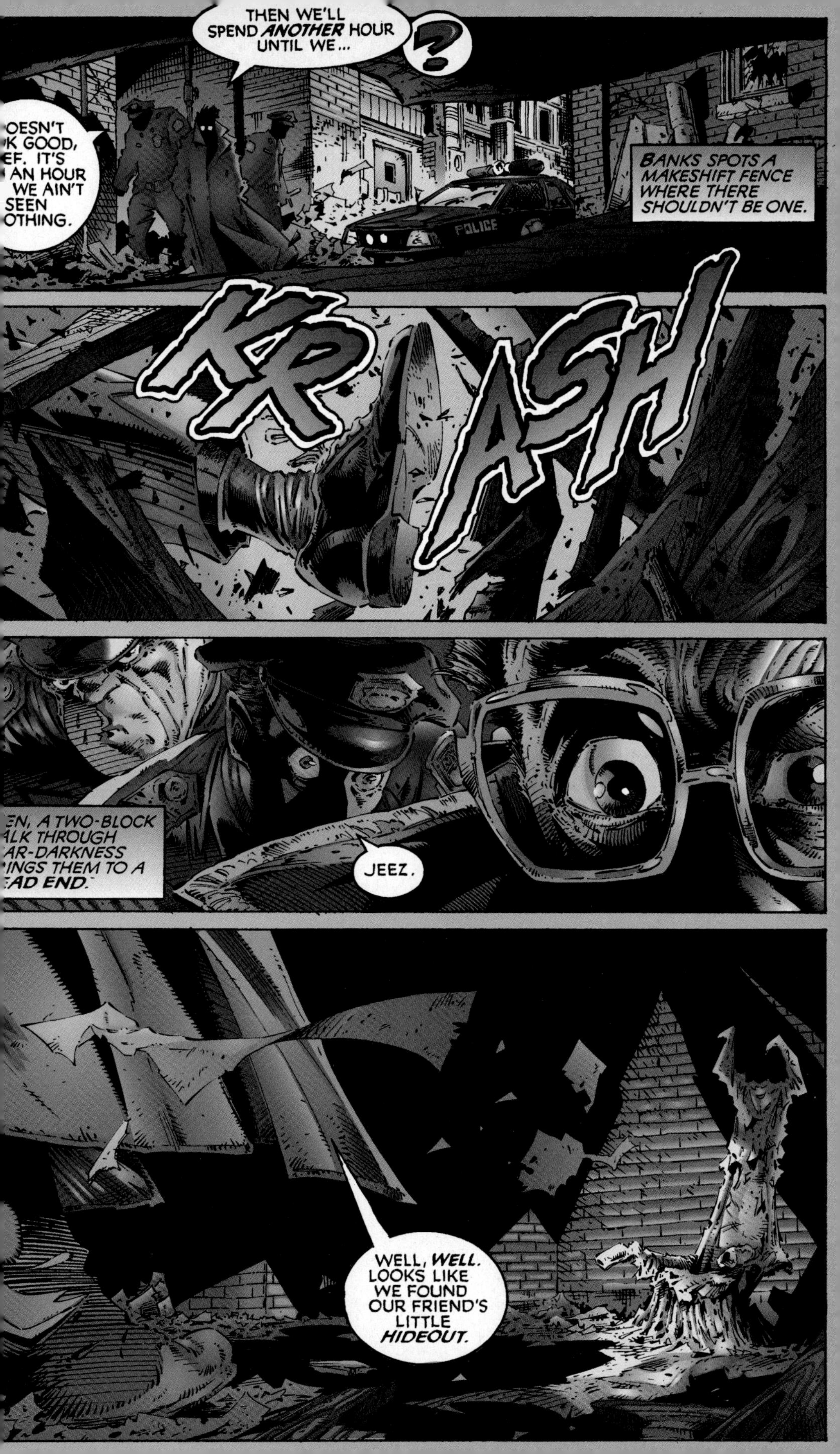

THEN WE'LL SPEND ANOTHER HOUR UNTIL WE...
?
OESN'T K GOOD, EF. IT'S AN HOUR WE AIN'T SEEN OTHING.
BANKS SPOTS A MAKESHIFT FENCE WHERE THERE SHOULDN'T BE ONE.
POLICE
KRASH
EN, A TWO-BLOCK ALK THROUGH AR-DARKNESS INGS THEM TO A EAD END.
JEEZ.
WELL, WELL. LOOKS LIKE WE FOUND OUR FRIEND'S LITTLE HIDEOUT.

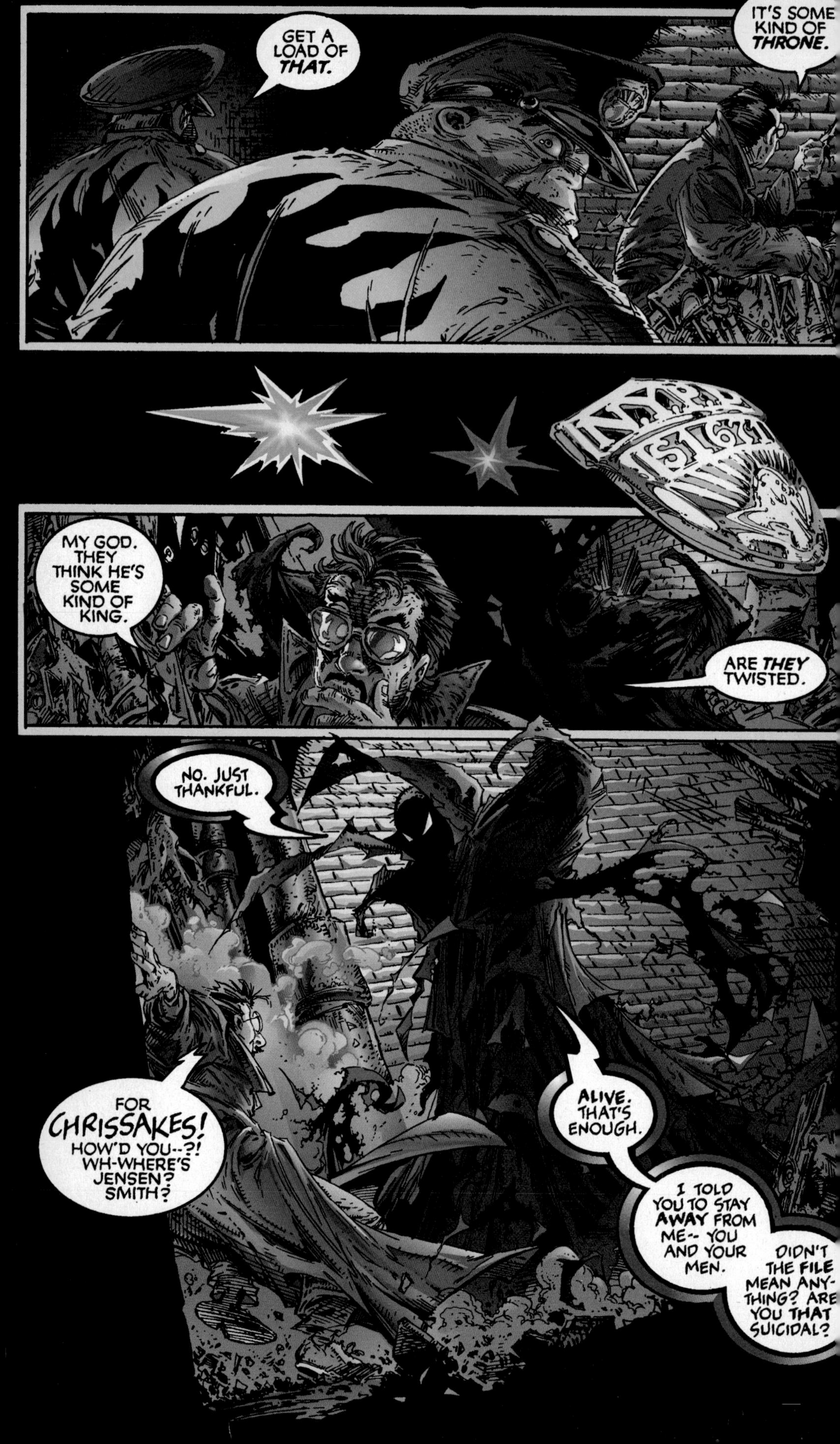
GET A LOAD OF THAT.
IT'S SOME KIND OF THRONE.
NYPD 5167
MY GOD. THEY THINK HE'S SOME KIND OF KING.
ARE THEY TWISTED.
NO. JUST THANKFUL.
FOR CHRISSAKES! HOW'D YOU--?! WH-WHERE'S JENSEN? SMITH?
ALIVE. THAT'S ENOUGH.
I TOLD YOU TO STAY AWAY FROM ME-- YOU AND YOUR MEN.
DIDN'T THE FILE MEAN ANY-THING? ARE YOU THAT SUICIDAL?

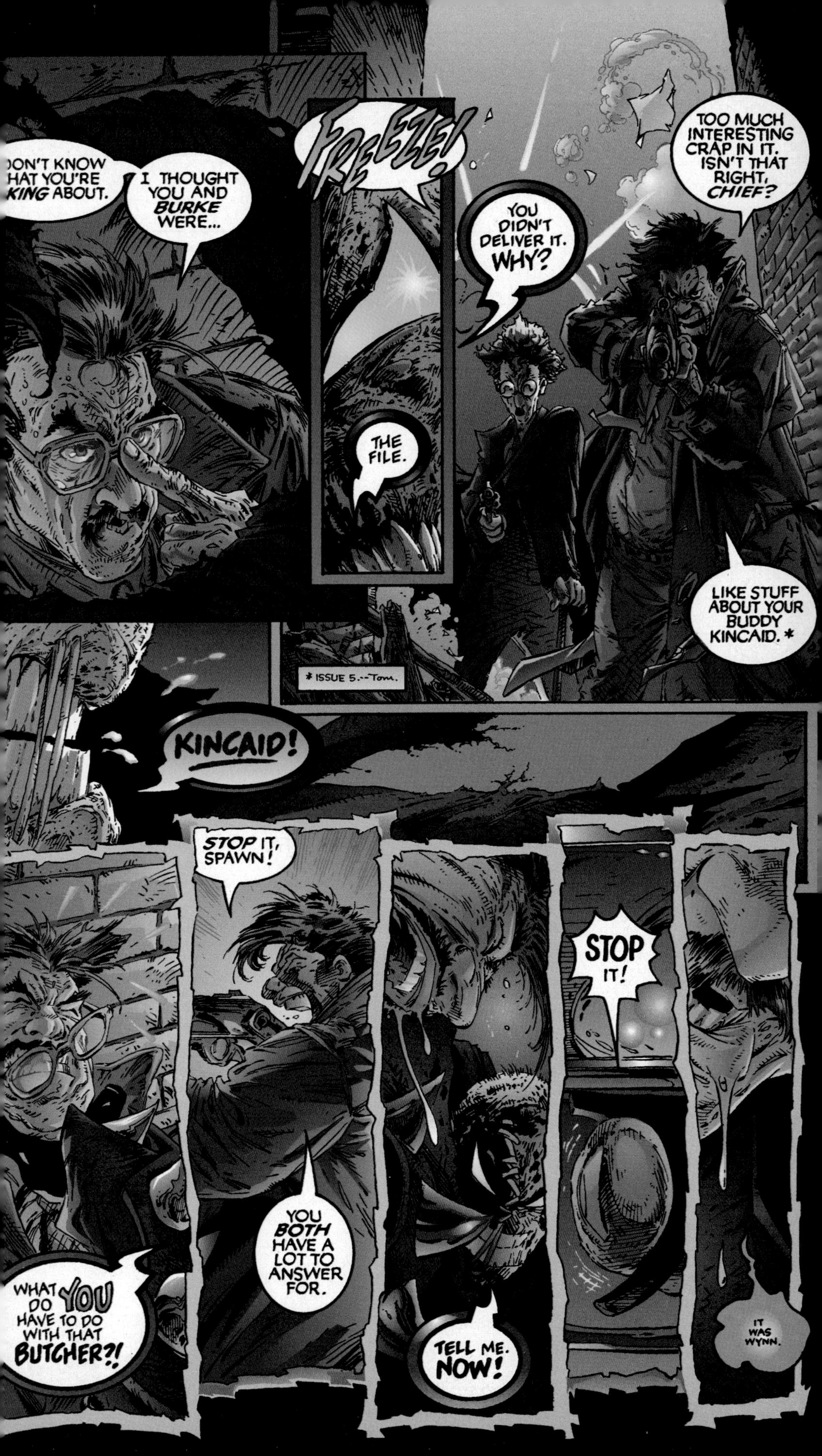

DON'T KNOW
HAT YOU'RE
KING ABOUT.
I THOUGHT YOU AND BURKE WERE...
FREEZE!
THE FILE.
YOU DIDN'T DELIVER IT. WHY?
TOO MUCH INTERESTING CRAP IN IT. ISN'T THAT RIGHT, CHIEF?
LIKE STUFF ABOUT YOUR BUDDY KINCAID. *
* ISSUE 5.--Tom.
KINCAID!
WHAT DO YOU HAVE TO DO WITH THAT BUTCHER?!
STOP IT, SPAWN!
YOU BOTH HAVE A LOT TO ANSWER FOR.
TELL ME. NOW!
STOP IT!
IT WAS WYNN.

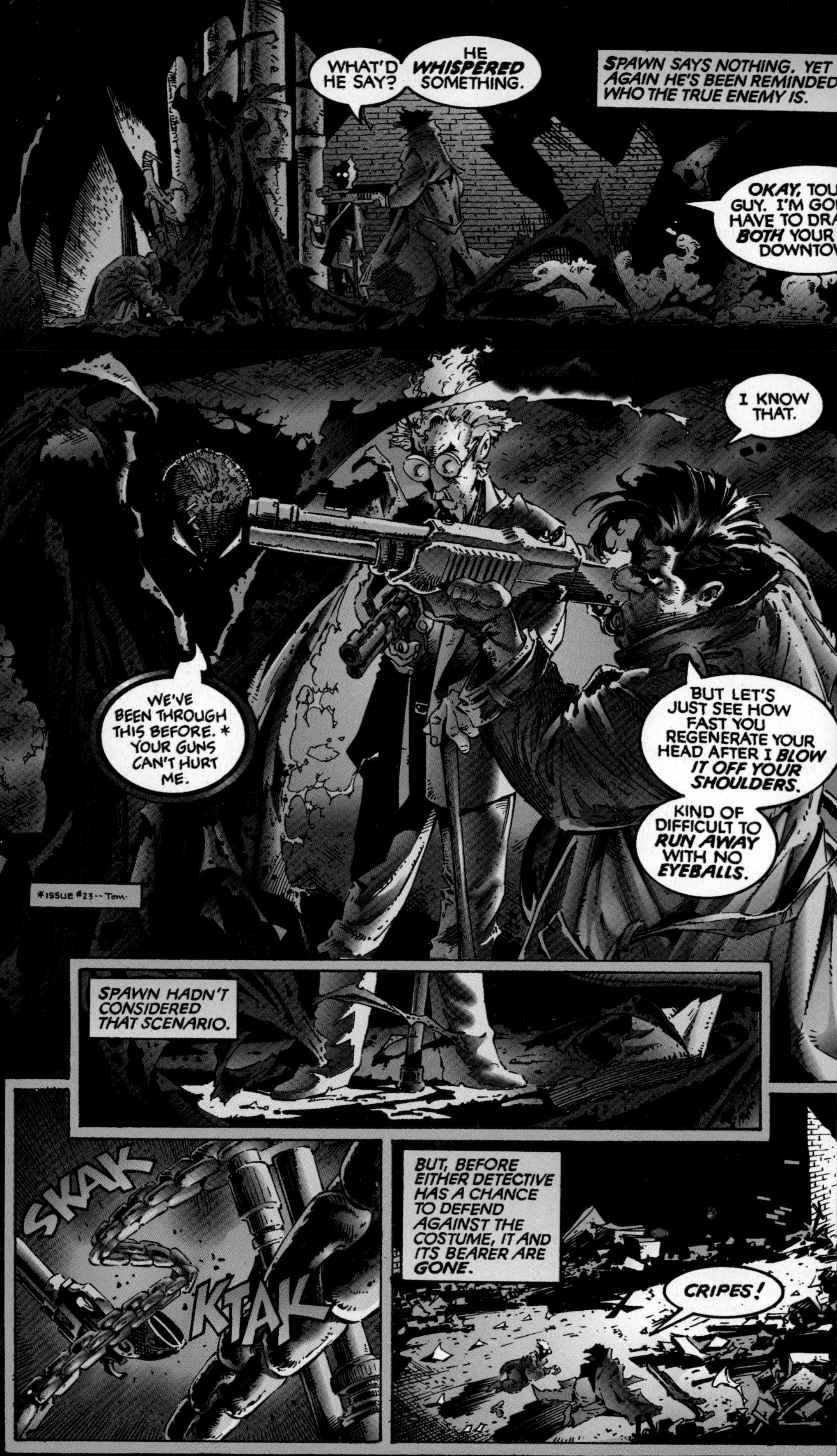

WHAT'D HE SAY?
HE *WHISPERED* SOMETHING.
SPAWN SAYS NOTHING. YET AGAIN HE'S BEEN REMINDED WHO THE TRUE ENEMY IS.
OKAY, TOU GUY. I'M GO HAVE TO DRA *BOTH* YOUR DOWNTOW
I KNOW THAT.
WE'VE BEEN THROUGH THIS BEFORE. * YOUR GUNS CAN'T HURT ME.
BUT LET'S JUST SEE HOW FAST YOU REGENERATE YOUR HEAD AFTER I *BLOW IT OFF YOUR SHOULDERS.*
KIND OF DIFFICULT TO *RUN AWAY* WITH NO *EYEBALLS.*
*ISSUE #23--Tom.
SPAWN HADN'T CONSIDERED THAT SCENARIO.
SKAK
KTAK
BUT, BEFORE EITHER DETECTIVE HAS A CHANCE TO DEFEND AGAINST THE COSTUME, IT AND ITS BEARER ARE GONE.
CRIPES!

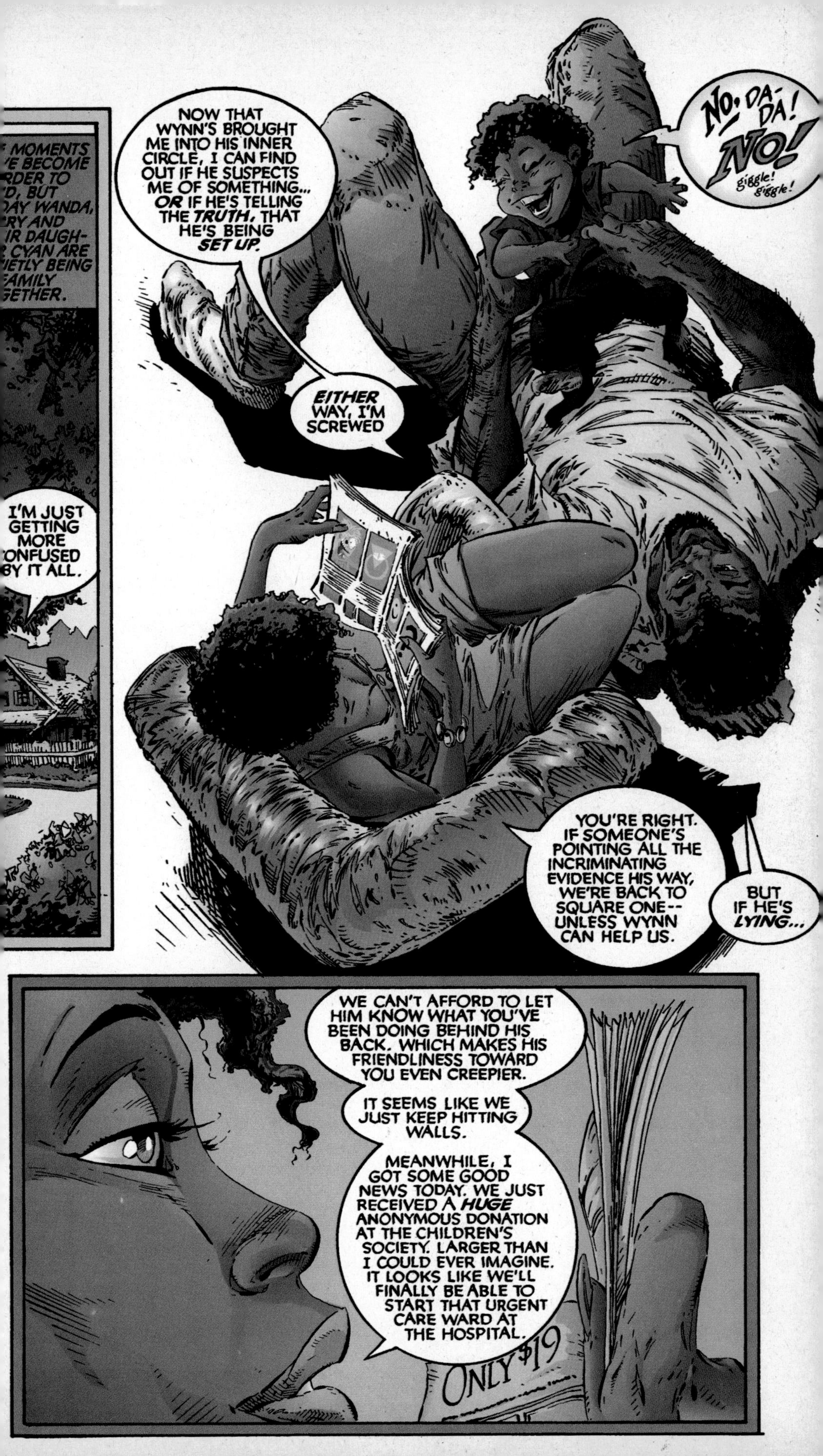
F MOMENTS VE BECOME RDER TO D, BUT DAY WANDA, RY AND IR DAUGH- CYAN ARE IETLY BEING FAMILY GETHER.
NOW THAT WYNN'S BROUGHT ME INTO HIS INNER CIRCLE, I CAN FIND OUT IF HE SUSPECTS ME OF SOMETHING... OR IF HE'S TELLING THE TRUTH, THAT HE'S BEING SET UP.
EITHER WAY, I'M SCREWED
NO, DA-DA! NO!
giggle! giggle!
I'M JUST GETTING MORE ONFUSED BY IT ALL.
YOU'RE RIGHT. IF SOMEONE'S POINTING ALL THE INCRIMINATING EVIDENCE HIS WAY, WE'RE BACK TO SQUARE ONE-- UNLESS WYNN CAN HELP US.
BUT IF HE'S LYING...
WE CAN'T AFFORD TO LET HIM KNOW WHAT YOU'VE BEEN DOING BEHIND HIS BACK, WHICH MAKES HIS FRIENDLINESS TOWARD YOU EVEN CREEPIER.
IT SEEMS LIKE WE JUST KEEP HITTING WALLS.
MEANWHILE, I GOT SOME GOOD NEWS TODAY. WE JUST RECEIVED A HUGE ANONYMOUS DONATION AT THE CHILDREN'S SOCIETY. LARGER THAN I COULD EVER IMAGINE. IT LOOKS LIKE WE'LL FINALLY BE ABLE TO START THAT URGENT CARE WARD AT THE HOSPITAL.
ONLY $19

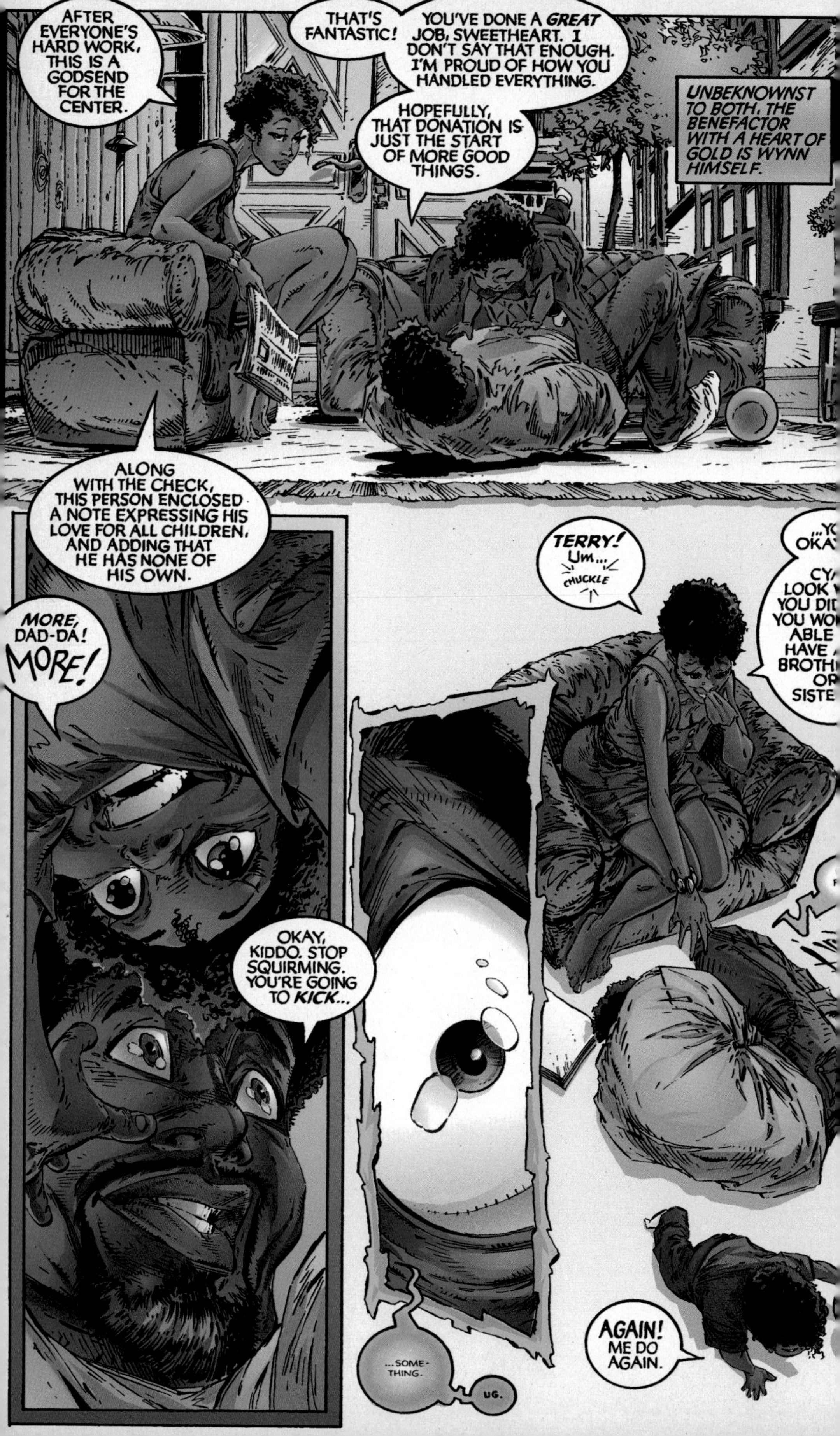

AFTER EVERYONE'S HARD WORK, THIS IS A GODSEND FOR THE CENTER.
THAT'S FANTASTIC!
YOU'VE DONE A *GREAT* JOB, SWEETHEART. I DON'T SAY THAT ENOUGH. I'M PROUD OF HOW YOU HANDLED EVERYTHING.
HOPEFULLY, THAT DONATION IS JUST THE START OF MORE GOOD THINGS.
UNBEKNOWNST TO BOTH, THE BENEFACTOR WITH A HEART OF GOLD IS WYNN HIMSELF.
ALONG WITH THE CHECK, THIS PERSON ENCLOSED A NOTE EXPRESSING HIS LOVE FOR ALL CHILDREN, AND ADDING THAT HE HAS NONE OF HIS OWN.
MORE, DAD-DA! MORE!
OKAY, KIDDO. STOP SQUIRMING. YOU'RE GOING TO *KICK*...
...SOME-THING.
UG.
TERRY! Um... CHUCKLE
...YO OKA
CYA LOOK YOU DID YOU WO ABLE HAVE BROTH OR SISTE
AGAIN! ME DO AGAIN.

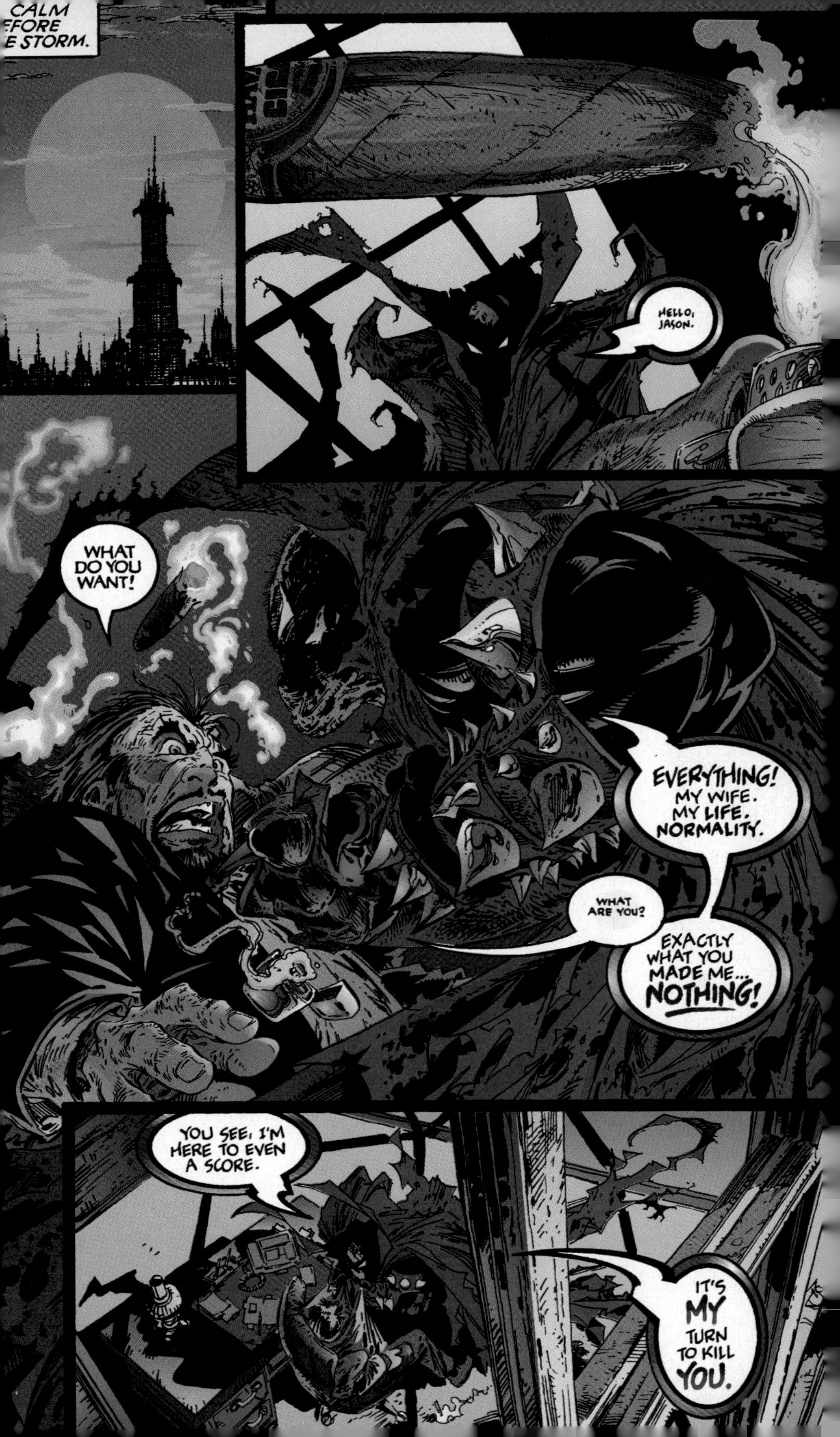

CALM
EFORE
E STORM.
HELLO, JASON.
WHAT DO YOU WANT!
EVERYTHING! MY WIFE. MY LIFE. NORMALITY.
WHAT ARE YOU?
EXACTLY WHAT YOU MADE ME... NOTHING!
YOU SEE, I'M HERE TO EVEN A SCORE.
IT'S MY TURN TO KILL YOU.

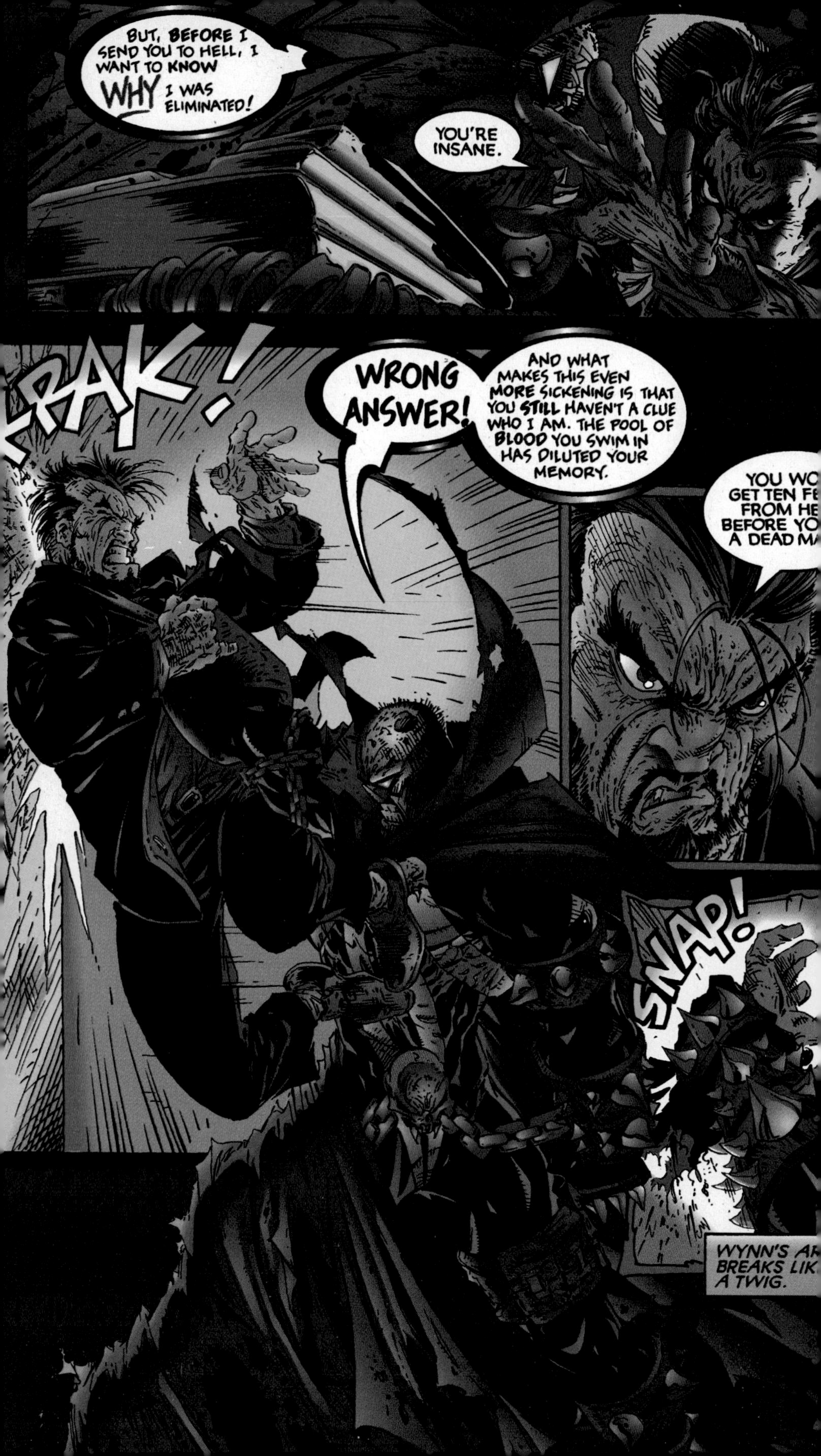

BUT, BEFORE I SEND YOU TO HELL, I WANT TO KNOW WHY I WAS ELIMINATED!
YOU'RE INSANE.
RAK!
WRONG ANSWER!
AND WHAT MAKES THIS EVEN MORE SICKENING IS THAT YOU STILL HAVEN'T A CLUE WHO I AM. THE POOL OF BLOOD YOU SWIM IN HAS DILUTED YOUR MEMORY.
YOU WO GET TEN FE FROM HE BEFORE YO A DEAD MA
SNAP!
WYNN'S AR BREAKS LIK A TWIG.

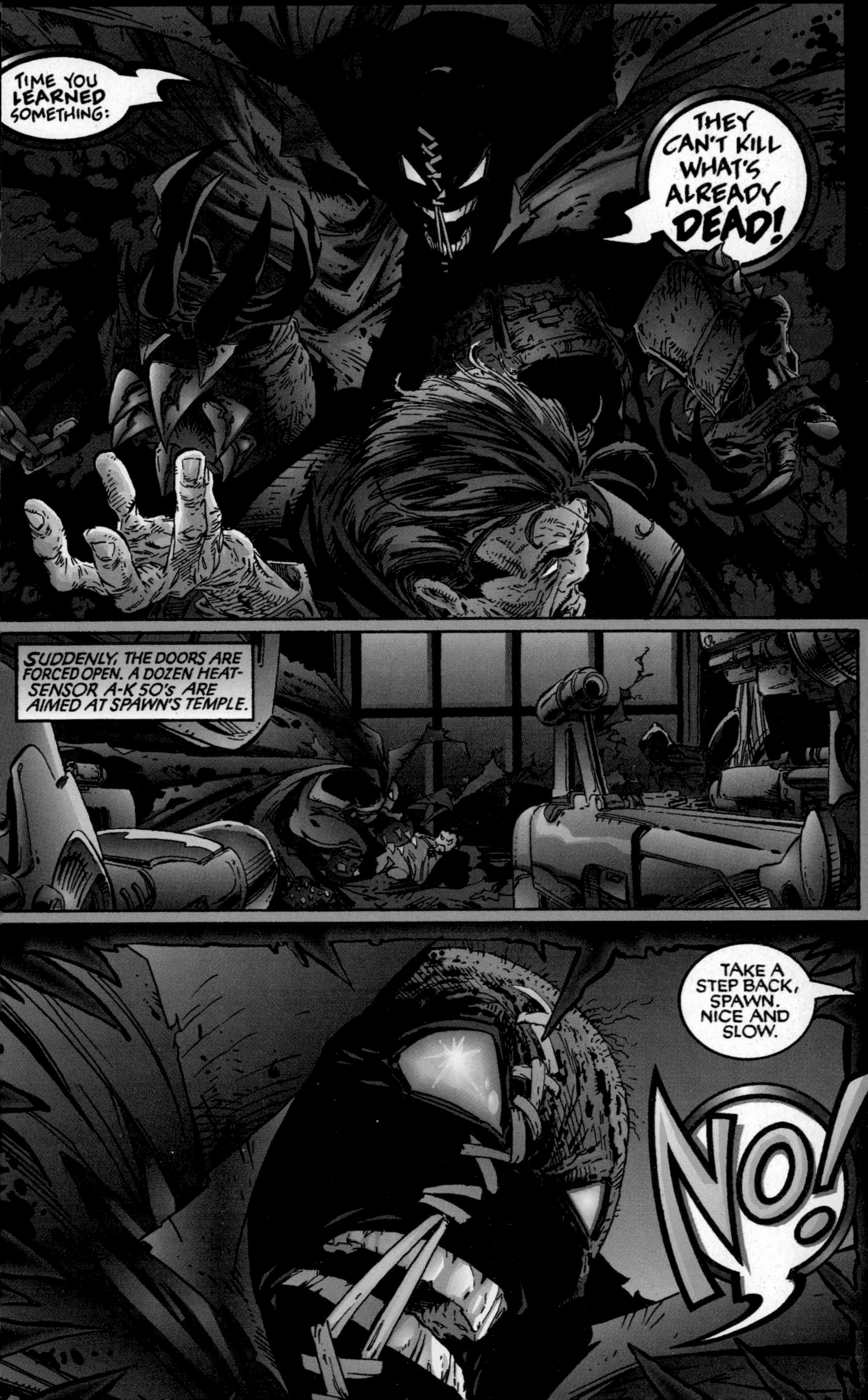
TIME YOU LEARNED SOMETHING:
THEY CAN'T KILL WHAT'S ALREADY DEAD!
SUDDENLY, THE DOORS ARE FORCED OPEN. A DOZEN HEAT-SENSOR A-K 50's ARE AIMED AT SPAWN'S TEMPLE.
TAKE A STEP BACK, SPAWN. NICE AND SLOW.
NO!

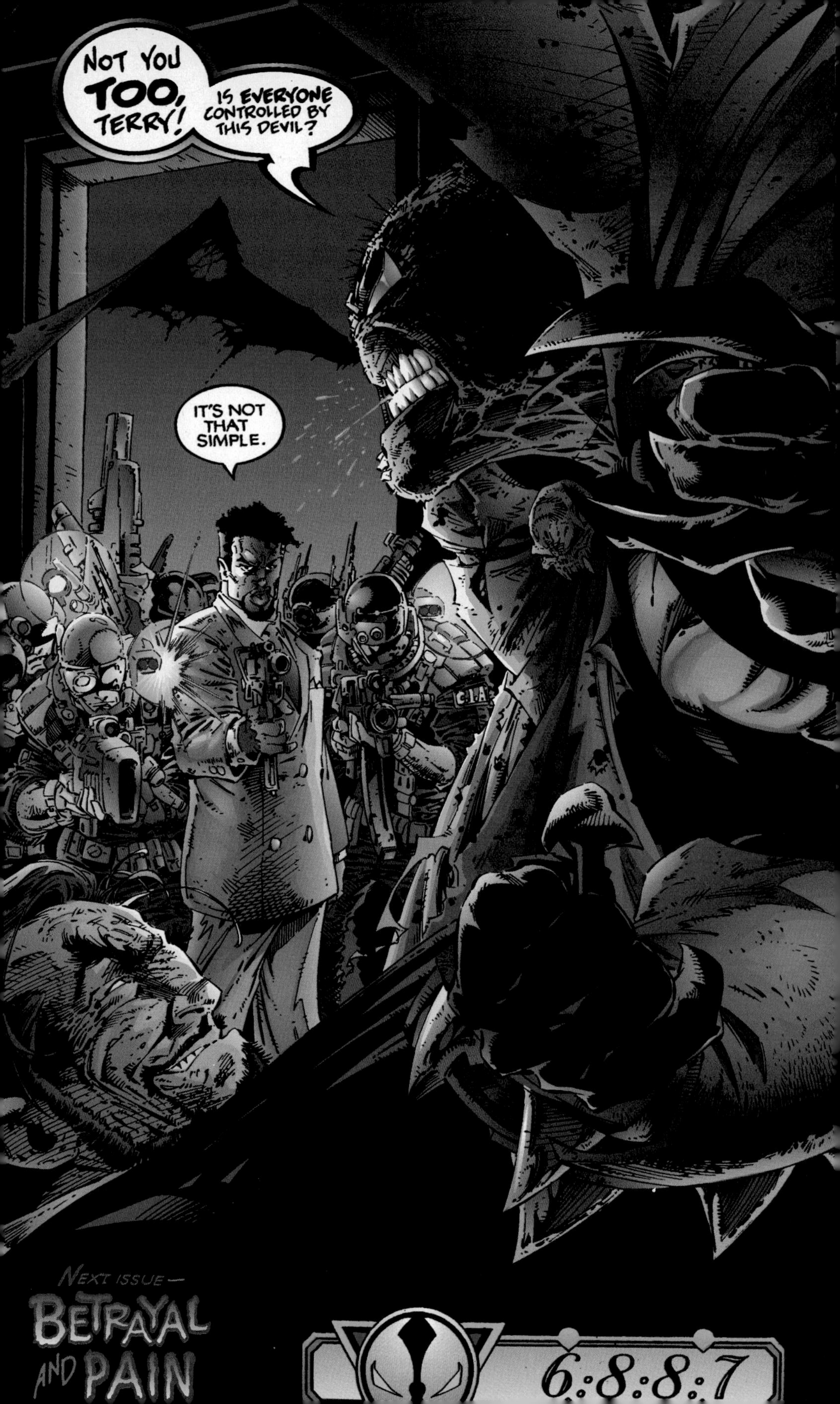
NOT YOU TOO, TERRY!
IS EVERYONE CONTROLLED BY THIS DEVIL?
IT'S NOT THAT SIMPLE.
C.I.A.
NEXT ISSUE—
BETRAYAL AND PAIN
6:8:8:7

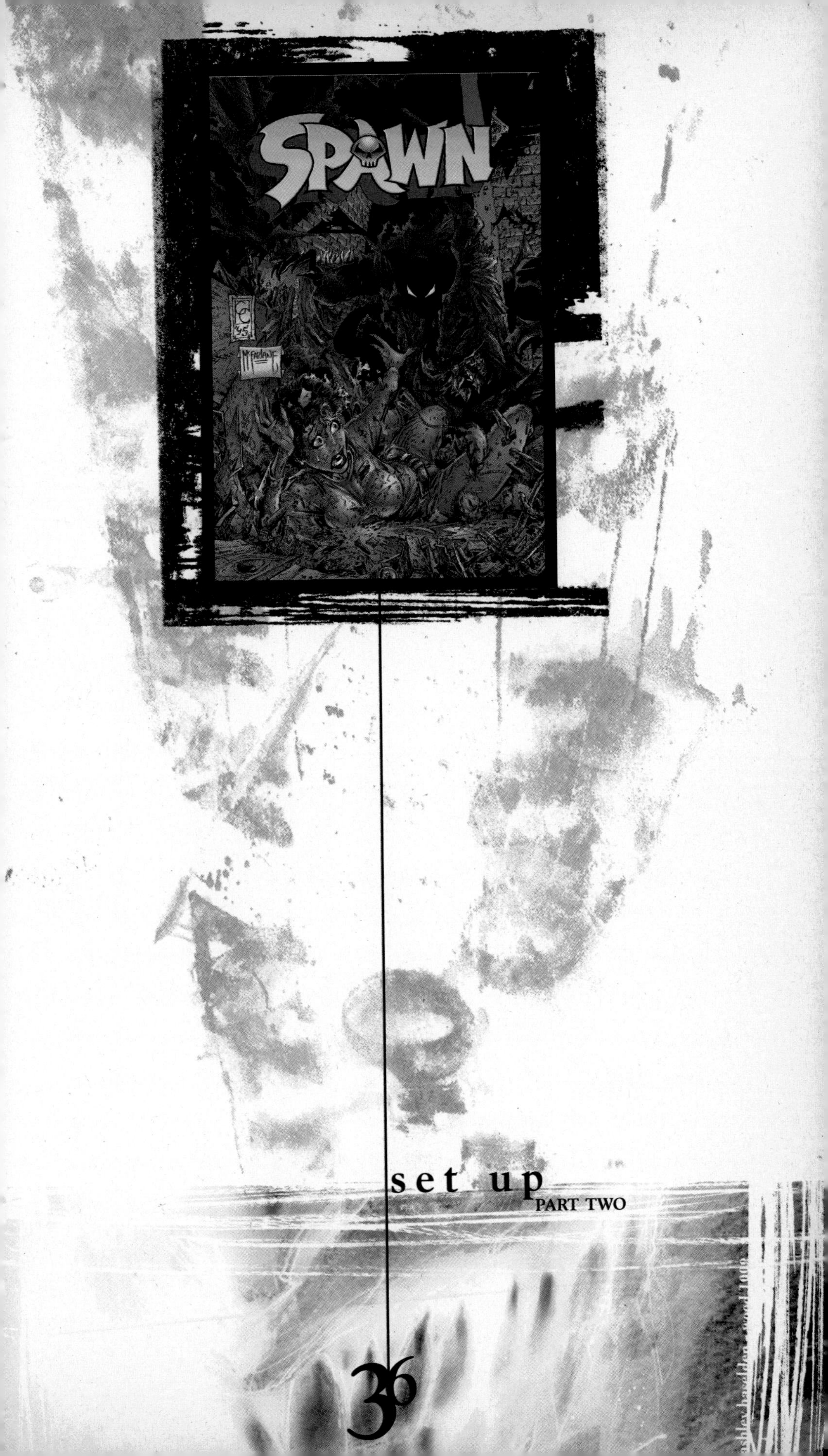
SPAWN

set up
PART TWO

SPAWN

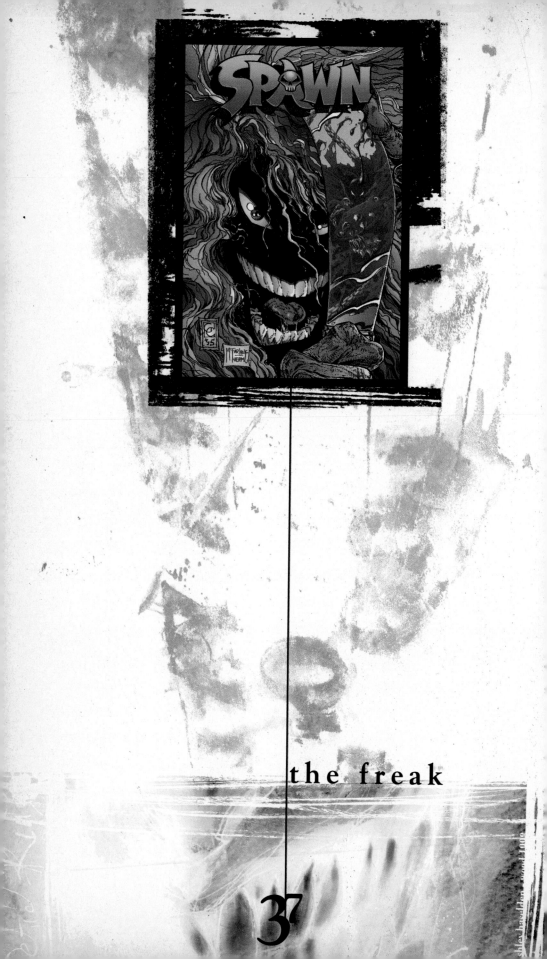

the freak

37

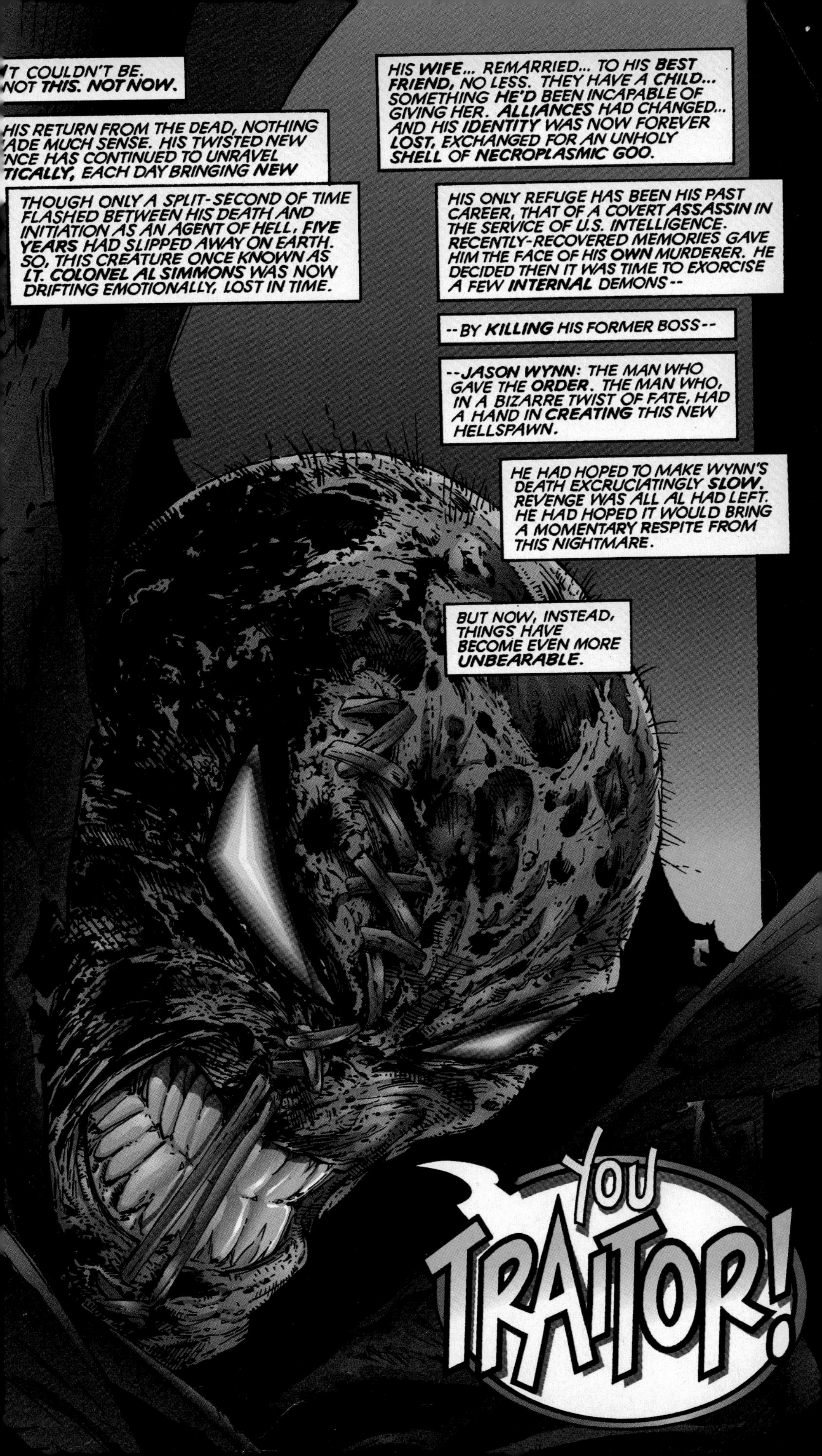
'T COULDN'T BE. NOT THIS. NOT NOW.
HIS RETURN FROM THE DEAD, NOTHING ADE MUCH SENSE. HIS TWISTED NEW NCE HAS CONTINUED TO UNRAVEL TICALLY, EACH DAY BRINGING NEW
THOUGH ONLY A SPLIT-SECOND OF TIME FLASHED BETWEEN HIS DEATH AND INITIATION AS AN AGENT OF HELL, FIVE YEARS HAD SLIPPED AWAY ON EARTH. SO, THIS CREATURE ONCE KNOWN AS LT. COLONEL AL SIMMONS WAS NOW DRIFTING EMOTIONALLY, LOST IN TIME.
HIS WIFE... REMARRIED... TO HIS BEST FRIEND, NO LESS. THEY HAVE A CHILD... SOMETHING HE'D BEEN INCAPABLE OF GIVING HER. ALLIANCES HAD CHANGED... AND HIS IDENTITY WAS NOW FOREVER LOST, EXCHANGED FOR AN UNHOLY SHELL OF NECROPLASMIC GOO.
HIS ONLY REFUGE HAS BEEN HIS PAST CAREER, THAT OF A COVERT ASSASSIN IN THE SERVICE OF U.S. INTELLIGENCE. RECENTLY-RECOVERED MEMORIES GAVE HIM THE FACE OF HIS OWN MURDERER. HE DECIDED THEN IT WAS TIME TO EXORCISE A FEW INTERNAL DEMONS--
--BY KILLING HIS FORMER BOSS--
--JASON WYNN: THE MAN WHO GAVE THE ORDER. THE MAN WHO, IN A BIZARRE TWIST OF FATE, HAD A HAND IN CREATING THIS NEW HELLSPAWN.
HE HAD HOPED TO MAKE WYNN'S DEATH EXCRUCIATINGLY SLOW. REVENGE WAS ALL AL HAD LEFT. HE HAD HOPED IT WOULD BRING A MOMENTARY RESPITE FROM THIS NIGHTMARE.
BUT NOW, INSTEAD, THINGS HAVE BECOME EVEN MORE UNBEARABLE.
YOU TRAITOR!

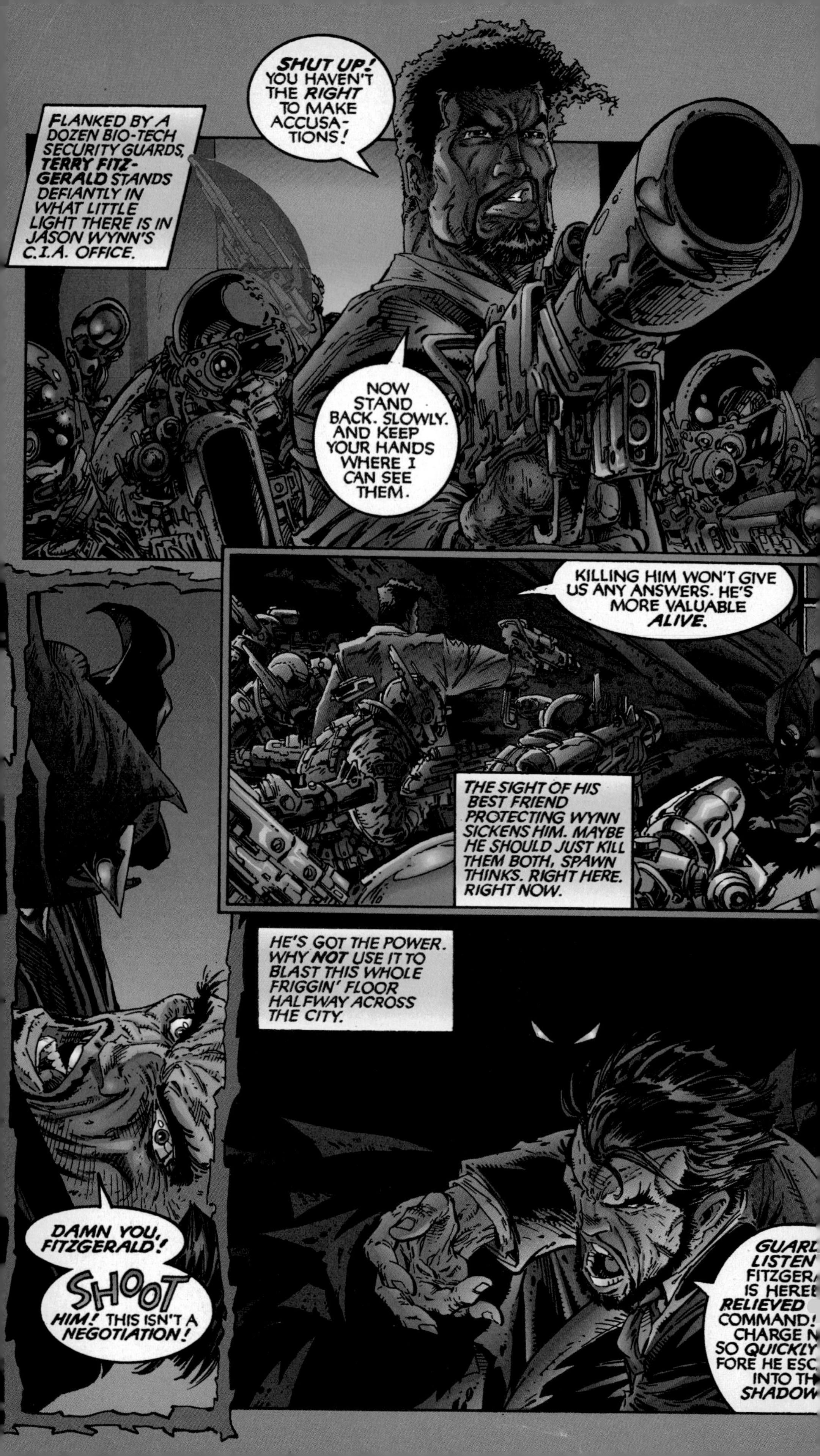
FLANKED BY A DOZEN BIO-TECH SECURITY GUARDS, TERRY FITZ-GERALD STANDS DEFIANTLY IN WHAT LITTLE LIGHT THERE IS IN JASON WYNN'S C.I.A. OFFICE.
SHUT UP! YOU HAVEN'T THE RIGHT TO MAKE ACCUSA-TIONS!
NOW STAND BACK. SLOWLY. AND KEEP YOUR HANDS WHERE I CAN SEE THEM.
KILLING HIM WON'T GIVE US ANY ANSWERS. HE'S MORE VALUABLE ALIVE.
THE SIGHT OF HIS BEST FRIEND PROTECTING WYNN SICKENS HIM. MAYBE HE SHOULD JUST KILL THEM BOTH, SPAWN THINKS. RIGHT HERE. RIGHT NOW.
HE'S GOT THE POWER. WHY NOT USE IT TO BLAST THIS WHOLE FRIGGIN' FLOOR HALFWAY ACROSS THE CITY.
DAMN YOU, FITZGERALD! SHOOT HIM! THIS ISN'T A NEGOTIATION!

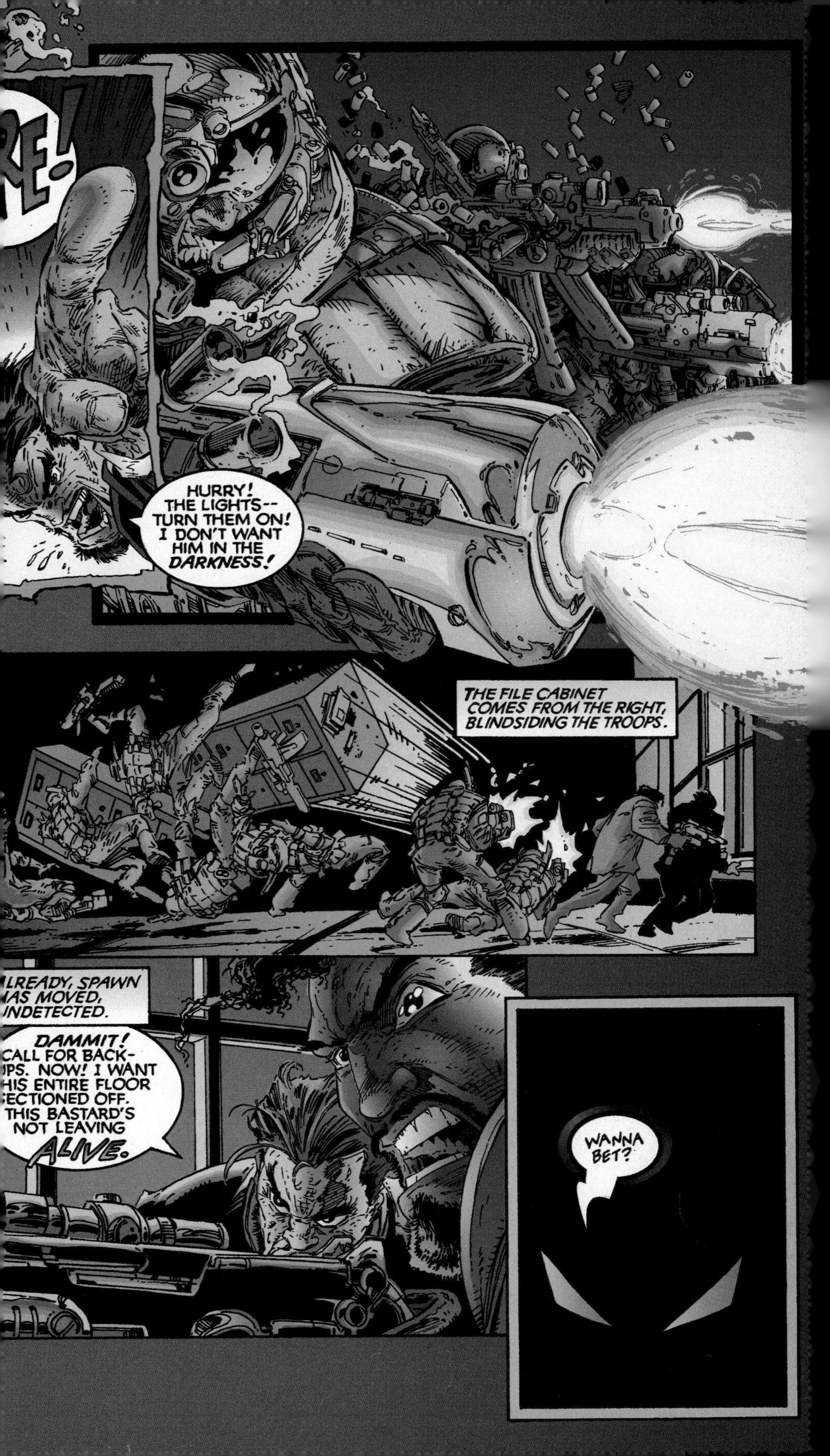
RE!
HURRY! THE LIGHTS-- TURN THEM ON! I DON'T WANT HIM IN THE DARKNESS!
THE FILE CABINET COMES FROM THE RIGHT, BLINDSIDING THE TROOPS.
LREADY, SPAWN AS MOVED, NDETECTED.
DAMMIT! CALL FOR BACK-UPS. NOW! I WANT HIS ENTIRE FLOOR ECTIONED OFF. THIS BASTARD'S NOT LEAVING ALIVE.
WANNA BET?

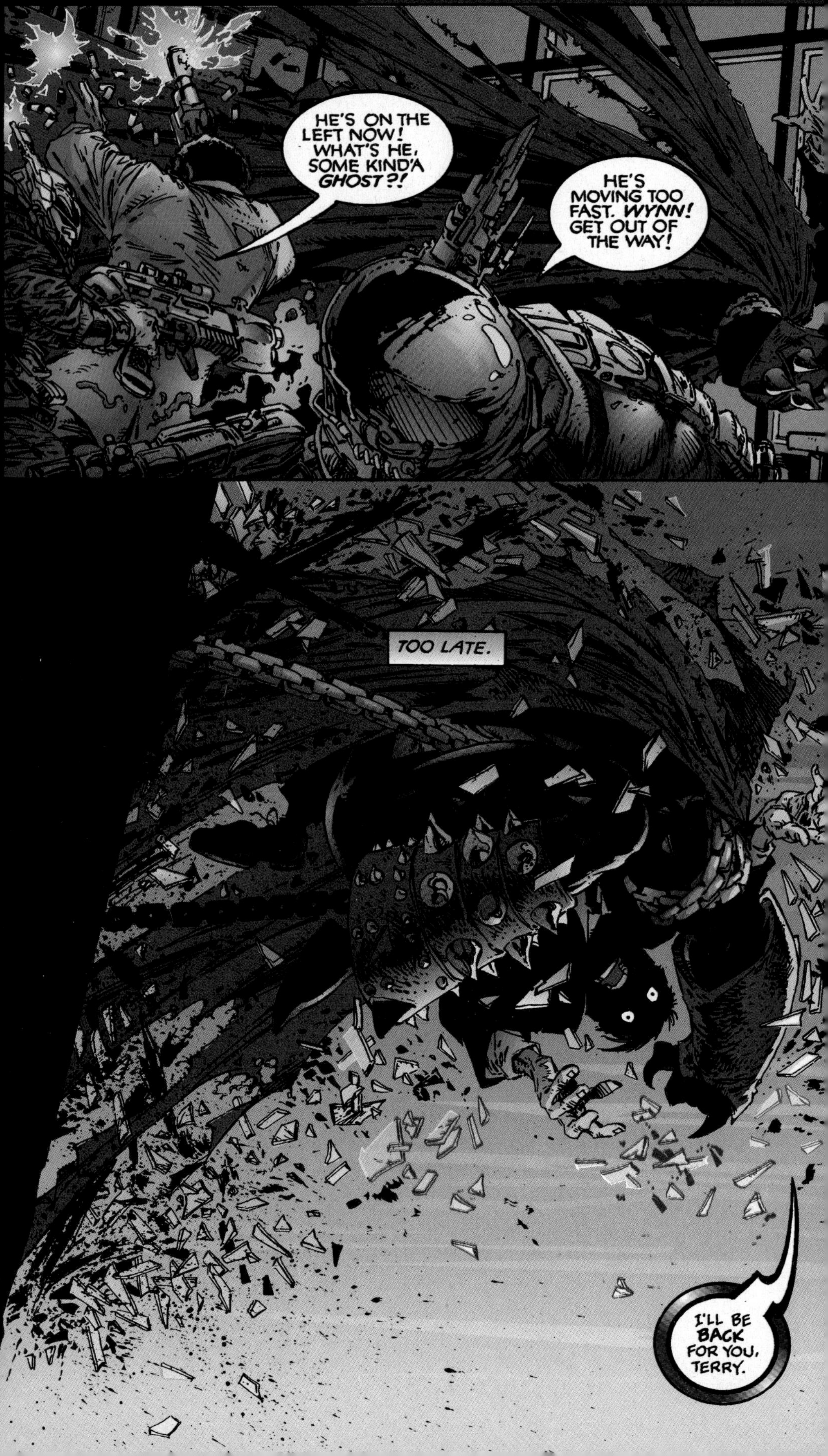
HE'S ON THE LEFT NOW! WHAT'S HE, SOME KIND'A GHOST?!
HE'S MOVING TOO FAST. WYNN! GET OUT OF THE WAY!
TOO LATE.
I'LL BE BACK FOR YOU, TERRY.

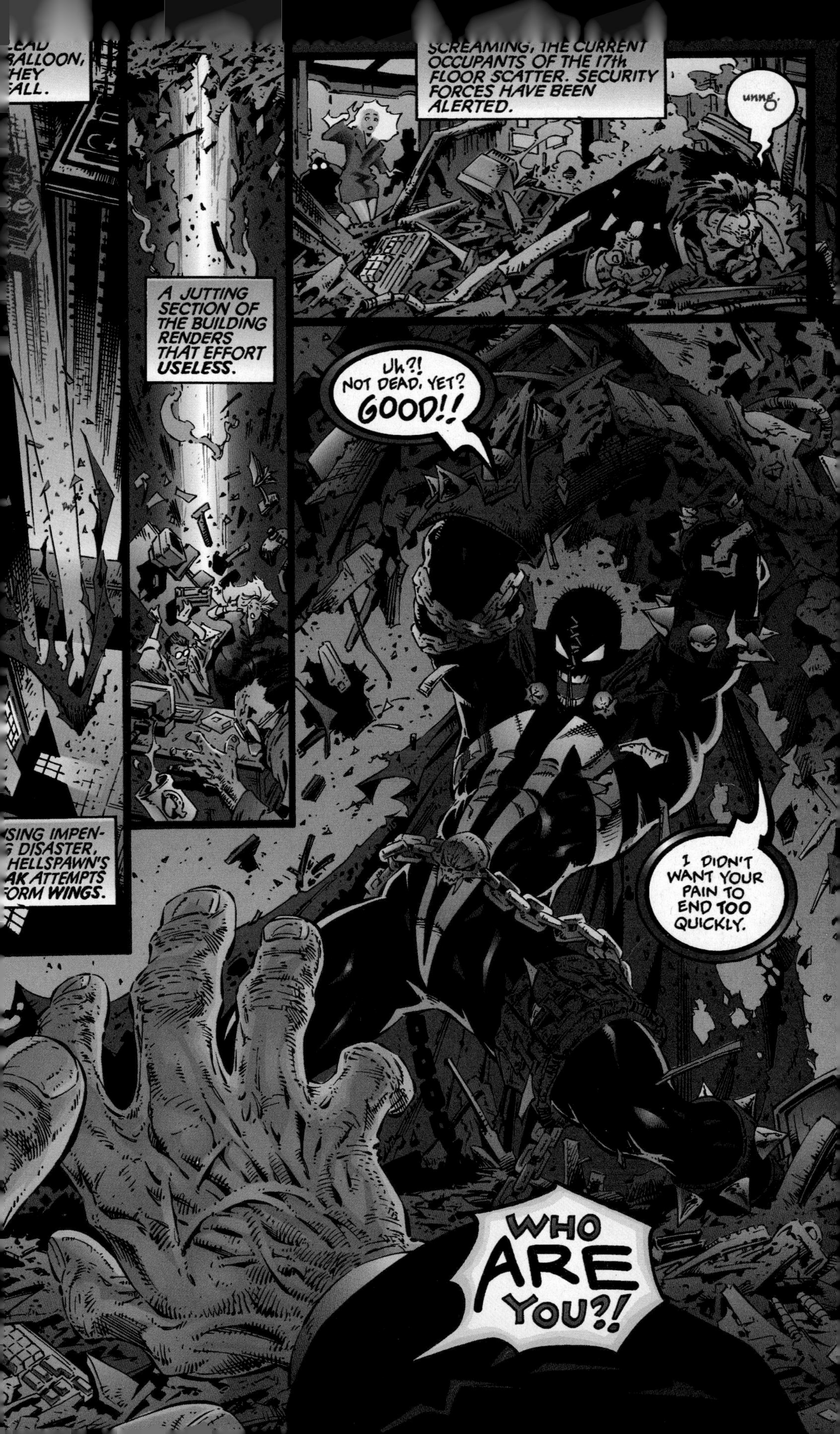

LEAD
BALLOON,
HEY
FALL.
SCREAMING, THE CURRENT OCCUPANTS OF THE 17th FLOOR SCATTER. SECURITY FORCES HAVE BEEN ALERTED.
unng.
A JUTTING SECTION OF THE BUILDING RENDERS THAT EFFORT USELESS.
SING IMPEN-
G DISASTER,
HELLSPAWN'S
AK ATTEMPTS
FORM WINGS.
UH?! NOT DEAD, YET? GOOD!!
I DIDN'T WANT YOUR PAIN TO END TOO QUICKLY.
WHO ARE YOU?!

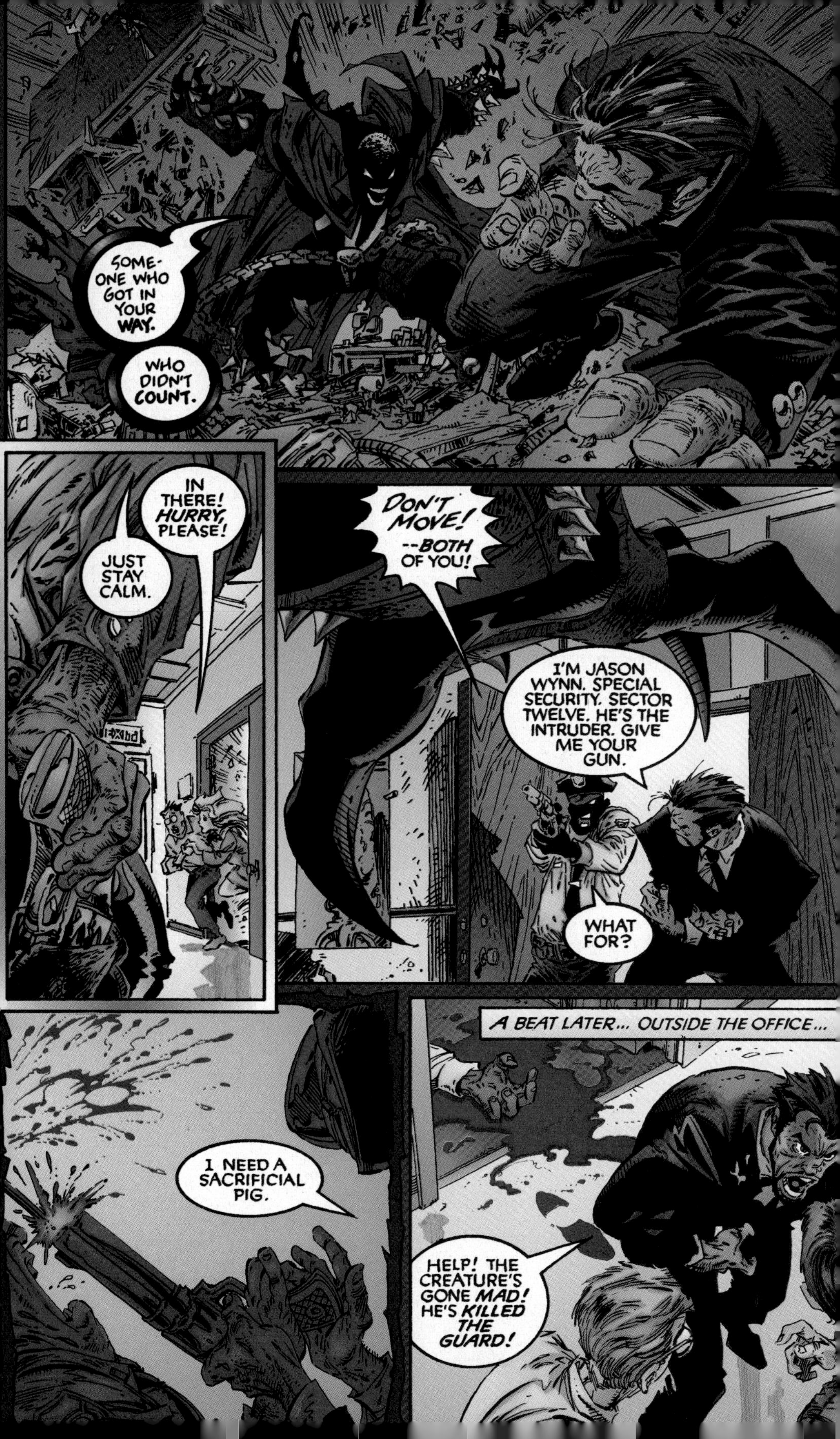
SOME-ONE WHO GOT IN YOUR WAY.
WHO DIDN'T COUNT.
IN THERE! HURRY, PLEASE!
JUST STAY CALM.
DON'T MOVE! --BOTH OF YOU!
I'M JASON WYNN. SPECIAL SECURITY. SECTOR TWELVE. HE'S THE INTRUDER. GIVE ME YOUR GUN.
WHAT FOR?
I NEED A SACRIFICIAL PIG.
A BEAT LATER... OUTSIDE THE OFFICE...
HELP! THE CREATURE'S GONE MAD! HE'S KILLED THE GUARD!

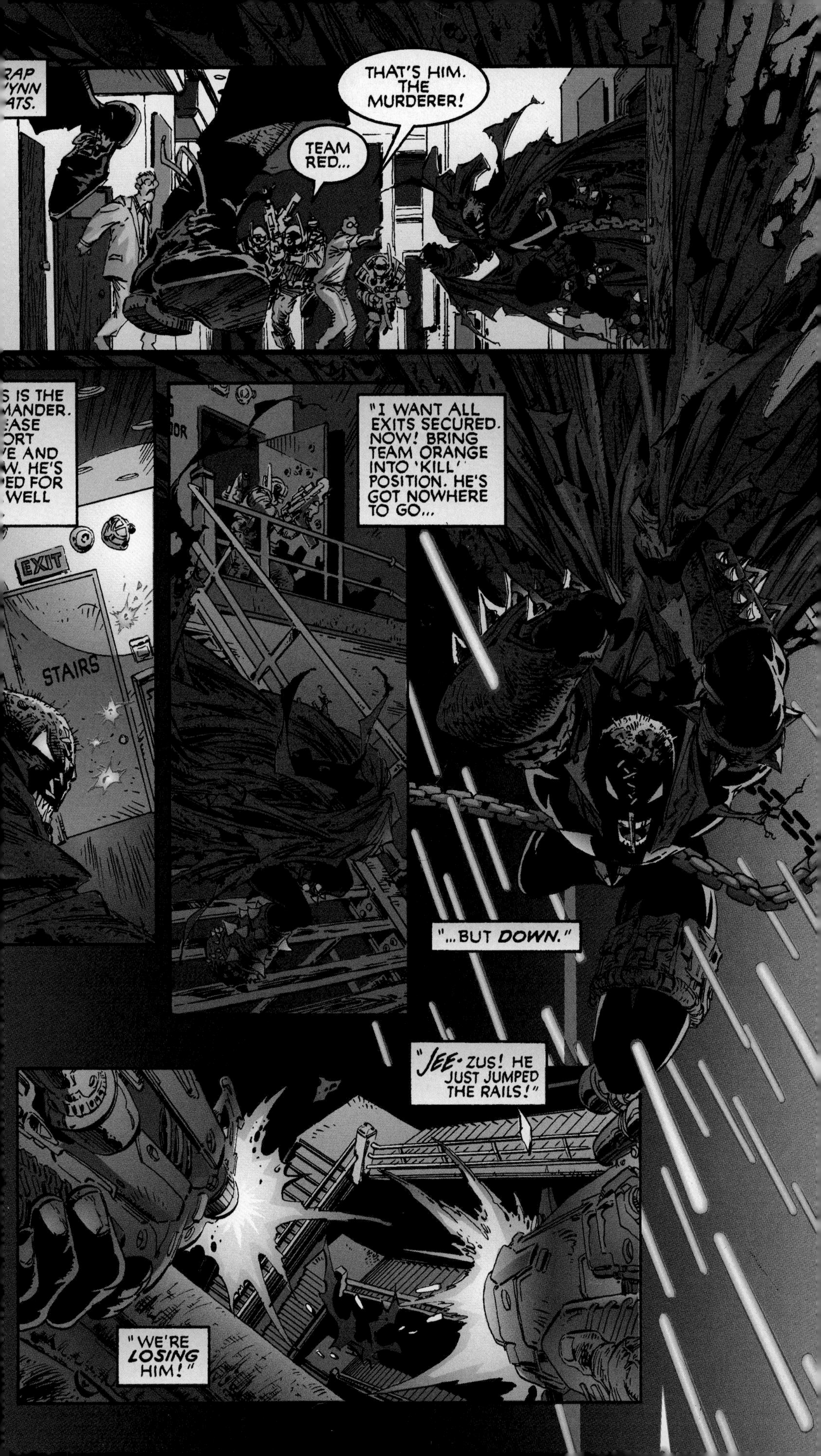

RAP
YNN
ATS.
THAT'S HIM. THE MURDERER!
TEAM RED...
S IS THE
MANDER.
EASE
ORT
VE AND
W. HE'S
PED FOR
WELL
STAIRS
EXIT
"I WANT ALL EXITS SECURED. NOW! BRING TEAM ORANGE INTO 'KILL' POSITION. HE'S GOT NOWHERE TO GO...
"...BUT DOWN."
"JEE-ZUS! HE JUST JUMPED THE RAILS!"
"WE'RE LOSING HIM!"

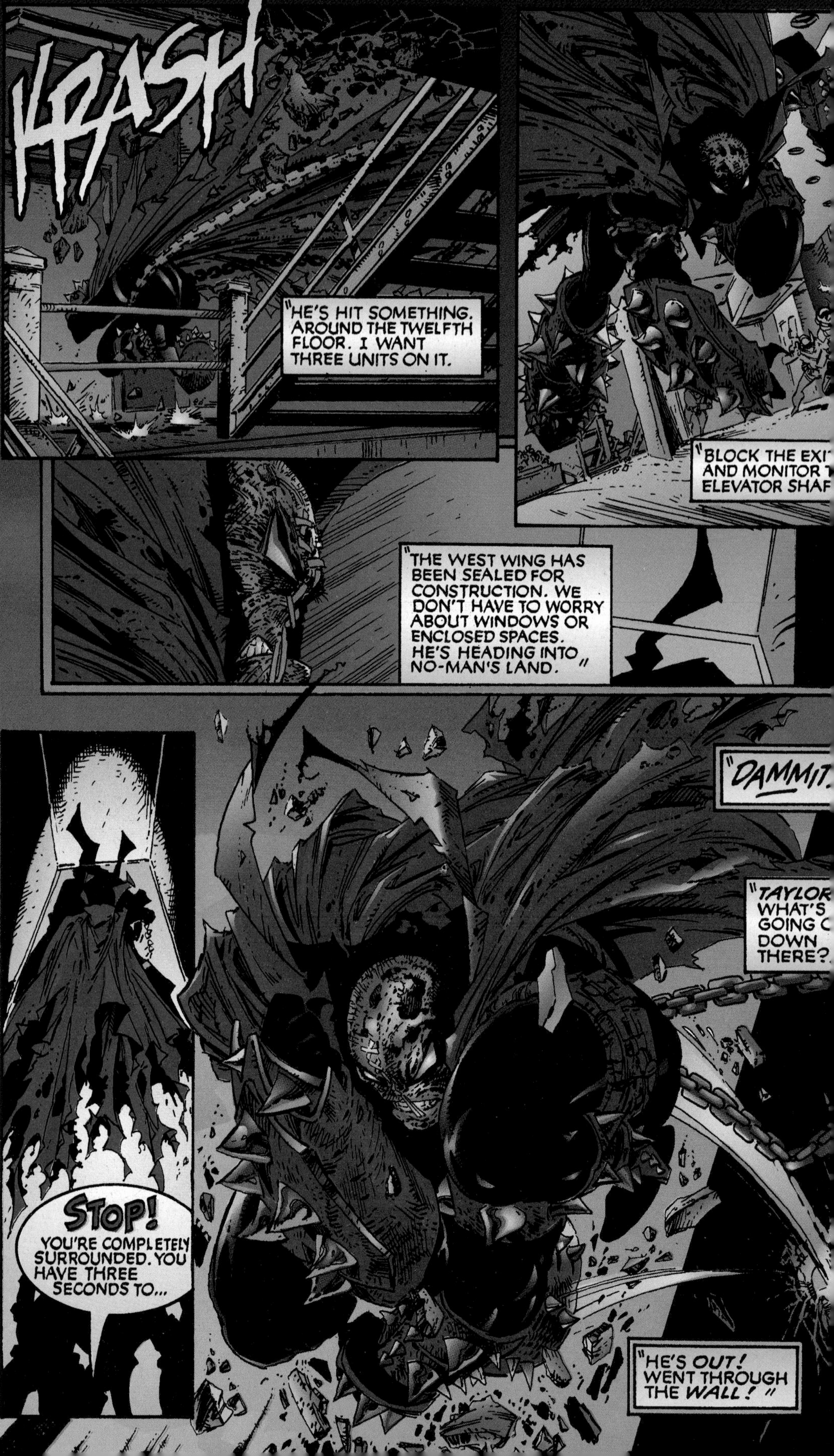
KRASH
"HE'S HIT SOMETHING. AROUND THE TWELFTH FLOOR. I WANT THREE UNITS ON IT.
"BLOCK THE EXI
AND MONITOR
ELEVATOR SHAF
"THE WEST WING HAS BEEN SEALED FOR CONSTRUCTION. WE DON'T HAVE TO WORRY ABOUT WINDOWS OR ENCLOSED SPACES. HE'S HEADING INTO NO-MAN'S LAND."
"DAMMIT.
"TAYLOR
WHAT'S GOING
DOWN THERE?
STOP! YOU'RE COMPLETELY SURROUNDED. YOU HAVE THREE SECONDS TO...
"HE'S OUT! WENT THROUGH THE WALL!"

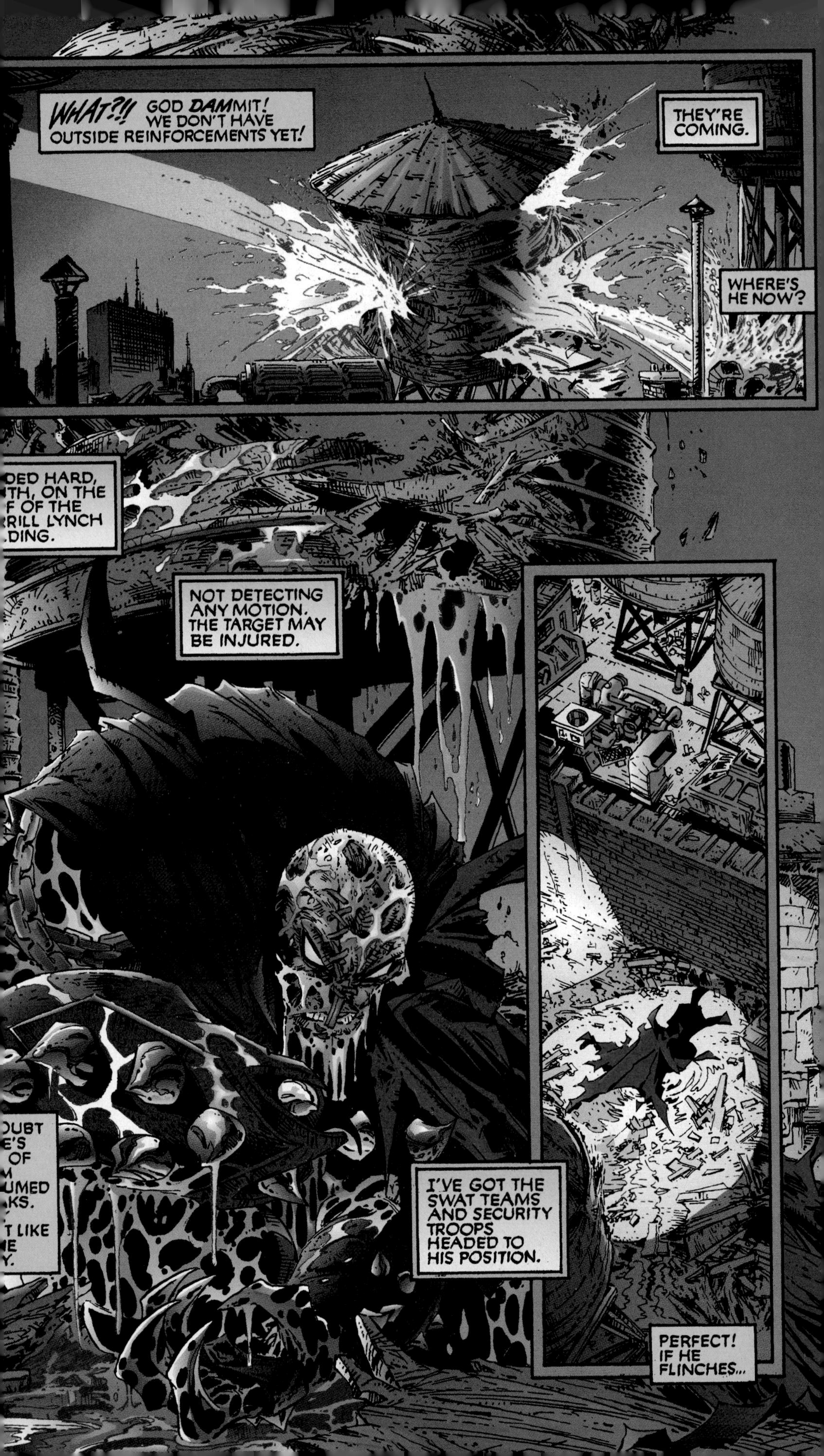

WHAT?!! GOD DAMMIT! WE DON'T HAVE OUTSIDE REINFORCEMENTS YET!
THEY'RE COMING.
WHERE'S HE NOW?
DED HARD, TH, ON THE F OF THE RRILL LYNCH DING.
NOT DETECTING ANY MOTION. THE TARGET MAY BE INJURED.
OUBT E'S OF M UMED KS. T LIKE E Y.
I'VE GOT THE SWAT TEAMS AND SECURITY TROOPS HEADED TO HIS POSITION.
PERFECT! IF HE FLINCHES...

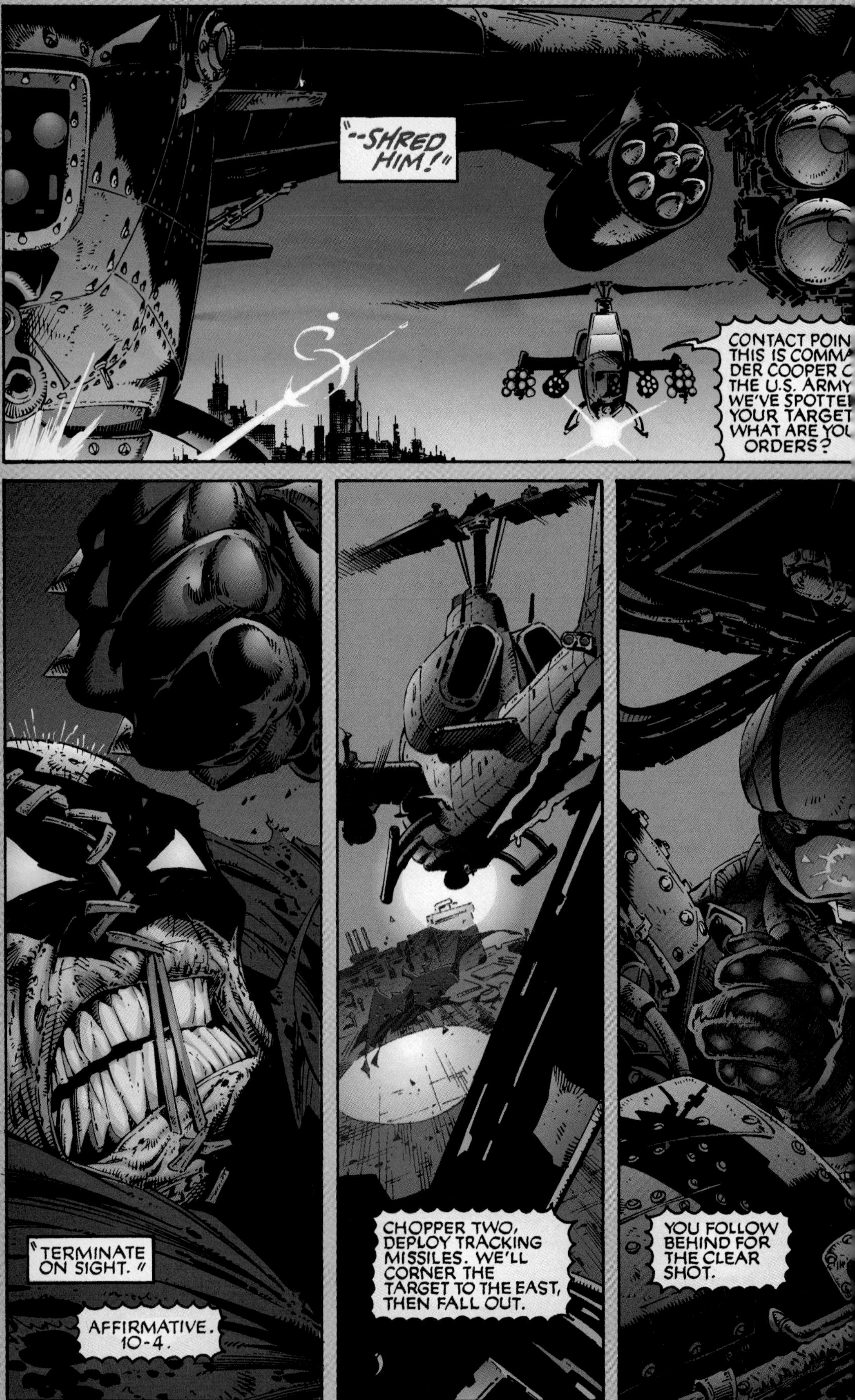
"--SHRED HIM!"
CONTACT POIN THIS IS COMMA DER COOPER O THE U.S. ARMY WE'VE SPOTTE YOUR TARGET WHAT ARE YOU ORDERS?
"TERMINATE ON SIGHT."
AFFIRMATIVE. 10-4.
CHOPPER TWO, DEPLOY TRACKING MISSILES. WE'LL CORNER THE TARGET TO THE EAST, THEN FALL OUT.
YOU FOLLOW BEHIND FOR THE CLEAR SHOT.

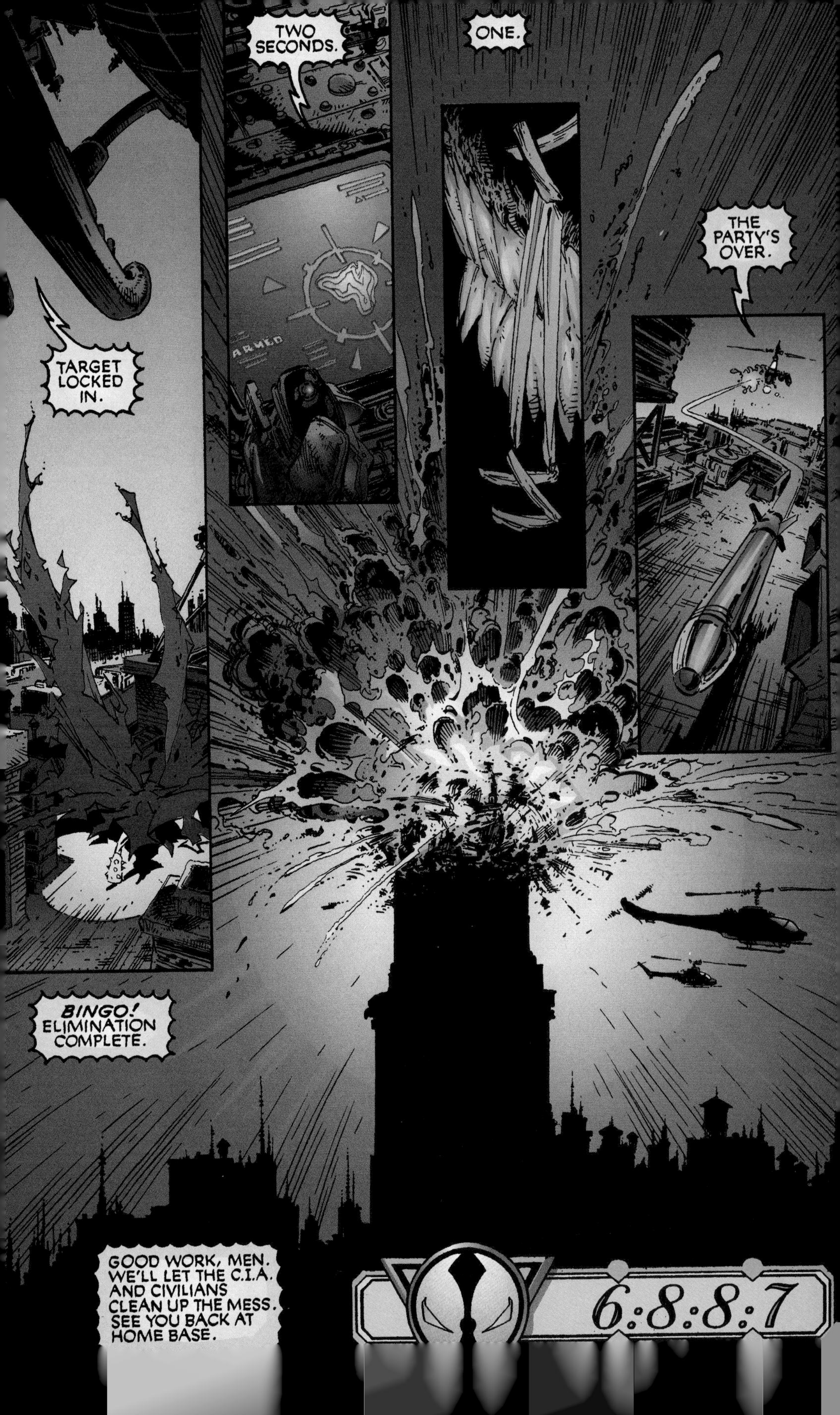
TARGET LOCKED IN.
TWO SECONDS.
ARMED
ONE.
THE PARTY'S OVER.
BINGO! ELIMINATION COMPLETE.
GOOD WORK, MEN. WE'LL LET THE C.I.A. AND CIVILIANS CLEAN UP THE MESS. SEE YOU BACK AT HOME BASE.
6:8:8:7

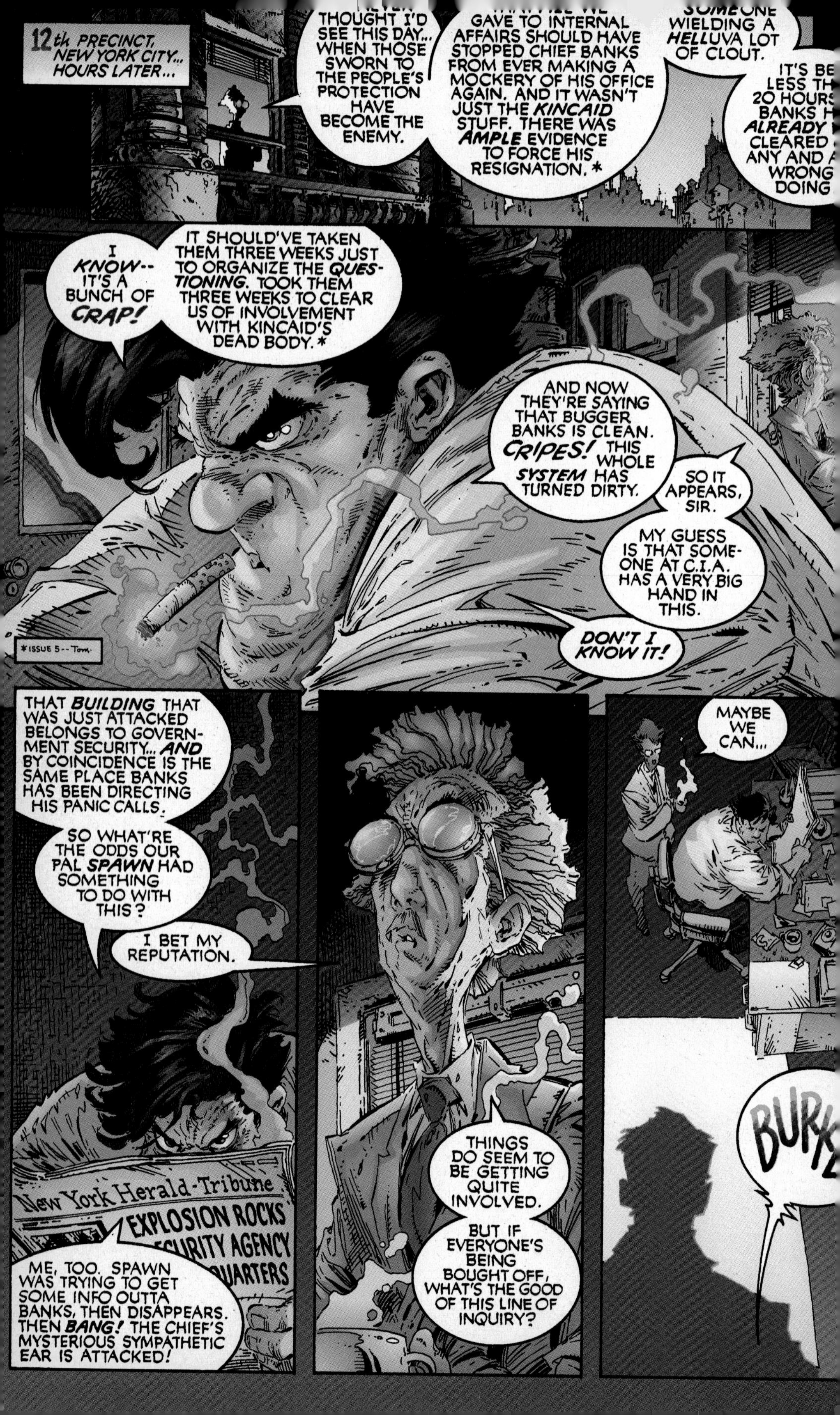
12th PRECINCT, NEW YORK CITY... HOURS LATER...
THOUGHT I'D SEE THIS DAY... WHEN THOSE SWORN TO THE PEOPLE'S PROTECTION HAVE BECOME THE ENEMY.
GAVE TO INTERNAL AFFAIRS SHOULD HAVE STOPPED CHIEF BANKS FROM EVER MAKING A MOCKERY OF HIS OFFICE AGAIN. AND IT WASN'T JUST THE KINCAID STUFF. THERE WAS AMPLE EVIDENCE TO FORCE HIS RESIGNATION. *
WIELDING A HELLUVA LOT OF CLOUT.
IT'S BE LESS TH 20 HOURS BANKS H ALREADY CLEARED ANY AND WRONG DOING
I KNOW-- IT'S A BUNCH OF CRAP!
IT SHOULD'VE TAKEN THEM THREE WEEKS JUST TO ORGANIZE THE QUESTIONING. TOOK THEM THREE WEEKS TO CLEAR US OF INVOLVEMENT WITH KINCAID'S DEAD BODY. *
AND NOW THEY'RE SAYING THAT BUGGER BANKS IS CLEAN. CRIPES! THIS WHOLE SYSTEM HAS TURNED DIRTY.
SO IT APPEARS, SIR.
MY GUESS IS THAT SOMEONE AT C.I.A. HAS A VERY BIG HAND IN THIS.
DON'T I KNOW IT!
*ISSUE 5 -- Tom.
THAT BUILDING THAT WAS JUST ATTACKED BELONGS TO GOVERNMENT SECURITY... AND BY COINCIDENCE IS THE SAME PLACE BANKS HAS BEEN DIRECTING HIS PANIC CALLS.
SO WHAT'RE THE ODDS OUR PAL SPAWN HAD SOMETHING TO DO WITH THIS?
I BET MY REPUTATION.
New York Herald-Tribune
EXPLOSION ROCKS
ME, TOO. SPAWN WAS TRYING TO GET SOME INFO OUTTA BANKS, THEN DISAPPEARS. THEN BANG! THE CHIEF'S MYSTERIOUS SYMPATHETIC EAR IS ATTACKED!
THINGS DO SEEM TO BE GETTING QUITE INVOLVED.
BUT IF EVERYONE'S BEING BOUGHT OFF, WHAT'S THE GOOD OF THIS LINE OF INQUIRY?
MAYBE WE CAN...

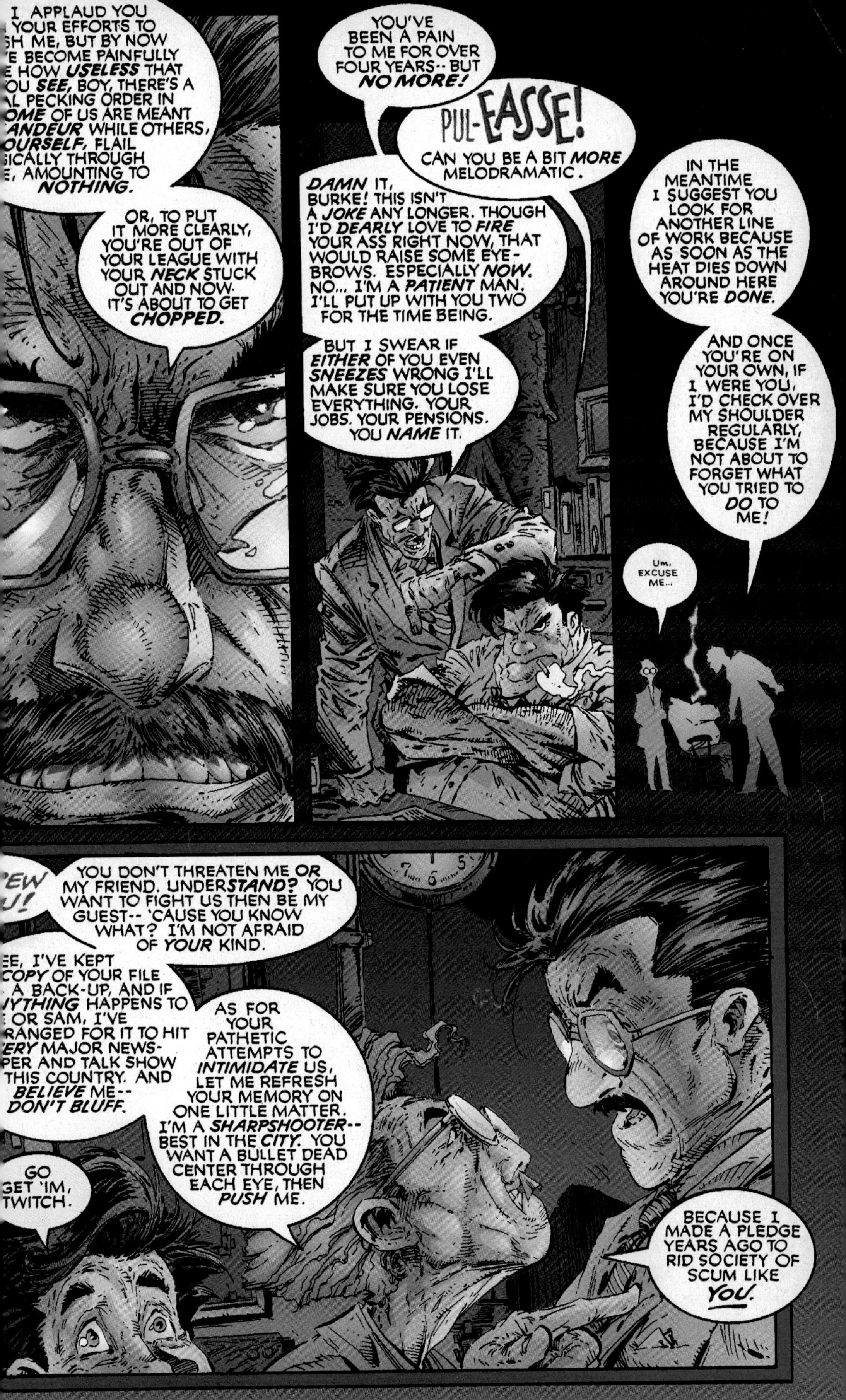
I APPLAUD YOU YOUR EFFORTS TO SH ME, BUT BY NOW E BECOME PAINFULLY E HOW USELESS THAT OU SEE, BOY, THERE'S A AL PECKING ORDER IN OME OF US ARE MEANT ANDEUR WHILE OTHERS, OURSELF, FLAIL ICALLY THROUGH E, AMOUNTING TO NOTHING.
OR, TO PUT IT MORE CLEARLY, YOU'RE OUT OF YOUR LEAGUE WITH YOUR NECK STUCK OUT AND NOW IT'S ABOUT TO GET CHOPPED.
YOU'VE BEEN A PAIN TO ME FOR OVER FOUR YEARS-- BUT NO MORE!
PUL-EASSE!
CAN YOU BE A BIT MORE MELODRAMATIC.
DAMN IT, BURKE! THIS ISN'T A JOKE ANY LONGER. THOUGH I'D DEARLY LOVE TO FIRE YOUR ASS RIGHT NOW, THAT WOULD RAISE SOME EYE-BROWS. ESPECIALLY NOW. NO... I'M A PATIENT MAN. I'LL PUT UP WITH YOU TWO FOR THE TIME BEING.
BUT I SWEAR IF EITHER OF YOU EVEN SNEEZES WRONG I'LL MAKE SURE YOU LOSE EVERYTHING. YOUR JOBS. YOUR PENSIONS. YOU NAME IT.
IN THE MEANTIME I SUGGEST YOU LOOK FOR ANOTHER LINE OF WORK BECAUSE AS SOON AS THE HEAT DIES DOWN AROUND HERE YOU'RE DONE.
AND ONCE YOU'RE ON YOUR OWN, IF I WERE YOU, I'D CHECK OVER MY SHOULDER REGULARLY, BECAUSE I'M NOT ABOUT TO FORGET WHAT YOU TRIED TO DO TO ME!
UM, EXCUSE ME...
EW U!
YOU DON'T THREATEN ME OR MY FRIEND. UNDERSTAND? YOU WANT TO FIGHT US THEN BE MY GUEST-- 'CAUSE YOU KNOW WHAT? I'M NOT AFRAID OF YOUR KIND.
EE, I'VE KEPT COPY OF YOUR FILE A BACK-UP, AND IF YTHING HAPPENS TO OR SAM, I'VE RANGED FOR IT TO HIT ERY MAJOR NEWS-PER AND TALK SHOW THIS COUNTRY. AND BELIEVE ME-- DON'T BLUFF.
AS FOR YOUR PATHETIC ATTEMPTS TO INTIMIDATE US, LET ME REFRESH YOUR MEMORY ON ONE LITTLE MATTER. I'M A SHARPSHOOTER-- BEST IN THE CITY. YOU WANT A BULLET DEAD CENTER THROUGH EACH EYE, THEN PUSH ME.
GO GET 'IM, TWITCH.
BECAUSE I MADE A PLEDGE YEARS AGO TO RID SOCIETY OF SCUM LIKE YOU.

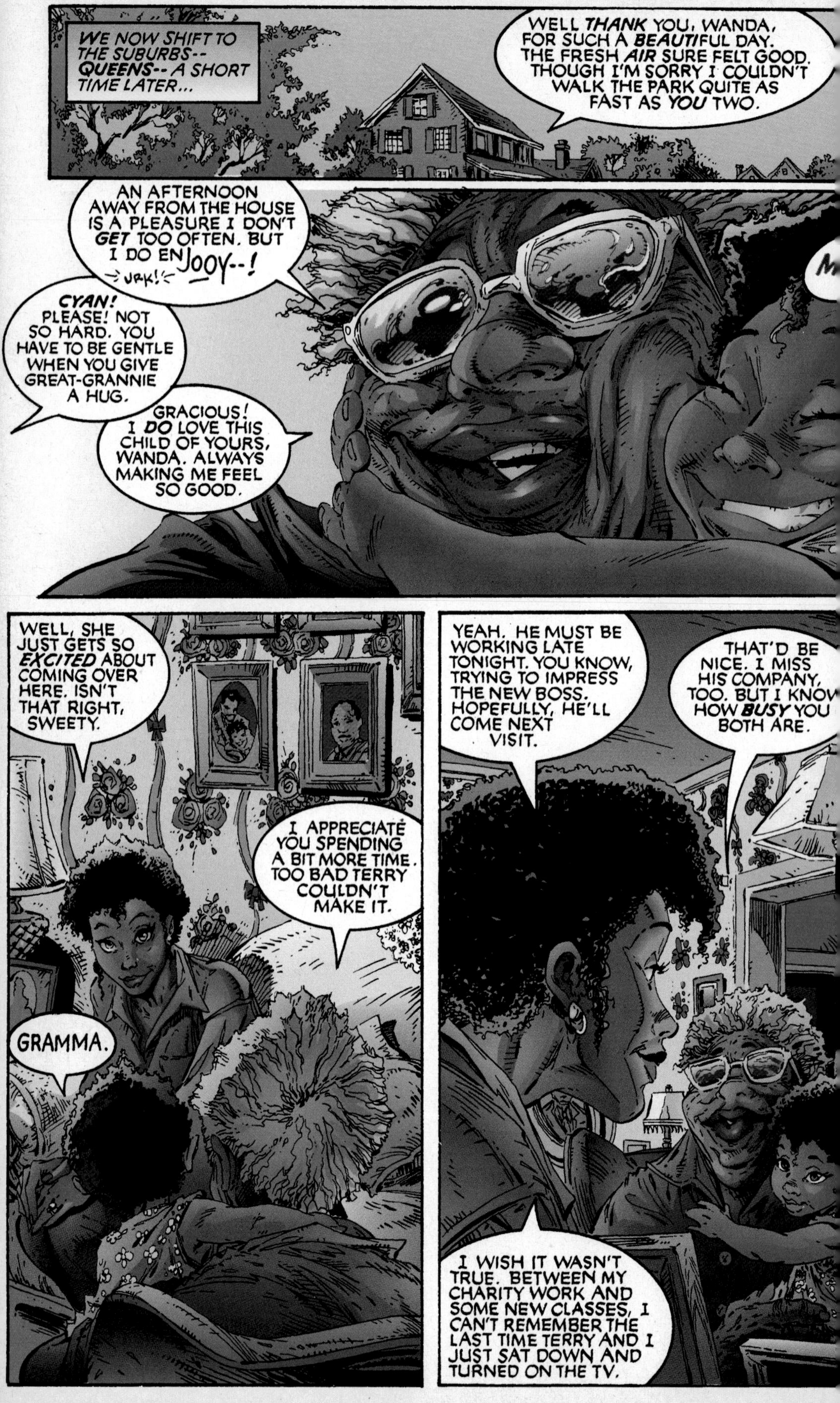
WE NOW SHIFT TO THE SUBURBS-- QUEENS-- A SHORT TIME LATER...
WELL THANK YOU, WANDA, FOR SUCH A BEAUTIFUL DAY. THE FRESH AIR SURE FELT GOOD. THOUGH I'M SORRY I COULDN'T WALK THE PARK QUITE AS FAST AS YOU TWO.
AN AFTERNOON AWAY FROM THE HOUSE IS A PLEASURE I DON'T GET TOO OFTEN. BUT I DO ENJOOY--!
URK!
CYAN! PLEASE! NOT SO HARD. YOU HAVE TO BE GENTLE WHEN YOU GIVE GREAT-GRANNIE A HUG.
GRACIOUS! I DO LOVE THIS CHILD OF YOURS, WANDA. ALWAYS MAKING ME FEEL SO GOOD.
WELL, SHE JUST GETS SO EXCITED ABOUT COMING OVER HERE. ISN'T THAT RIGHT, SWEETY.
GRAMMA.
I APPRECIATE YOU SPENDING A BIT MORE TIME. TOO BAD TERRY COULDN'T MAKE IT.
YEAH. HE MUST BE WORKING LATE TONIGHT. YOU KNOW, TRYING TO IMPRESS THE NEW BOSS. HOPEFULLY, HE'LL COME NEXT VISIT.
THAT'D BE NICE. I MISS HIS COMPANY, TOO. BUT I KNOW HOW BUSY YOU BOTH ARE.
I WISH IT WASN'T TRUE. BETWEEN MY CHARITY WORK AND SOME NEW CLASSES, I CAN'T REMEMBER THE LAST TIME TERRY AND I JUST SAT DOWN AND TURNED ON THE TV.

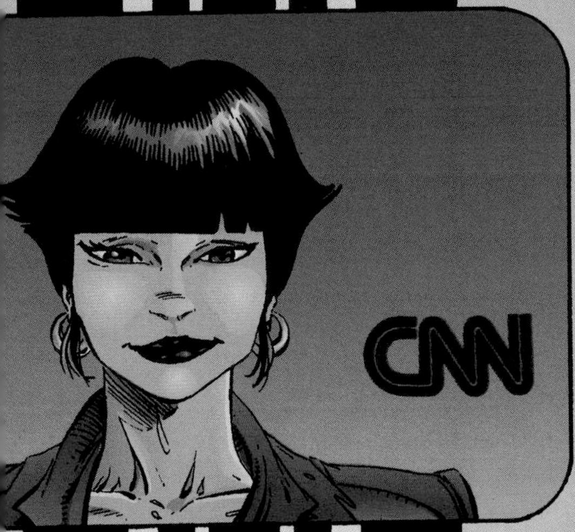
CNN

...CONTINUE OUR LIVE COVERAGE OF TONIGHT'S BOMBING AT NEW YORK CITY'S MERRILL-LYNCH BUILDING, AND THE REPORTED ASSAULT ON THE C.I.A HEADQUARTERS NEXT DOOR. POLICE SOURCES ARE CAUTIOUSLY OPTIMISTIC THAT NO ONE DIED IN THIS ATTACK ON THE NATION'S LARGEST BROKERAGE INSTITUTION. THE UPPER TWO STORIES OF THIS BUILDING, WHICH HOUSE THE GYM AND CAFETERIA, HAD ALREADY BEEN SECURED FOR THE NIGHT. IT IS BELIEVED THAT NO EMPLOYEES WERE WORKING LATE IN ANY OTHER AREAS, AND MOST HAVE BEEN LOCATED AT THEIR HOMES. THE WHITE HOUSE DENIES REPORTS THAT AN AS-YET UNIDENTIFIED TERRORIST GROUP HAD STAGED THE EVENT AS A REJECTION OF THE ADMINSTRATION'S PEACE NEGOTIATIONS IN THE MIDDLE EAST.

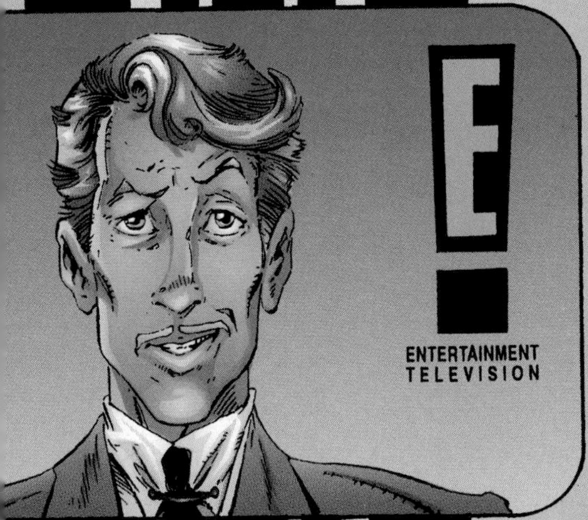
E!
ENTERTAINMENT TELEVISION

OFF THE RECORD SPECULATION FROM ***MY*** ANONYMOUS SOURCES IS THAT A ***HOME-GROWN*** TERRORIST GROUP WAS BLOWING A LOUD RASPBERY AT THE PRESIDENT'S MIDDLE EAST PEACE EFFORT. AT THE SAME TIME, FRENZIED SPIN DOCTORS ARE QUICK TO DISPEL ANY ***HINT*** OF A CONNECTION TO THE OKLAHOMA CITY INCIDENT. *"JUST THE ACTIONS OF ANOTHER DERANGED INDIVIDUAL"*, THEY TELL US, WHICH IS TO SAY, NOBODY HAS A ***CLUE.*** CONFUSING MATTERS EVEN FURTHER IS THE RAPID INVOLVEMENT OF OUR NATION'S MILITARY FORCES. SOME EYE-WITNESSES SAY IT WAS THE ***PRESENCE*** OF THE HELICOPTERS THAT TRIGGERED THE BOMBINGS, WHILE OTHERS MAINTAIN THE DAMAGE WAS DONE ***BEFORE*** THEIR ARRIVAL. IN EITHER CASE, EVERY AGENCY IN THE CITY IS NOW ON ALERT FOR POSSIBLE FOLLOW-UP ACTION. MEANWHILE, ALL EYES TURN TO THE WHITE HOUSE FOR SOMEONE -- ***ANY***ONE -- TO EXPLAIN IT ALL FOR US.

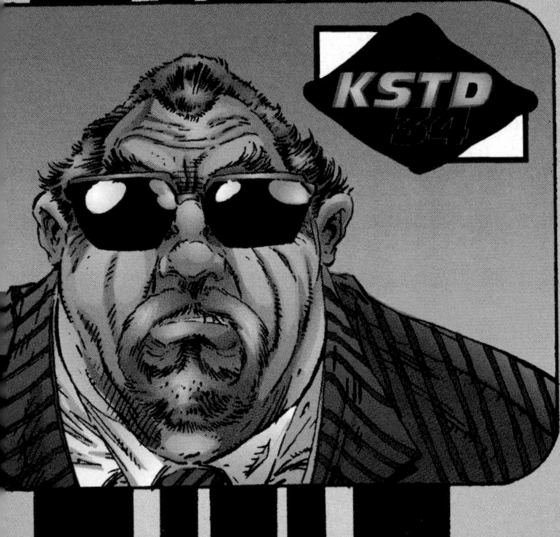
KSTD 34

ARE YOU ***KIDDING*** ME?! THIS ISN'T A CASE OF WHACKED-OUT IDIOTS LOOKING FOR ATTENTION, ***NO*** SIR! WHAT WE'RE LOOKING AT IS ***RETALIATION.*** SOME GROUP IS SENDING A MESSAGE TO THOSE WHO HIDE IN THE SHADOWS, PLAYING DOPEY SPY GAMES WITH OUR TAX DOLLARS. NO ONE IS ADMITTING ANYTHING, BUT ANYONE WHO THINKS THE C.I.A. ATTACK AND THE MERRILL-LYNCH BOMBING ARE UNRELATED IS EITHER ***IGNORANT*** OR ***STUPID.*** THIS WHOLE ***THING*** SMELLS ROTTEN. WORSE THAN THAT, THE PRESIDENT AND HIS AIDES ARE STONEWALLING. DIDN'T WE ELECT THESE GUYS BECAUSE THE ***PREVIOUS*** BUNCH WERE CLAIMING "DENIABILITY" TOO OFTEN?! SO NOW WE HAVE THE ***ARMY,*** THE ***FINANCIAL*** COMMUNITY AND THE ***CENTRAL INTELLIGENCE*** BOYS RUNNING AROUND IN AN ANT FARM, BUT FOR A CHANGE WE'VE GOT A MAGNIFYING GLASS ON 'EM. I GUARANTEE THAT ***SOME***ONE'S HIDING SOMETHING, AND THIS TIME WE JUST MIGHT FIND OUT WHAT IT IS.

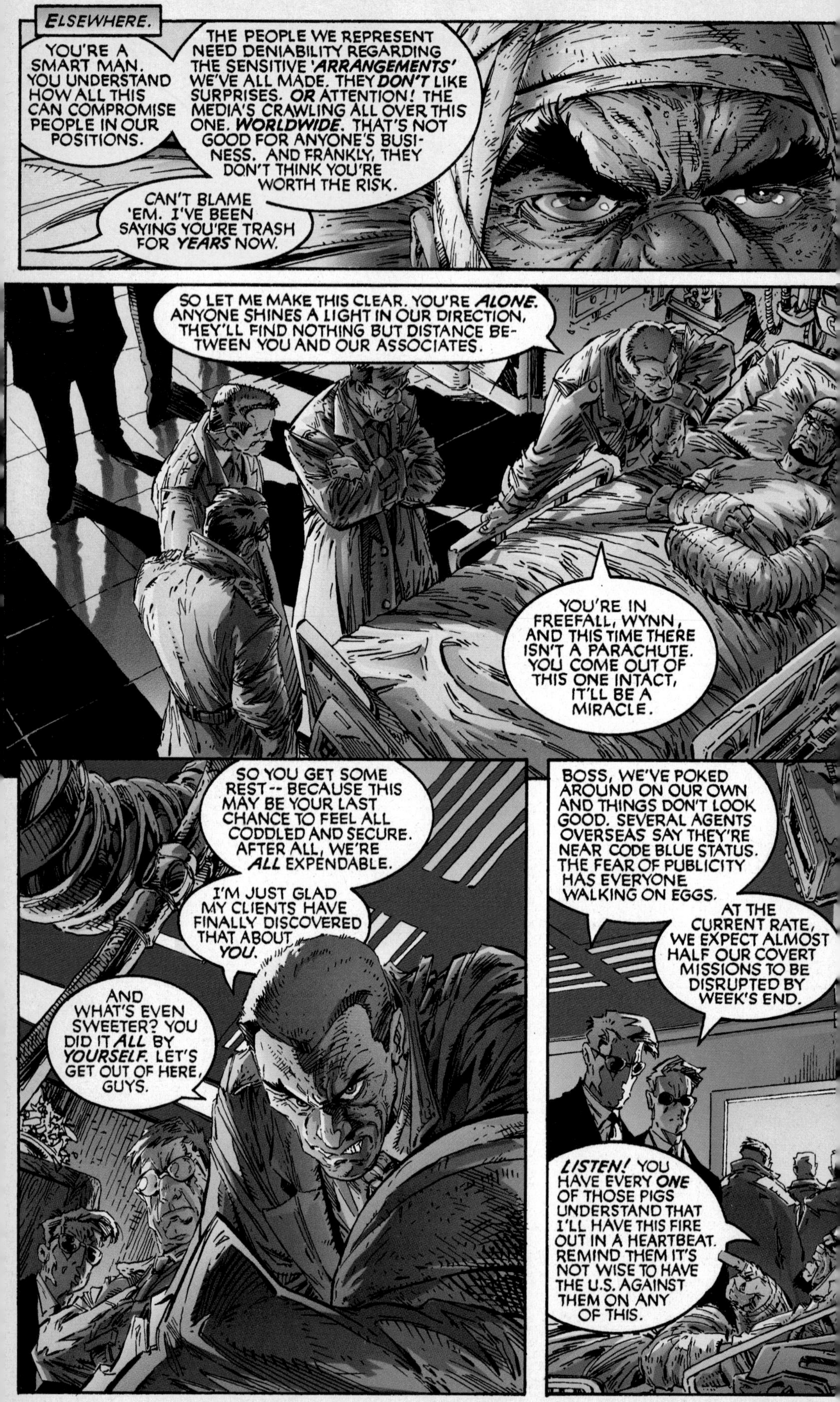
ELSEWHERE.
YOU'RE A SMART MAN. YOU UNDERSTAND HOW ALL THIS CAN COMPROMISE PEOPLE IN OUR POSITIONS.
THE PEOPLE WE REPRESENT NEED DENIABILITY REGARDING THE SENSITIVE 'ARRANGEMENTS' WE'VE ALL MADE. THEY DON'T LIKE SURPRISES. OR ATTENTION! THE MEDIA'S CRAWLING ALL OVER THIS ONE. WORLDWIDE. THAT'S NOT GOOD FOR ANYONE'S BUSINESS. AND FRANKLY, THEY DON'T THINK YOU'RE WORTH THE RISK.
CAN'T BLAME 'EM. I'VE BEEN SAYING YOU'RE TRASH FOR YEARS NOW.
SO LET ME MAKE THIS CLEAR. YOU'RE ALONE. ANYONE SHINES A LIGHT IN OUR DIRECTION, THEY'LL FIND NOTHING BUT DISTANCE BETWEEN YOU AND OUR ASSOCIATES.
YOU'RE IN FREEFALL, WYNN, AND THIS TIME THERE ISN'T A PARACHUTE. YOU COME OUT OF THIS ONE INTACT, IT'LL BE A MIRACLE.
SO YOU GET SOME REST -- BECAUSE THIS MAY BE YOUR LAST CHANCE TO FEEL ALL CODDLED AND SECURE. AFTER ALL, WE'RE ALL EXPENDABLE.
I'M JUST GLAD MY CLIENTS HAVE FINALLY DISCOVERED THAT ABOUT YOU.
AND WHAT'S EVEN SWEETER? YOU DID IT ALL BY YOURSELF. LET'S GET OUT OF HERE, GUYS.
BOSS, WE'VE POKED AROUND ON OUR OWN AND THINGS DON'T LOOK GOOD. SEVERAL AGENTS OVERSEAS SAY THEY'RE NEAR CODE BLUE STATUS. THE FEAR OF PUBLICITY HAS EVERYONE WALKING ON EGGS.
AT THE CURRENT RATE, WE EXPECT ALMOST HALF OUR COVERT MISSIONS TO BE DISRUPTED BY WEEK'S END.
LISTEN! YOU HAVE EVERY ONE OF THOSE PIGS UNDERSTAND THAT I'LL HAVE THIS FIRE OUT IN A HEARTBEAT. REMIND THEM IT'S NOT WISE TO HAVE THE U.S. AGAINST THEM ON ANY OF THIS.

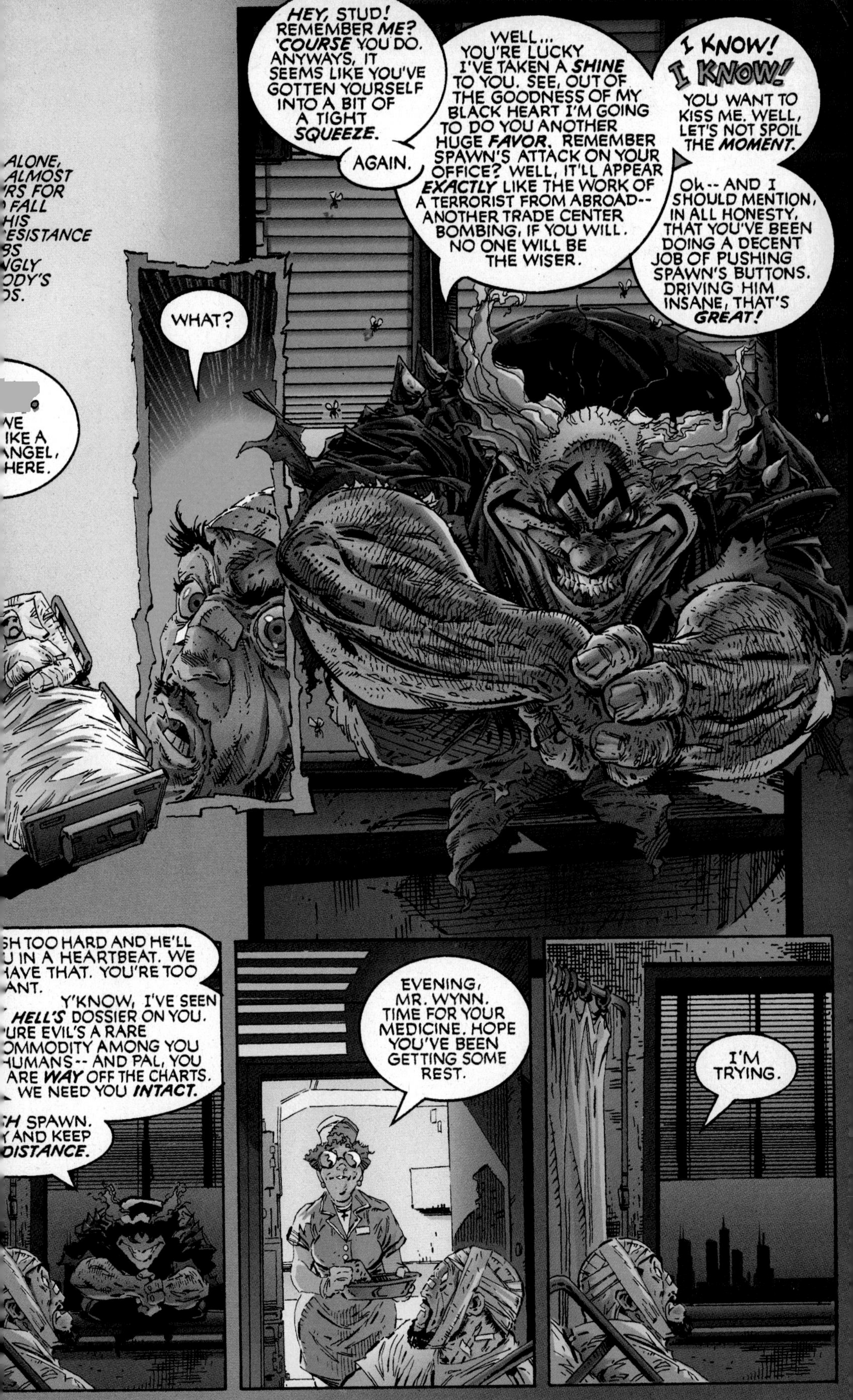
HEY, STUD! REMEMBER ME? 'COURSE YOU DO. ANYWAYS, IT SEEMS LIKE YOU'VE GOTTEN YOURSELF INTO A BIT OF A TIGHT SQUEEZE.
AGAIN.
WELL... YOU'RE LUCKY I'VE TAKEN A SHINE TO YOU. SEE, OUT OF THE GOODNESS OF MY BLACK HEART I'M GOING TO DO YOU ANOTHER HUGE FAVOR. REMEMBER SPAWN'S ATTACK ON YOUR OFFICE? WELL, IT'LL APPEAR EXACTLY LIKE THE WORK OF A TERRORIST FROM ABROAD-- ANOTHER TRADE CENTER BOMBING, IF YOU WILL. NO ONE WILL BE THE WISER.
I KNOW! I KNOW! YOU WANT TO KISS ME. WELL, LET'S NOT SPOIL THE MOMENT.
Oh-- AND I SHOULD MENTION, IN ALL HONESTY, THAT YOU'VE BEEN DOING A DECENT JOB OF PUSHING SPAWN'S BUTTONS. DRIVING HIM INSANE, THAT'S GREAT!
WHAT?
Y'KNOW, I'VE SEEN HELL'S DOSSIER ON YOU.
EVENING, MR. WYNN. TIME FOR YOUR MEDICINE. HOPE YOU'VE BEEN GETTING SOME REST.
I'M TRYING.

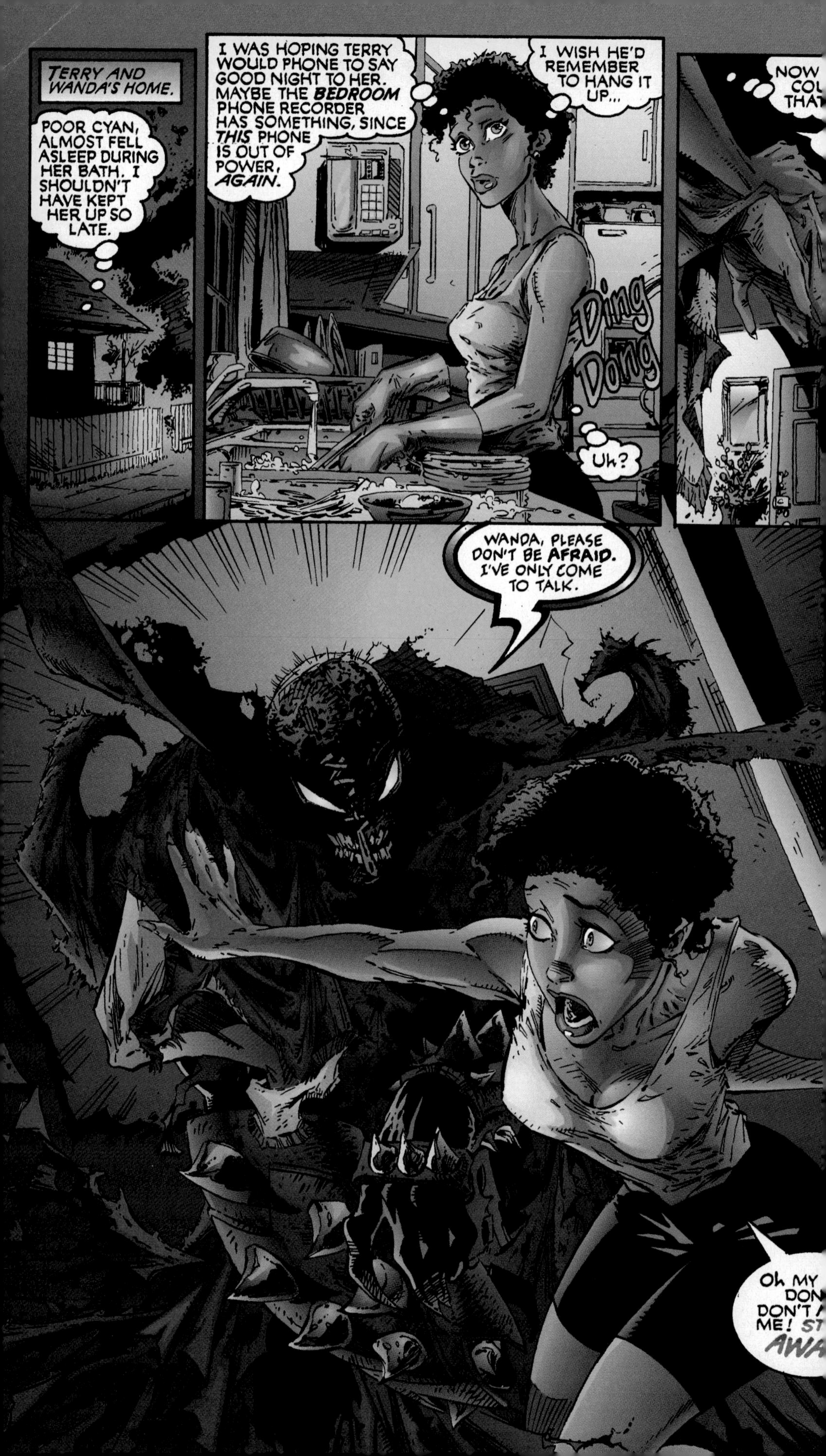

TERRY AND WANDA'S HOME.
POOR CYAN, ALMOST FELL ASLEEP DURING HER BATH. I SHOULDN'T HAVE KEPT HER UP SO LATE.
I WAS HOPING TERRY WOULD PHONE TO SAY GOOD NIGHT TO HER. MAYBE THE BEDROOM PHONE RECORDER HAS SOMETHING, SINCE THIS PHONE IS OUT OF POWER, AGAIN.
I WISH HE'D REMEMBER TO HANG IT UP...
Ding Dong
Uh?
WANDA, PLEASE DON'T BE AFRAID. I'VE ONLY COME TO TALK.

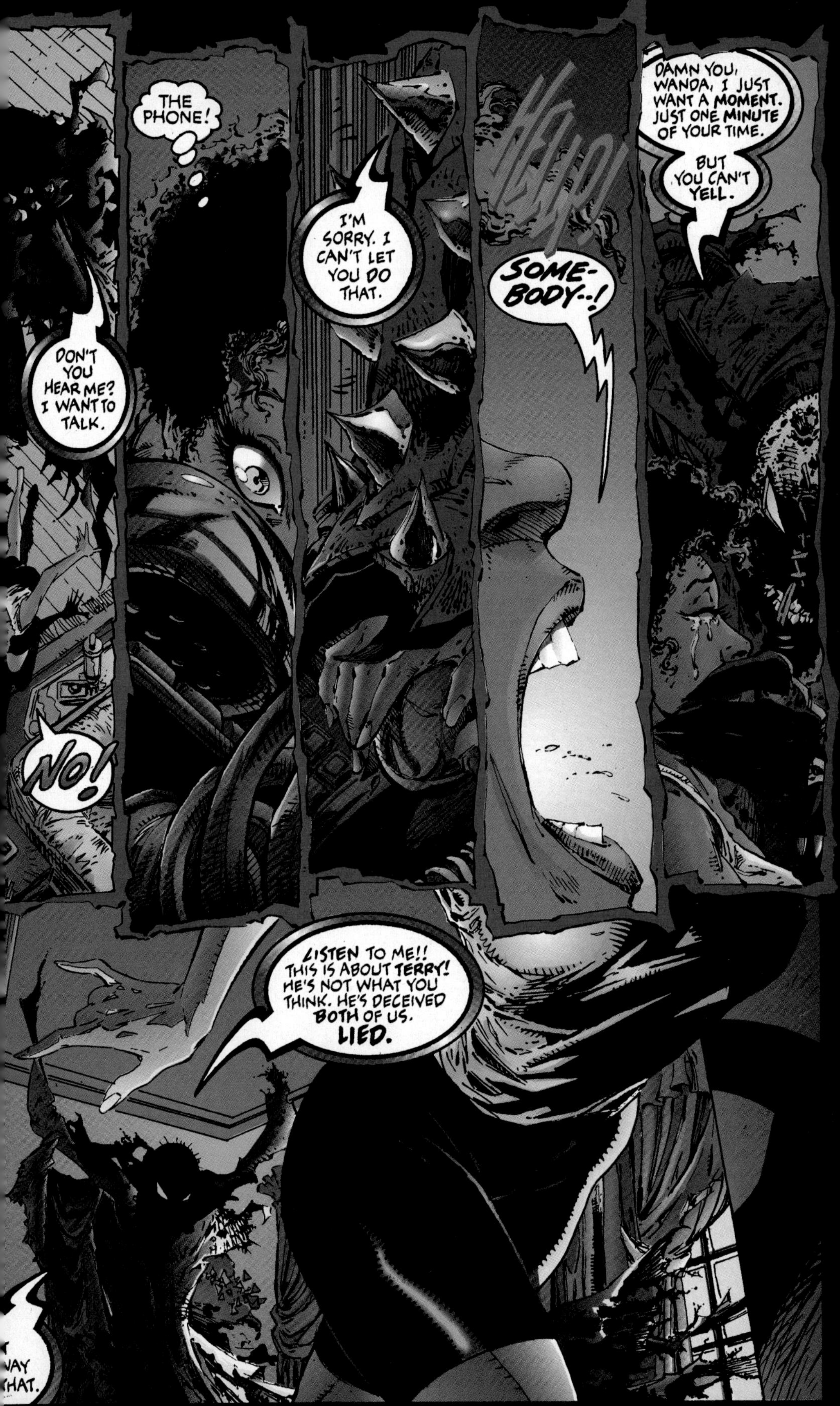
DON'T YOU HEAR ME? I WANT TO TALK.
NO!
THE PHONE!
I'M SORRY. I CAN'T LET YOU DO THAT.
HELP!
SOME-BODY--!
DAMN YOU, WANDA, I JUST WANT A MOMENT. JUST ONE MINUTE OF YOUR TIME.
BUT YOU CAN'T YELL.
LISTEN TO ME!! THIS IS ABOUT TERRY! HE'S NOT WHAT YOU THINK. HE'S DECEIVED BOTH OF US. LIED.

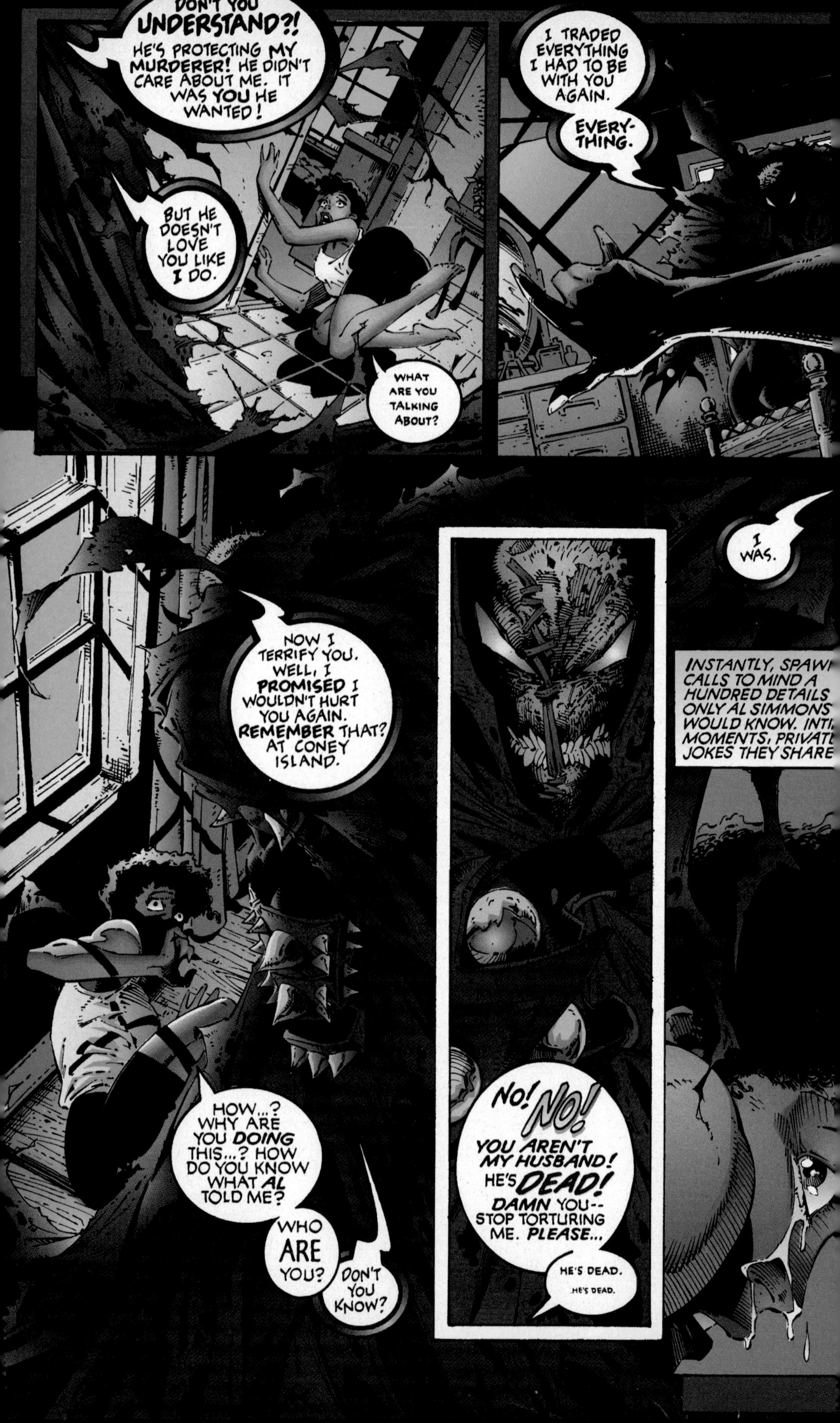
DON'T YOU UNDERSTAND?! HE'S PROTECTING MY MURDERER! HE DIDN'T CARE ABOUT ME. IT WAS YOU HE WANTED!
BUT HE DOESN'T LOVE YOU LIKE I DO.
WHAT ARE YOU TALKING ABOUT?
I TRADED EVERYTHING I HAD TO BE WITH YOU AGAIN.
EVERY-THING.
NOW I TERRIFY YOU. WELL, I PROMISED I WOULDN'T HURT YOU AGAIN. REMEMBER THAT? AT CONEY ISLAND.
HOW...? WHY ARE YOU DOING THIS...? HOW DO YOU KNOW WHAT AL TOLD ME?
WHO ARE YOU?
DON'T YOU KNOW?
NO! NO! YOU AREN'T MY HUSBAND! HE'S DEAD! DAMN YOU-- STOP TORTURING ME. PLEASE...
HE'S DEAD.
HE'S DEAD.
I WAS.
INSTANTLY, SPAWN CALLS TO MIND A HUNDRED DETAILS ONLY AL SIMMONS WOULD KNOW. INTI MOMENTS, PRIVATE JOKES THEY SHARE

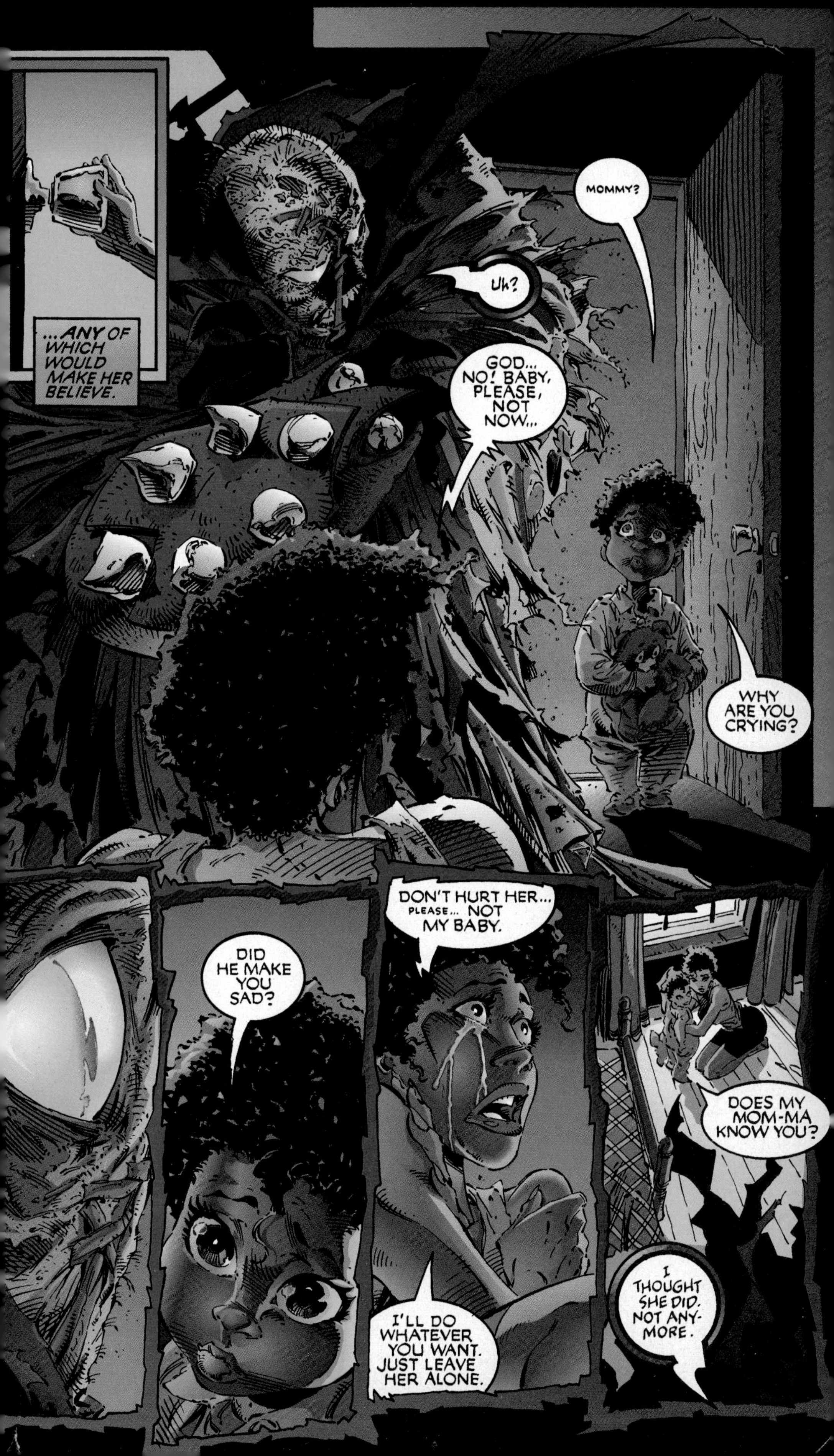
...ANY OF WHICH WOULD MAKE HER BELIEVE.
MOMMY?
Uh?
GOD... NO! BABY, PLEASE, NOT NOW...
WHY ARE YOU CRYING?
DID HE MAKE YOU SAD?
DON'T HURT HER... PLEASE... NOT MY BABY.
I'LL DO WHATEVER YOU WANT. JUST LEAVE HER ALONE.
DOES MY MOM-MA KNOW YOU?
I THOUGHT SHE DID. NOT ANY-MORE.

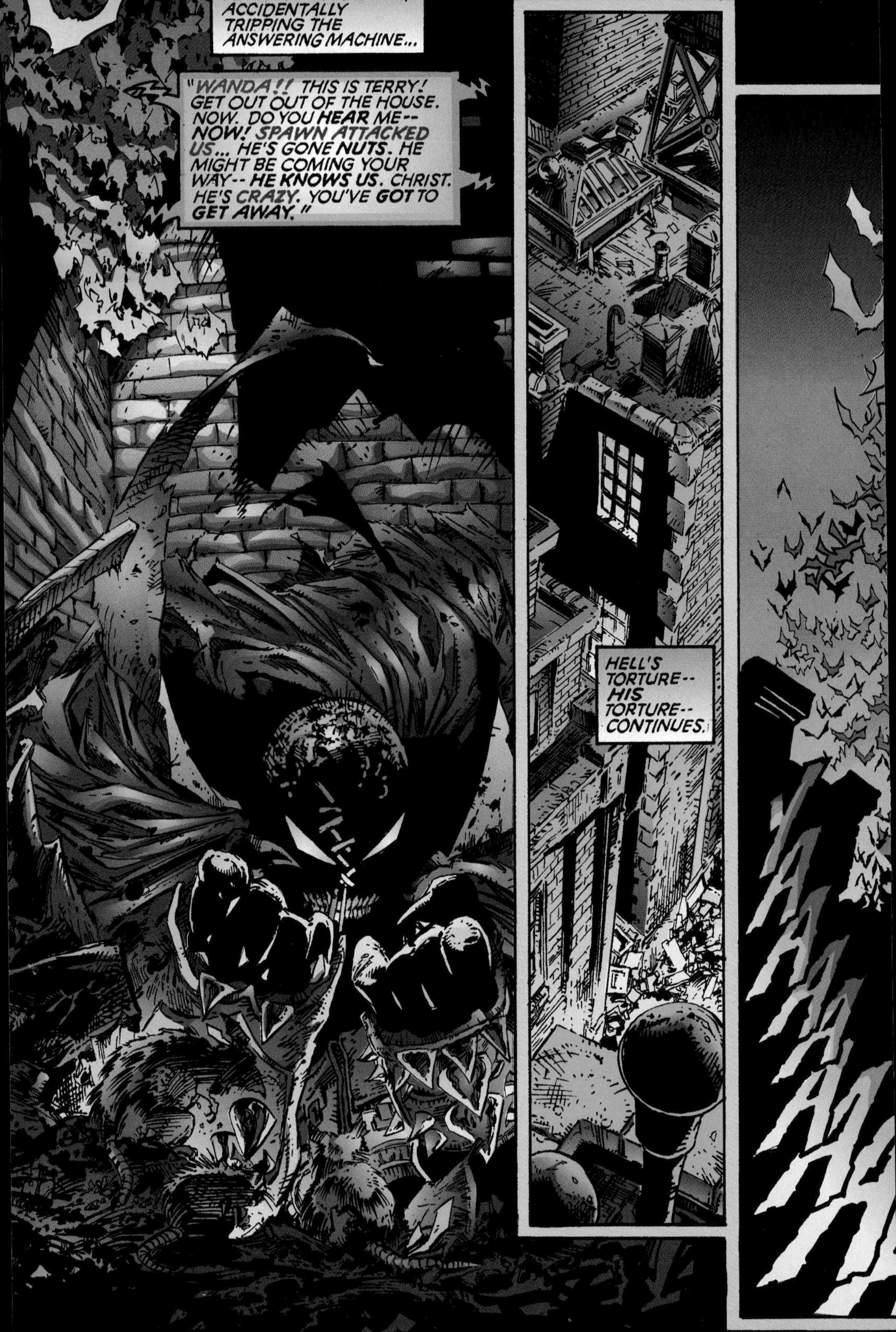
ACCIDENTALLY TRIPPING THE ANSWERING MACHINE...
"WANDA!! THIS IS TERRY! GET OUT OUT OF THE HOUSE. NOW. DO YOU HEAR ME-- NOW! SPAWN ATTACKED US... HE'S GONE NUTS. HE MIGHT BE COMING YOUR WAY-- HE KNOWS US. CHRIST. HE'S CRAZY. YOU'VE GOT TO GET AWAY."
HELL'S TORTURE-- HIS TORTURE-- CONTINUES.

SPAWN

mind games

38

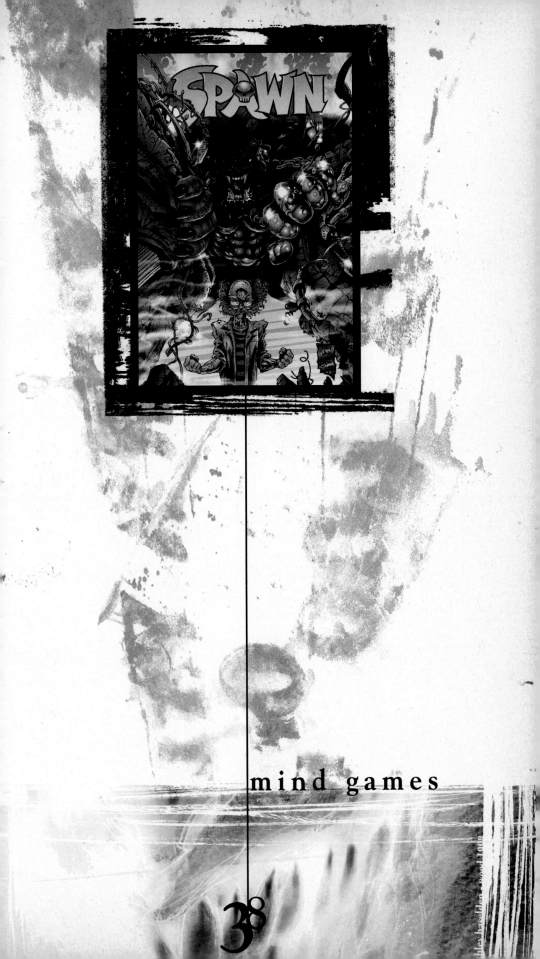

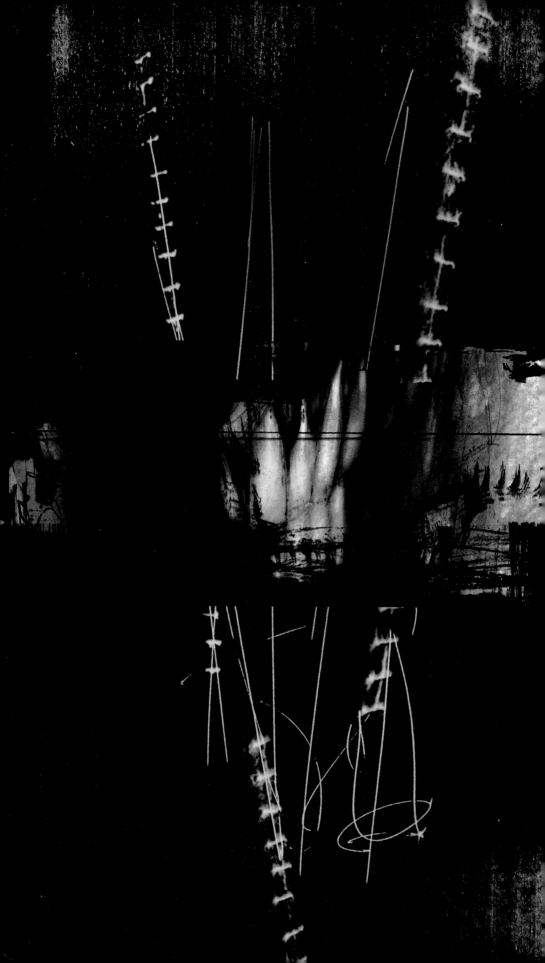

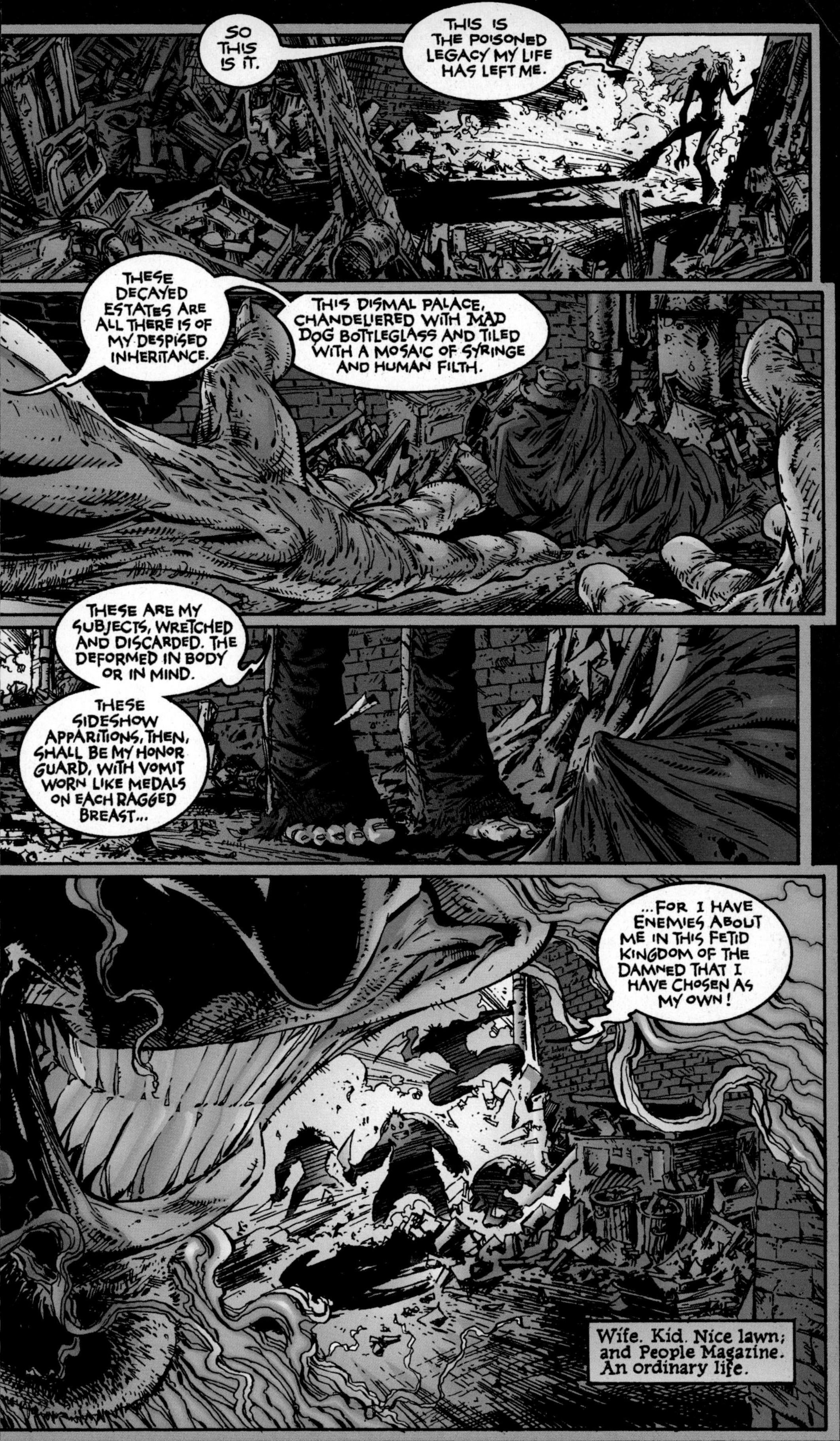
SO THIS IS IT.
THIS IS THE POISONED LEGACY MY LIFE HAS LEFT ME.
THESE DECAYED ESTATES ARE ALL THERE IS OF MY DESPISED INHERITANCE.
THIS DISMAL PALACE, CHANDELIERED WITH MAD DOG BOTTLEGLASS AND TILED WITH A MOSAIC OF SYRINGE AND HUMAN FILTH.
THESE ARE MY SUBJECTS, WRETCHED AND DISCARDED. THE DEFORMED IN BODY OR IN MIND.
THESE SIDESHOW APPARITIONS, THEN, SHALL BE MY HONOR GUARD, WITH VOMIT WORN LIKE MEDALS ON EACH RAGGED BREAST...
...FOR I HAVE ENEMIES ABOUT ME IN THIS FETID KINGDOM OF THE DAMNED THAT I HAVE CHOSEN AS MY OWN!
Wife. Kid. Nice lawn; and People Magazine. An ordinary life.

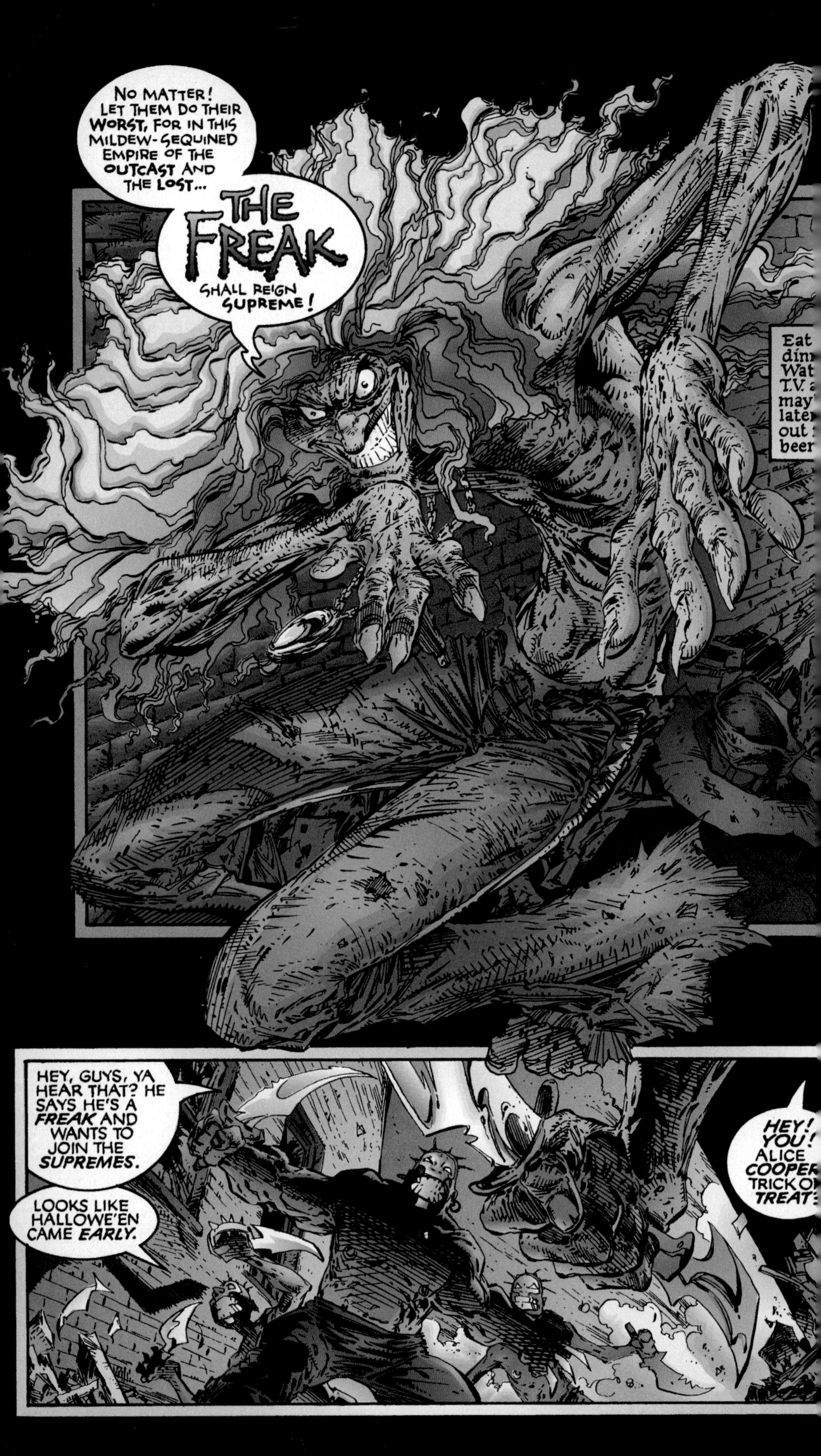
NO MATTER! LET THEM DO THEIR WORST, FOR IN THIS MILDEW-SEQUINED EMPIRE OF THE OUTCAST AND THE LOST...
THE FREAK SHALL REIGN SUPREME!
Eat dinn Wat T.V. a may later out beer
HEY, GUYS, YA HEAR THAT? HE SAYS HE'S A FREAK AND WANTS TO JOIN THE SUPREMES.
LOOKS LIKE HALLOWE'EN CAME EARLY.
HEY! YOU! ALICE COOPER TRICK O TREAT

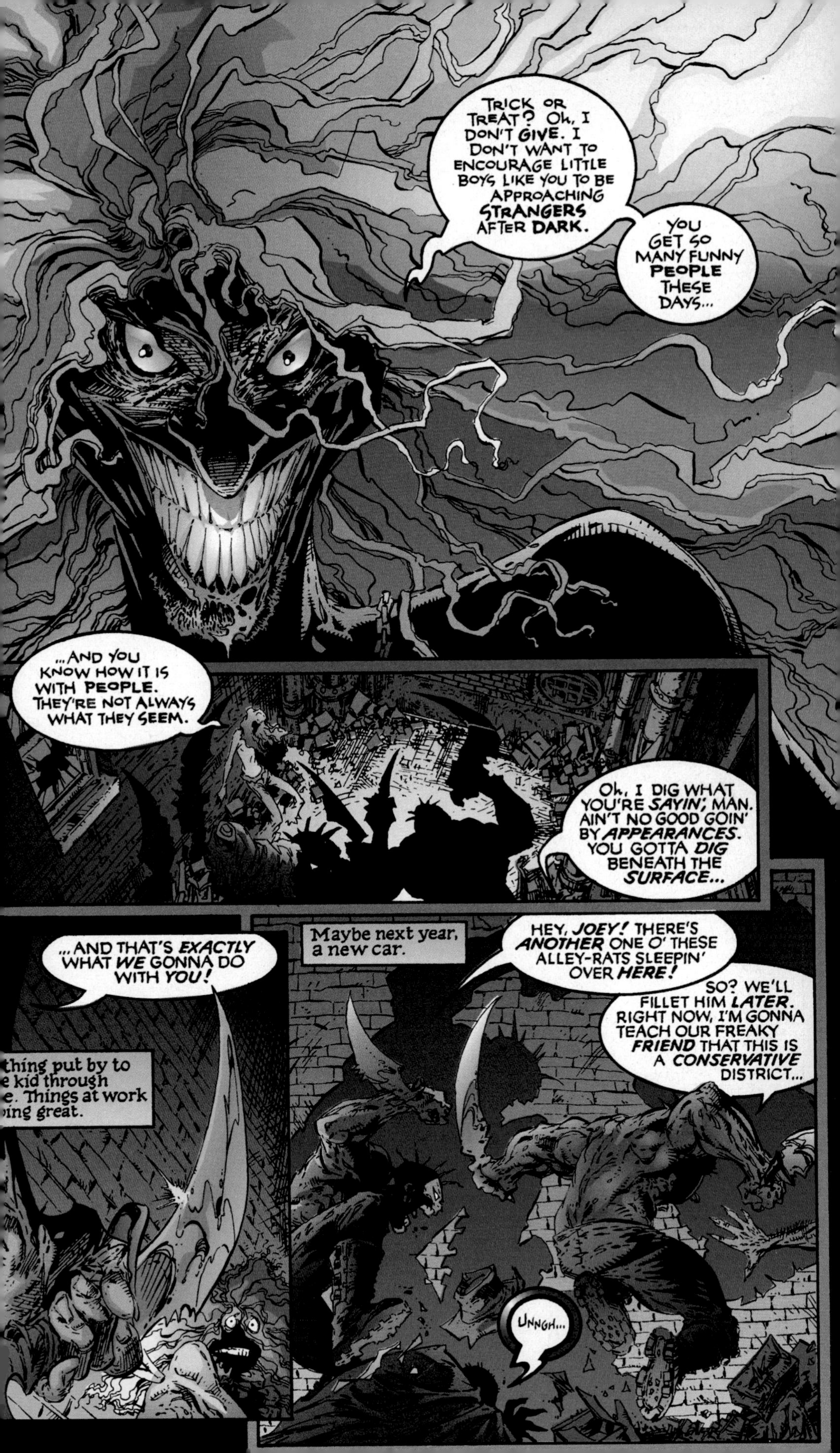
TRICK OR TREAT? Oh, I DON'T GIVE. I DON'T WANT TO ENCOURAGE LITTLE BOYS LIKE YOU TO BE APPROACHING STRANGERS AFTER DARK.
YOU GET SO MANY FUNNY PEOPLE THESE DAYS...
...AND YOU KNOW HOW IT IS WITH PEOPLE. THEY'RE NOT ALWAYS WHAT THEY SEEM.
Oh, I DIG WHAT YOU'RE SAYIN', MAN. AIN'T NO GOOD GOIN' BY APPEARANCES. YOU GOTTA DIG BENEATH THE SURFACE...
...AND THAT'S EXACTLY WHAT WE GONNA DO WITH YOU!
thing put by to
e kid through
e. Things at work
oing great.
Maybe next year, a new car.
HEY, JOEY! THERE'S ANOTHER ONE O' THESE ALLEY-RATS SLEEPIN' OVER HERE!
SO? WE'LL FILLET HIM LATER. RIGHT NOW, I'M GONNA TEACH OUR FREAKY FRIEND THAT THIS IS A CONSERVATIVE DISTRICT...
UNNGH...

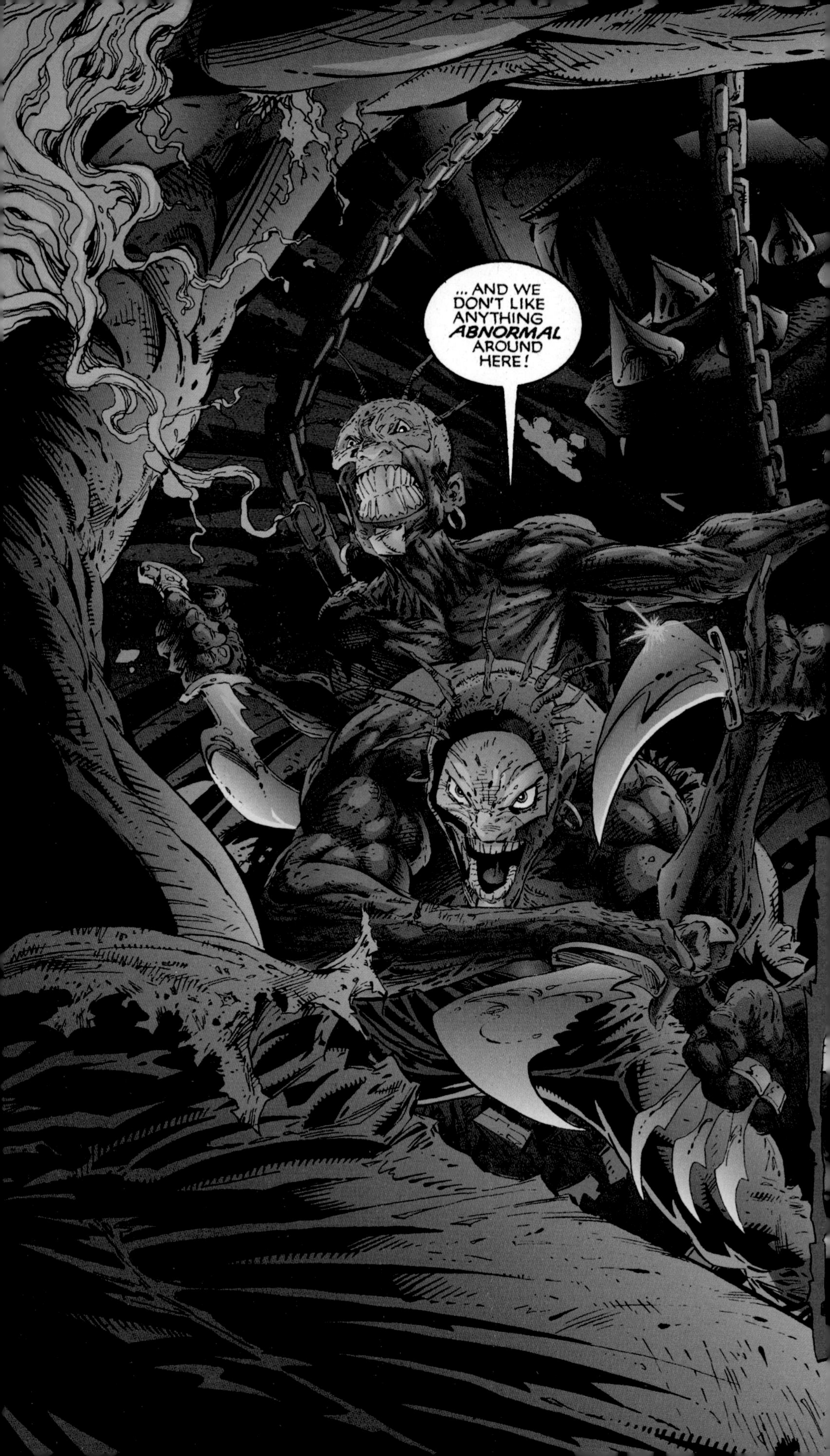
...AND WE DON'T LIKE ANYTHING ABNORMAL AROUND HERE!

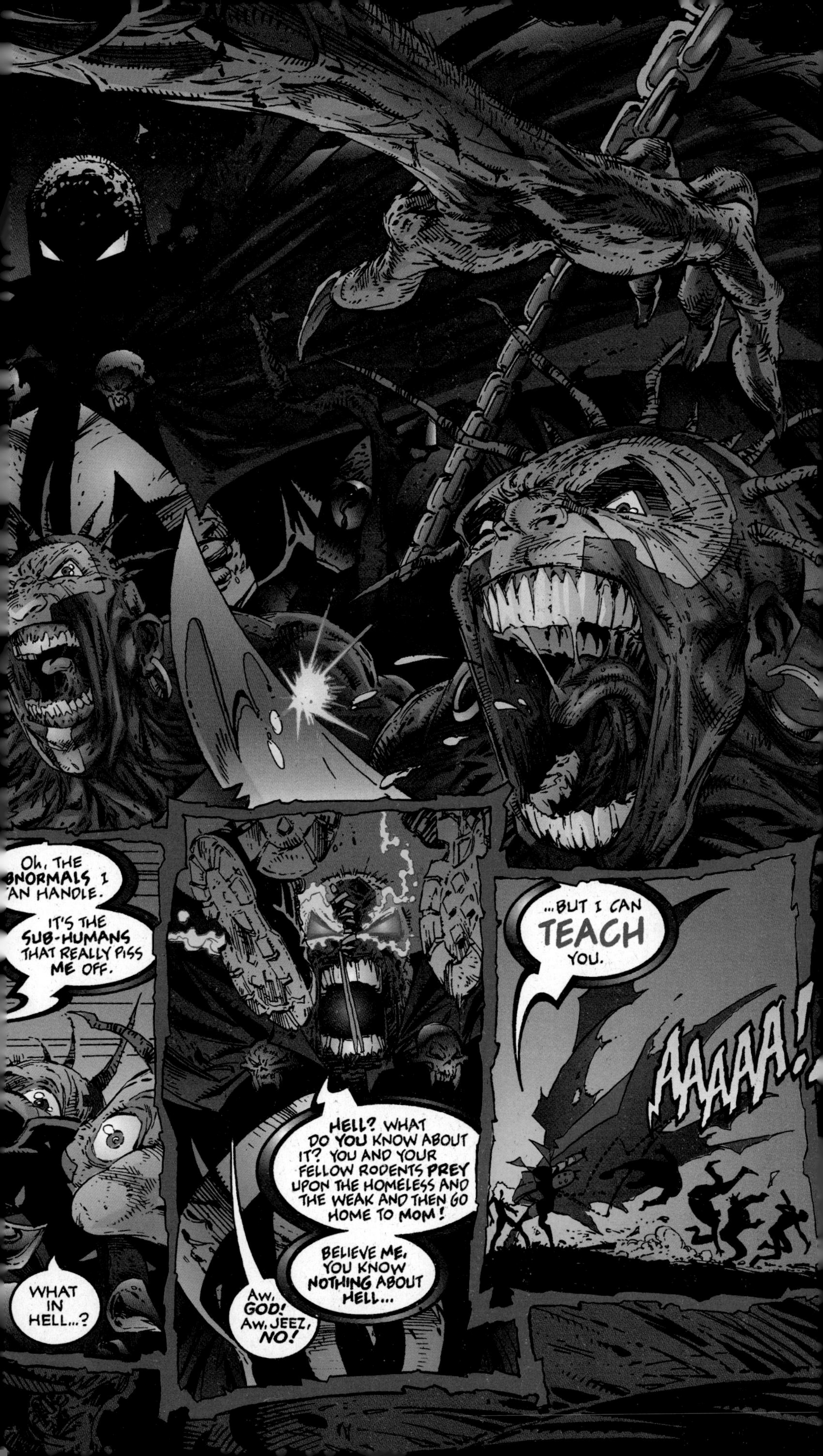

Oh, THE BNORMALS I CAN HANDLE.
IT'S THE SUB-HUMANS THAT REALLY PISS ME OFF.
WHAT IN HELL...?
HELL? WHAT DO YOU KNOW ABOUT IT? YOU AND YOUR FELLOW RODENTS PREY UPON THE HOMELESS AND THE WEAK AND THEN GO HOME TO MOM!
BELIEVE ME, YOU KNOW NOTHING ABOUT HELL...
AW, GOD! AW, JEEZ, NO!
...BUT I CAN TEACH YOU.
AAAAA!

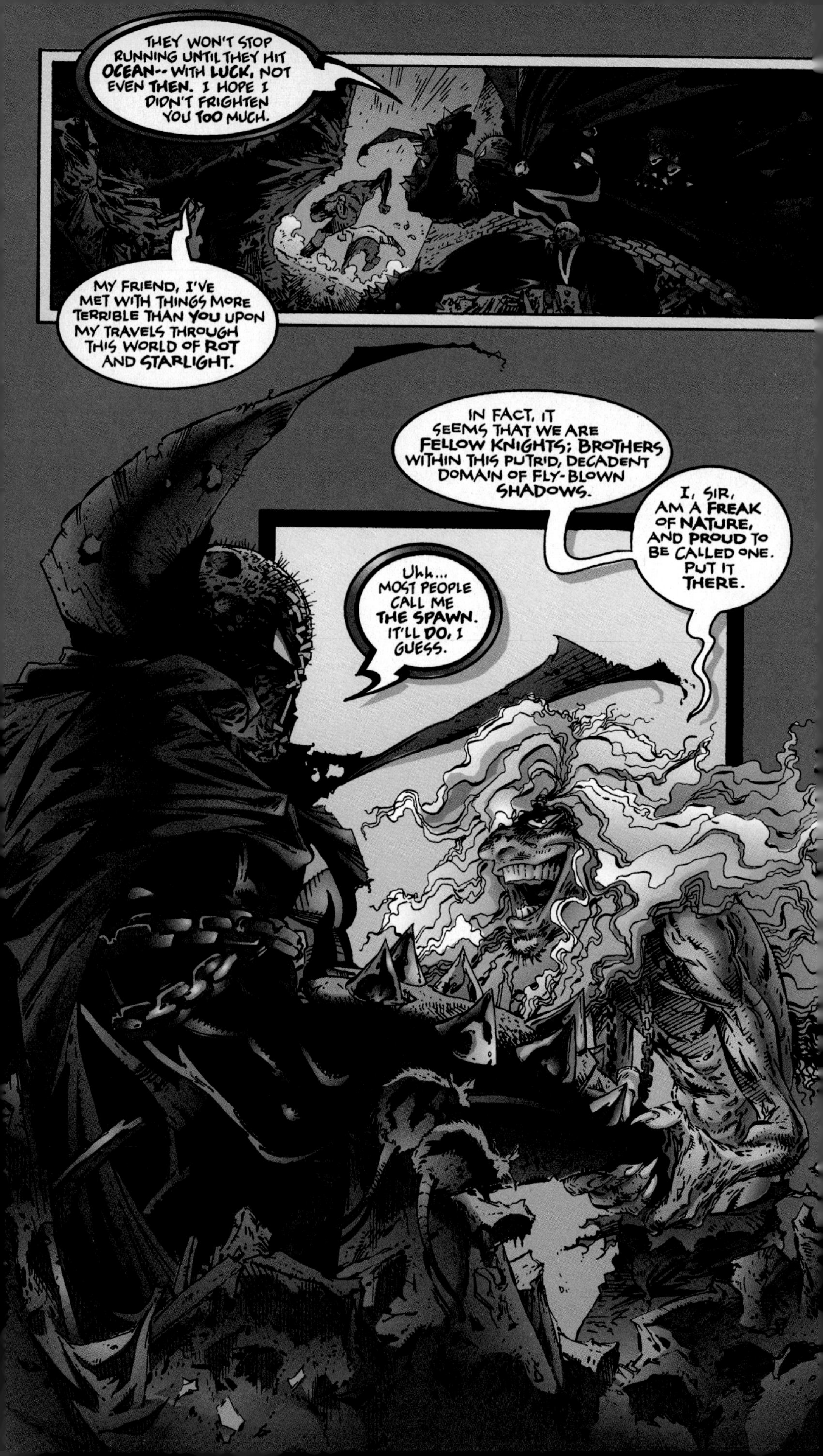
THEY WON'T STOP RUNNING UNTIL THEY HIT OCEAN-- WITH LUCK, NOT EVEN THEN. I HOPE I DIDN'T FRIGHTEN YOU TOO MUCH.
MY FRIEND, I'VE MET WITH THINGS MORE TERRIBLE THAN YOU UPON MY TRAVELS THROUGH THIS WORLD OF ROT AND STARLIGHT.
IN FACT, IT SEEMS THAT WE ARE FELLOW KNIGHTS; BROTHERS WITHIN THIS PUTRID, DECADENT DOMAIN OF FLY-BLOWN SHADOWS.
I, SIR, AM A FREAK OF NATURE, AND PROUD TO BE CALLED ONE. PUT IT THERE.
Uhh... MOST PEOPLE CALL ME THE SPAWN. IT'LL DO, I GUESS.

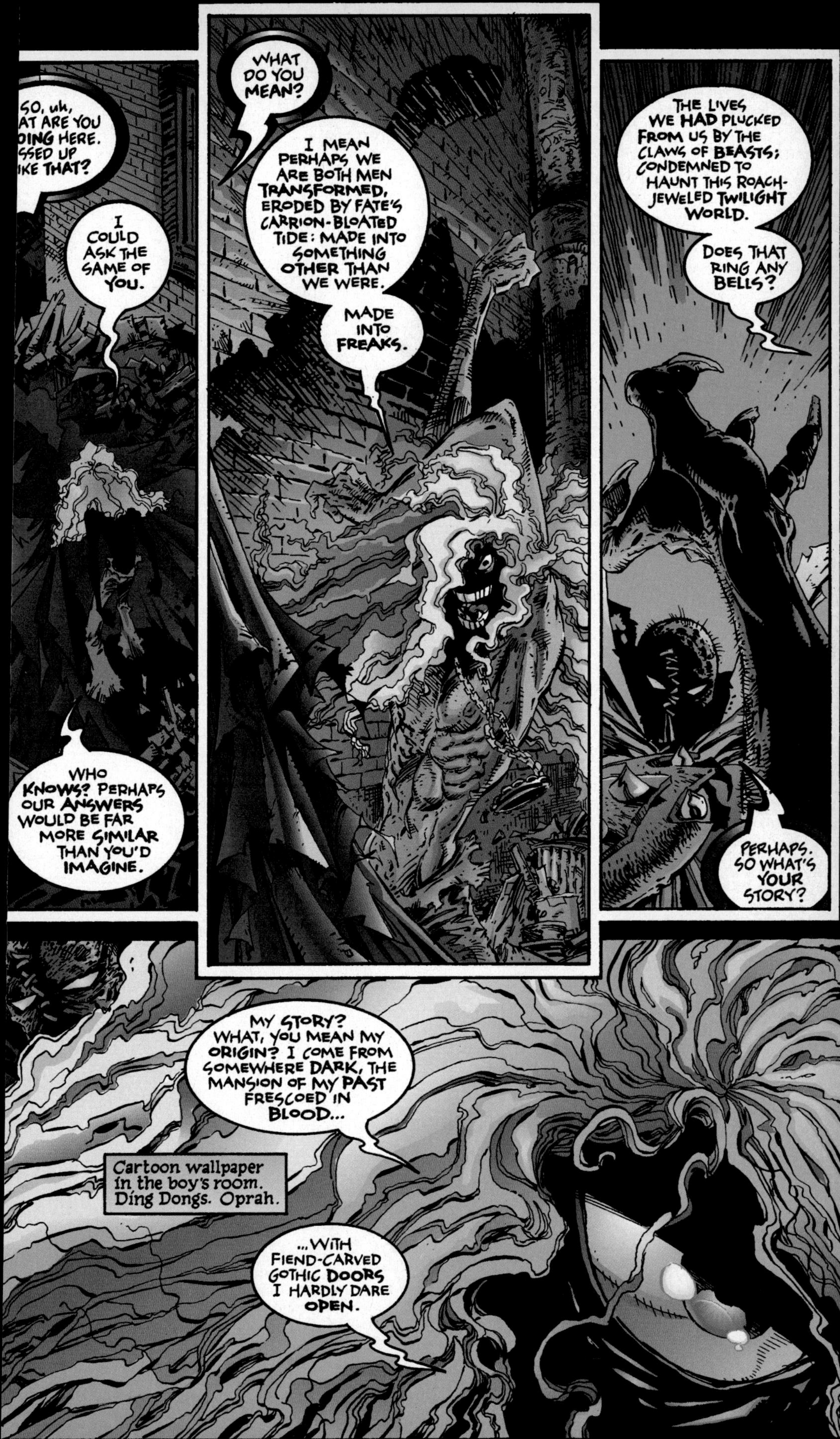
SO, uh,
AT ARE YOU
OING HERE.
SSED UP
IKE THAT?
I COULD ASK THE SAME OF YOU.
WHO KNOWS? PERHAPS OUR ANSWERS WOULD BE FAR MORE SIMILAR THAN YOU'D IMAGINE.
WHAT DO YOU MEAN?
I MEAN PERHAPS WE ARE BOTH MEN TRANSFORMED, ERODED BY FATE'S CARRION-BLOATED TIDE: MADE INTO SOMETHING OTHER THAN WE WERE.
MADE INTO FREAKS.
THE LIVES WE HAD PLUCKED FROM US BY THE CLAWS OF BEASTS; CONDEMNED TO HAUNT THIS ROACH-JEWELED TWILIGHT WORLD.
DOES THAT RING ANY BELLS?
PERHAPS. SO WHAT'S YOUR STORY?
MY STORY? WHAT, YOU MEAN MY ORIGIN? I COME FROM SOMEWHERE DARK, THE MANSION OF MY PAST FRESCOED IN BLOOD...
Cartoon wallpaper in the boy's room. Ding Dongs. Oprah.
...WITH FIEND-CARVED GOTHIC DOORS I HARDLY DARE OPEN.

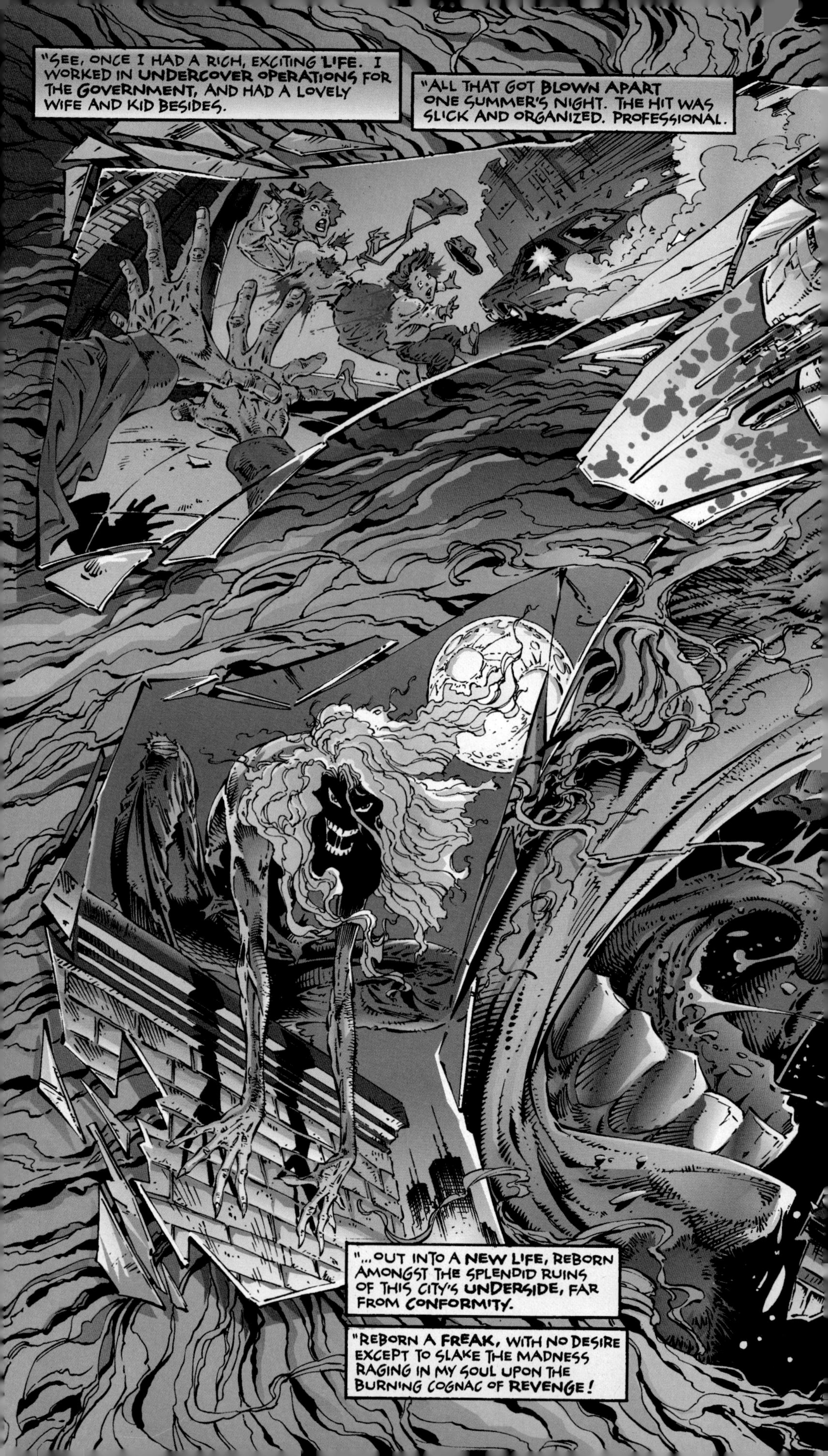
"SEE, ONCE I HAD A RICH, EXCITING LIFE. I WORKED IN UNDERCOVER OPERATIONS FOR THE GOVERNMENT, AND HAD A LOVELY WIFE AND KID BESIDES.
"ALL THAT GOT BLOWN APART ONE SUMMER'S NIGHT. THE HIT WAS SLICK AND ORGANIZED. PROFESSIONAL.
"...OUT INTO A NEW LIFE, REBORN AMONGST THE SPLENDID RUINS OF THIS CITY'S UNDERSIDE, FAR FROM CONFORMITY.
"REBORN A FREAK, WITH NO DESIRE EXCEPT TO SLAKE THE MADNESS RAGING IN MY SOUL UPON THE BURNING COGNAC OF REVENGE!

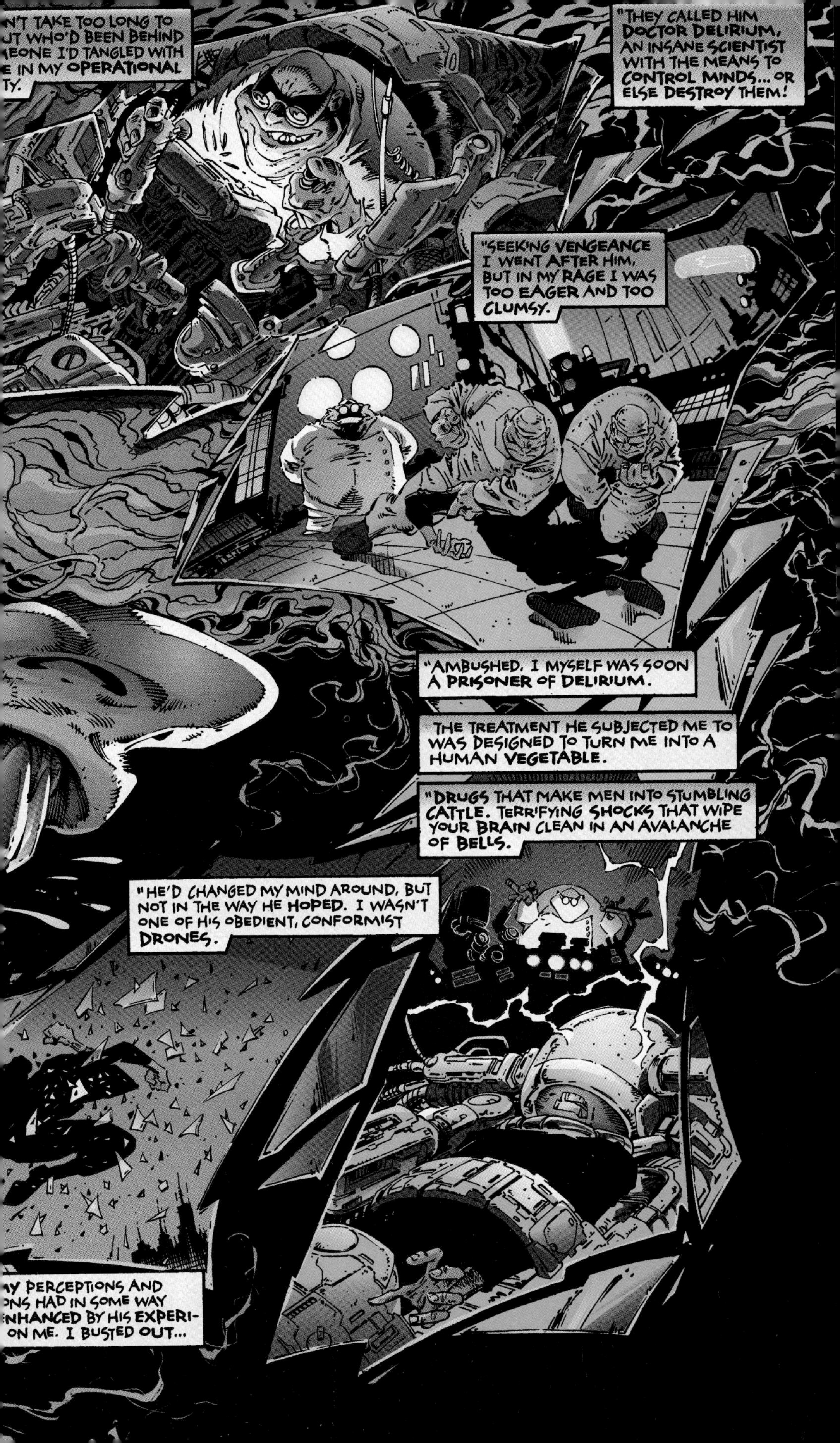

N'T TAKE TOO LONG TO UT WHO'D BEEN BEHIND IEONE I'D TANGLED WITH E IN MY OPERATIONAL TY.
"THEY CALLED HIM DOCTOR DELIRIUM, AN INSANE SCIENTIST WITH THE MEANS TO CONTROL MINDS... OR ELSE DESTROY THEM!
"SEEKING VENGEANCE I WENT AFTER HIM, BUT IN MY RAGE I WAS TOO EAGER AND TOO CLUMSY.
"AMBUSHED, I MYSELF WAS SOON A PRISONER OF DELIRIUM.
THE TREATMENT HE SUBJECTED ME TO WAS DESIGNED TO TURN ME INTO A HUMAN VEGETABLE.
"DRUGS THAT MAKE MEN INTO STUMBLING CATTLE. TERRIFYING SHOCKS THAT WIPE YOUR BRAIN CLEAN IN AN AVALANCHE OF BELLS.
"HE'D CHANGED MY MIND AROUND, BUT NOT IN THE WAY HE HOPED. I WASN'T ONE OF HIS OBEDIENT, CONFORMIST DRONES.
MY PERCEPTIONS AND ONS HAD IN SOME WAY ENHANCED BY HIS EXPERI- ON ME. I BUSTED OUT...

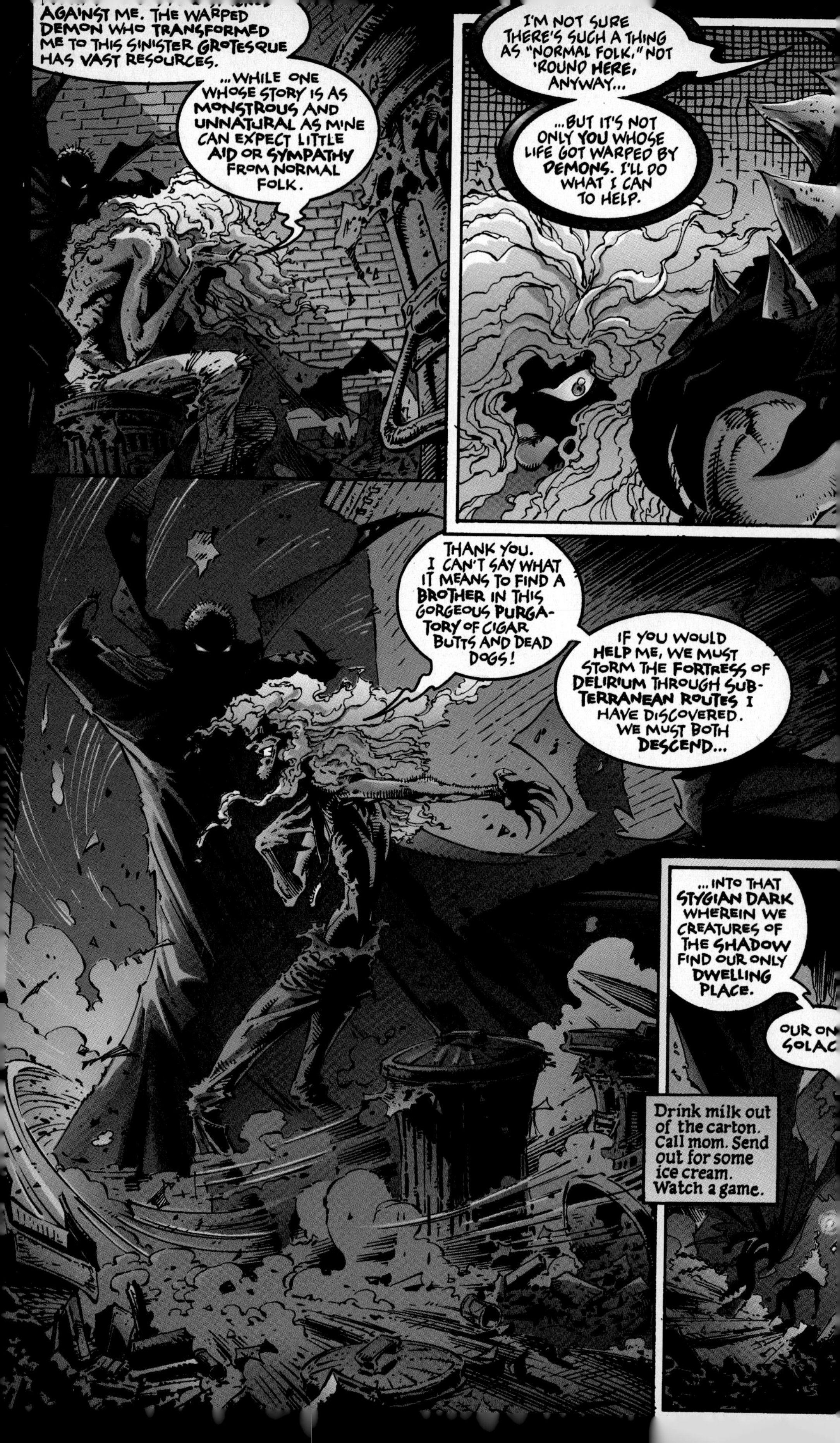
AGAINST ME. THE WARPED DEMON WHO TRANSFORMED ME TO THIS SINISTER GROTESQUE HAS VAST RESOURCES.
...WHILE ONE WHOSE STORY IS AS MONSTROUS AND UNNATURAL AS MINE CAN EXPECT LITTLE AID OR SYMPATHY FROM NORMAL FOLK.
I'M NOT SURE THERE'S SUCH A THING AS "NORMAL FOLK," NOT 'ROUND HERE, ANYWAY...
...BUT IT'S NOT ONLY YOU WHOSE LIFE GOT WARPED BY DEMONS. I'LL DO WHAT I CAN TO HELP.
THANK YOU. I CAN'T SAY WHAT IT MEANS TO FIND A BROTHER IN THIS GORGEOUS PURGATORY OF CIGAR BUTTS AND DEAD DOGS!
IF YOU WOULD HELP ME, WE MUST STORM THE FORTRESS OF DELIRIUM THROUGH SUBTERRANEAN ROUTES I HAVE DISCOVERED. WE MUST BOTH DESCEND...
...INTO THAT STYGIAN DARK WHEREIN WE CREATURES OF THE SHADOW FIND OUR ONLY DWELLING PLACE.
Drink milk out of the carton. Call mom. Send out for some ice cream. Watch a game.

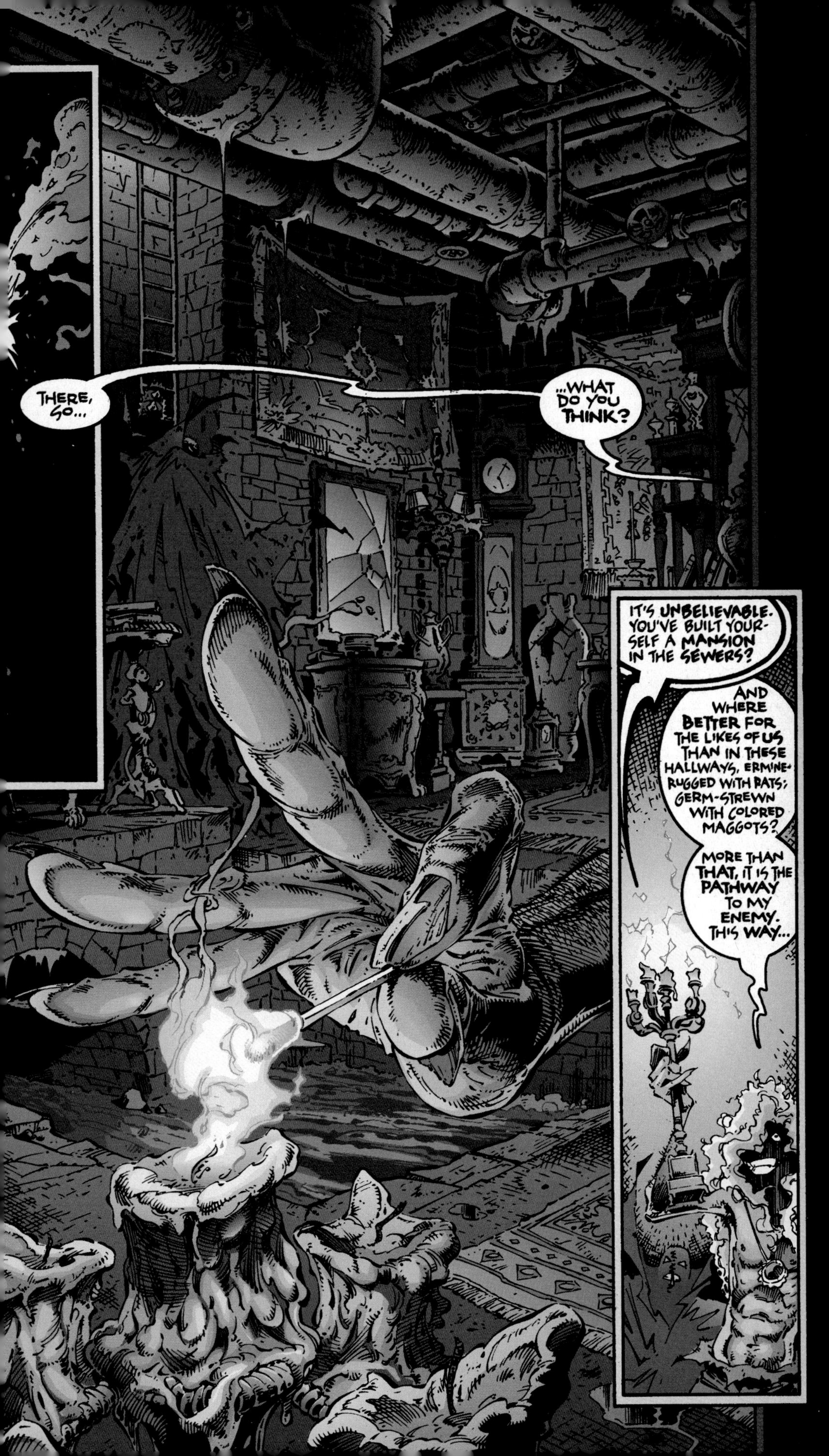
THERE, SO...
...WHAT DO YOU THINK?
IT'S UNBELIEVABLE. YOU'VE BUILT YOURSELF A MANSION IN THE SEWERS?
AND WHERE BETTER FOR THE LIKES OF US THAN IN THESE HALLWAYS, ERMINE-RUGGED WITH RATS; GERM-STREWN WITH COLORED MAGGOTS?
MORE THAN THAT, IT IS THE PATHWAY TO MY ENEMY. THIS WAY...

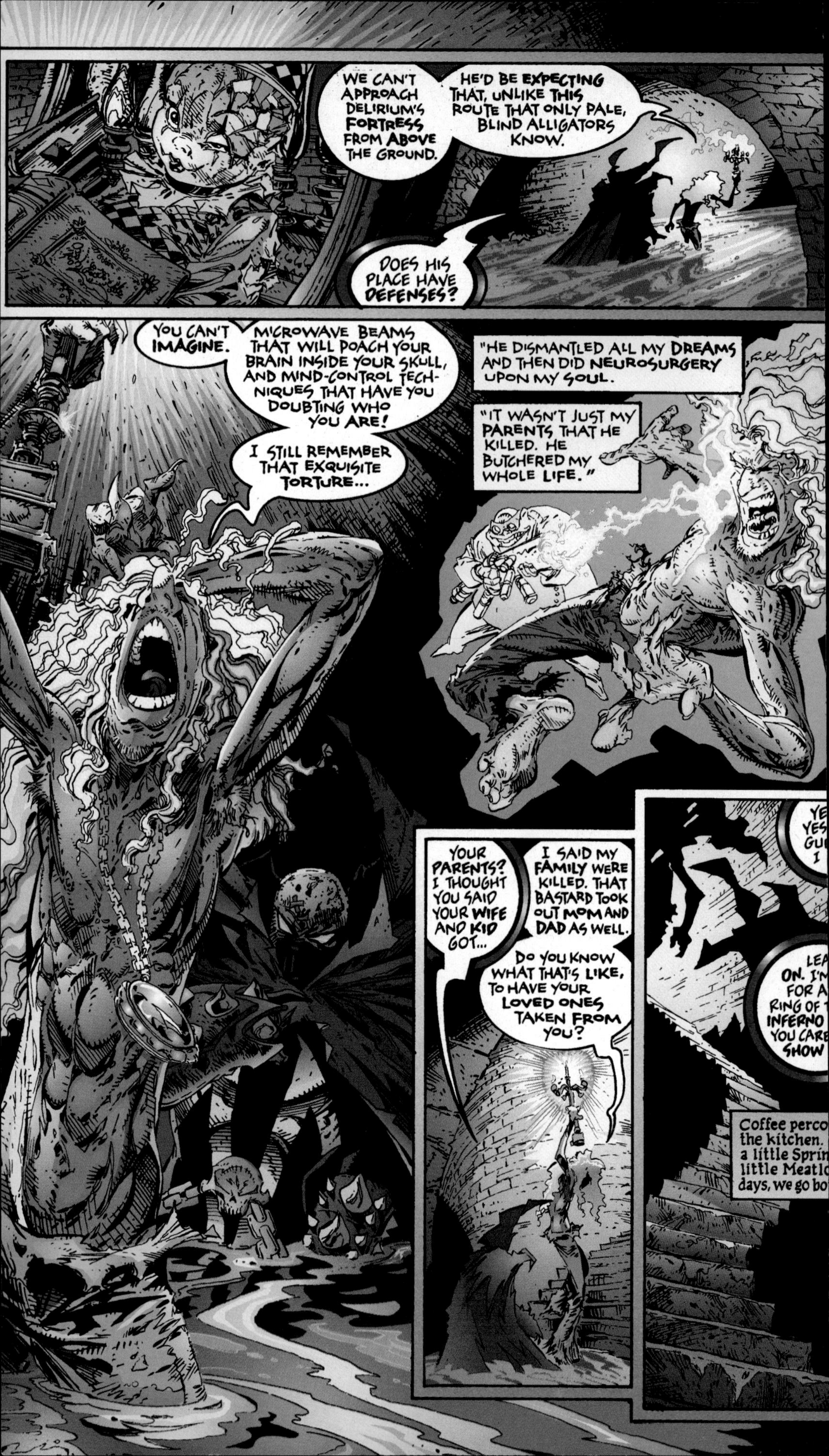
WE CAN'T APPROACH DELIRIUM'S FORTRESS FROM ABOVE THE GROUND.
HE'D BE EXPECTING THAT, UNLIKE THIS ROUTE THAT ONLY PALE, BLIND ALLIGATORS KNOW.
DOES HIS PLACE HAVE DEFENSES?
YOU CAN'T IMAGINE.
MICROWAVE BEAMS THAT WILL POACH YOUR BRAIN INSIDE YOUR SKULL, AND MIND-CONTROL TECH-NIQUES THAT HAVE YOU DOUBTING WHO YOU ARE!
I STILL REMEMBER THAT EXQUISITE TORTURE...
"HE DISMANTLED ALL MY DREAMS AND THEN DID NEUROSURGERY UPON MY SOUL.
"IT WASN'T JUST MY PARENTS THAT HE KILLED. HE BUTCHERED MY WHOLE LIFE."
YOUR PARENTS? I THOUGHT YOU SAID YOUR WIFE AND KID GOT...
I SAID MY FAMILY WERE KILLED. THAT BASTARD TOOK OUT MOM AND DAD AS WELL.
DO YOU KNOW WHAT THAT'S LIKE, TO HAVE YOUR LOVED ONES TAKEN FROM YOU?
YE YES GU I
LEA ON. I'M FOR A RING OF INFERNO YOU CARE SHOW
Coffee perco the kitchen. a little Sprin little Meatlo days, we go bo

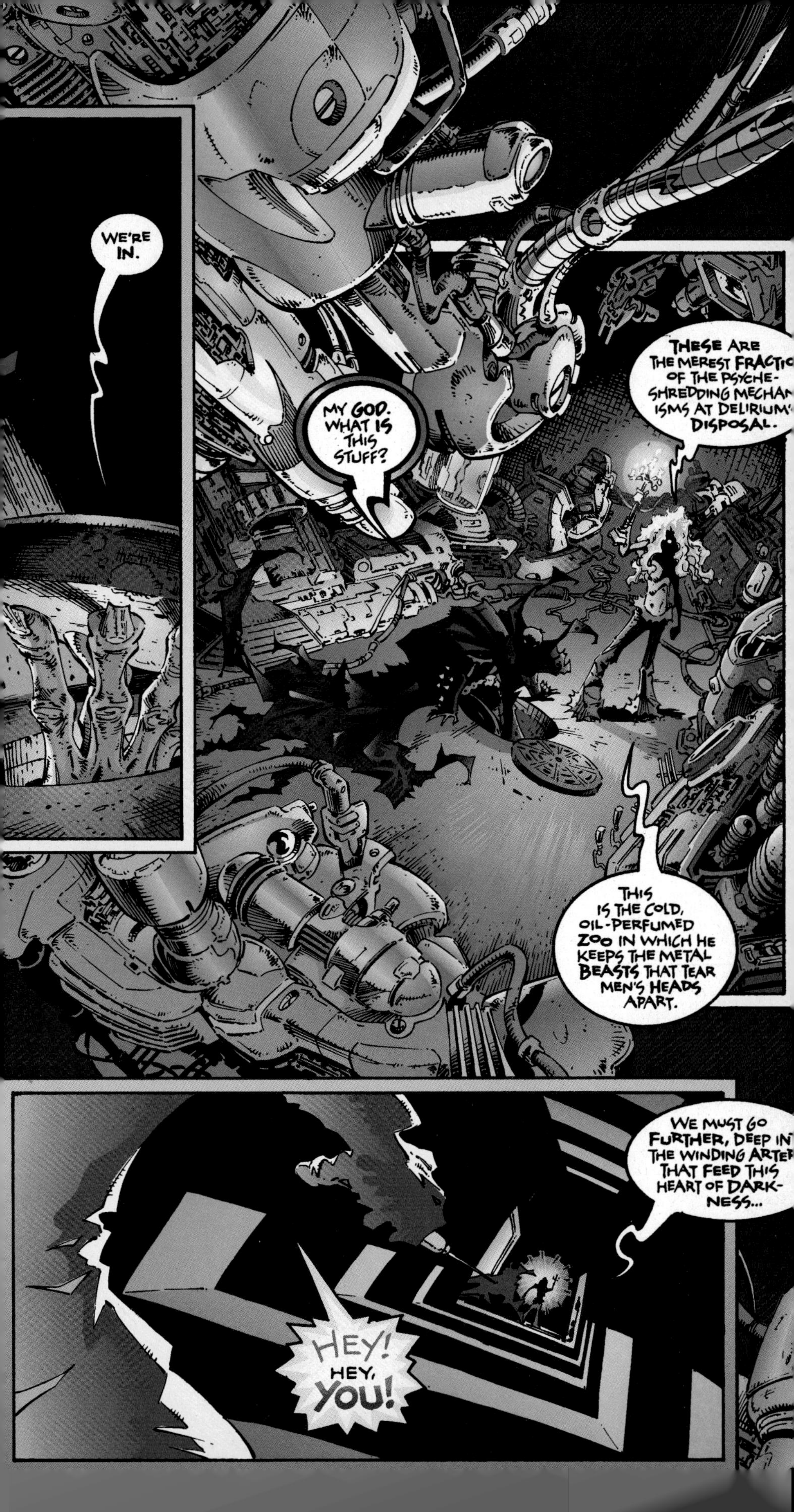
WE'RE IN.
THESE ARE THE MEREST FRACTIO OF THE PSYCHE-SHREDDING MECHAN ISMS AT DELIRIUM'S DISPOSAL.
MY GOD. WHAT IS THIS STUFF?
THIS IS THE COLD, OIL-PERFUMED ZOO IN WHICH HE KEEPS THE METAL BEASTS THAT TEAR MEN'S HEADS APART.
WE MUST GO FURTHER, DEEP INT THE WINDING ARTEF THAT FEED THIS HEART OF DARK-NESS...
HEY! HEY, YOU!

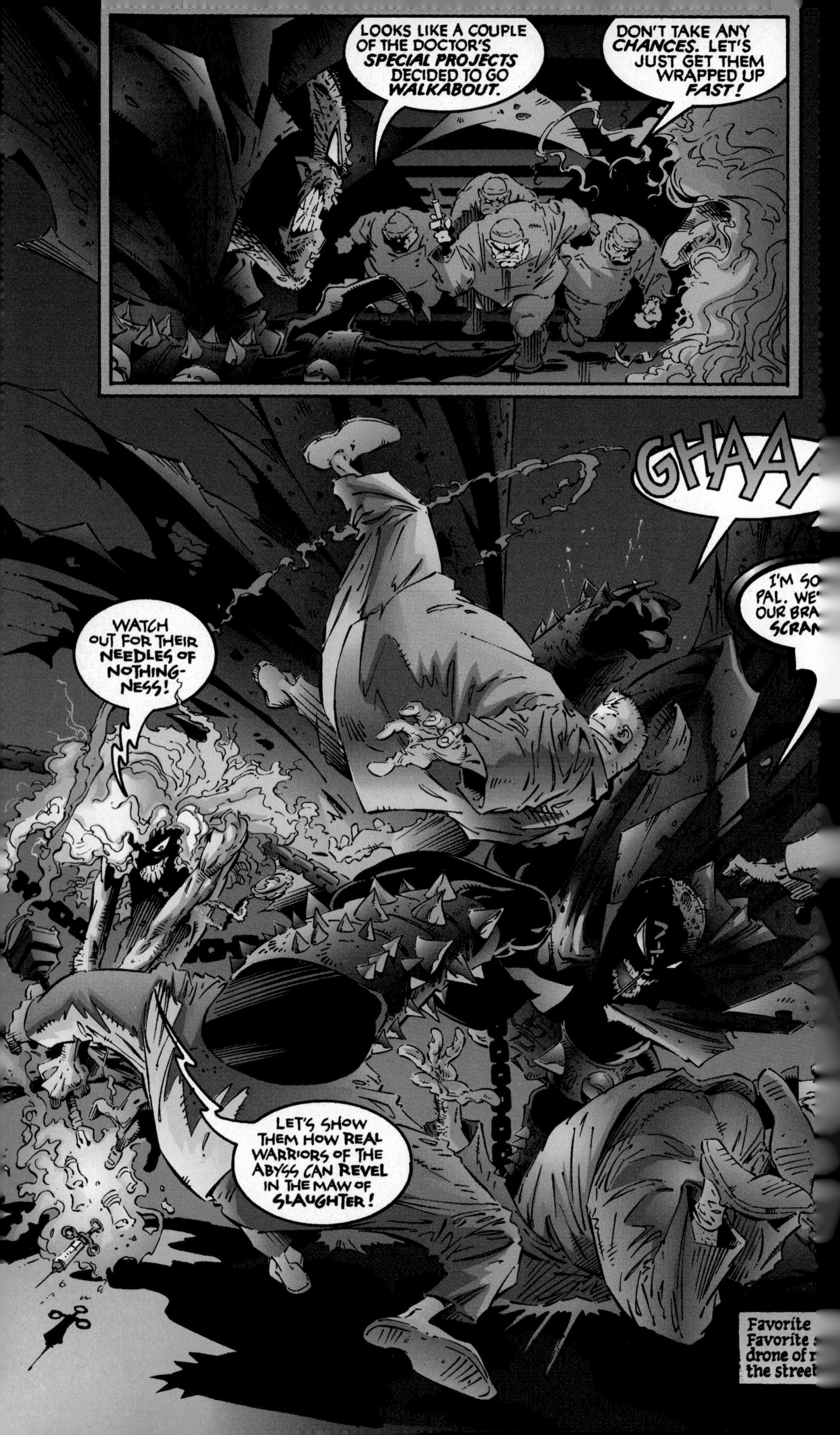
LOOKS LIKE A COUPLE OF THE DOCTOR'S SPECIAL PROJECTS DECIDED TO GO WALKABOUT.
DON'T TAKE ANY CHANCES. LET'S JUST GET THEM WRAPPED UP FAST!
GHAAA
I'M SO PAL. WE' OUR BRA SCRAM
WATCH OUT FOR THEIR NEEDLES OF NOTHING-NESS!
LET'S SHOW THEM HOW REAL WARRIORS OF THE ABYSS CAN REVEL IN THE MAW OF SLAUGHTER!
Favorite Favorite drone of the street

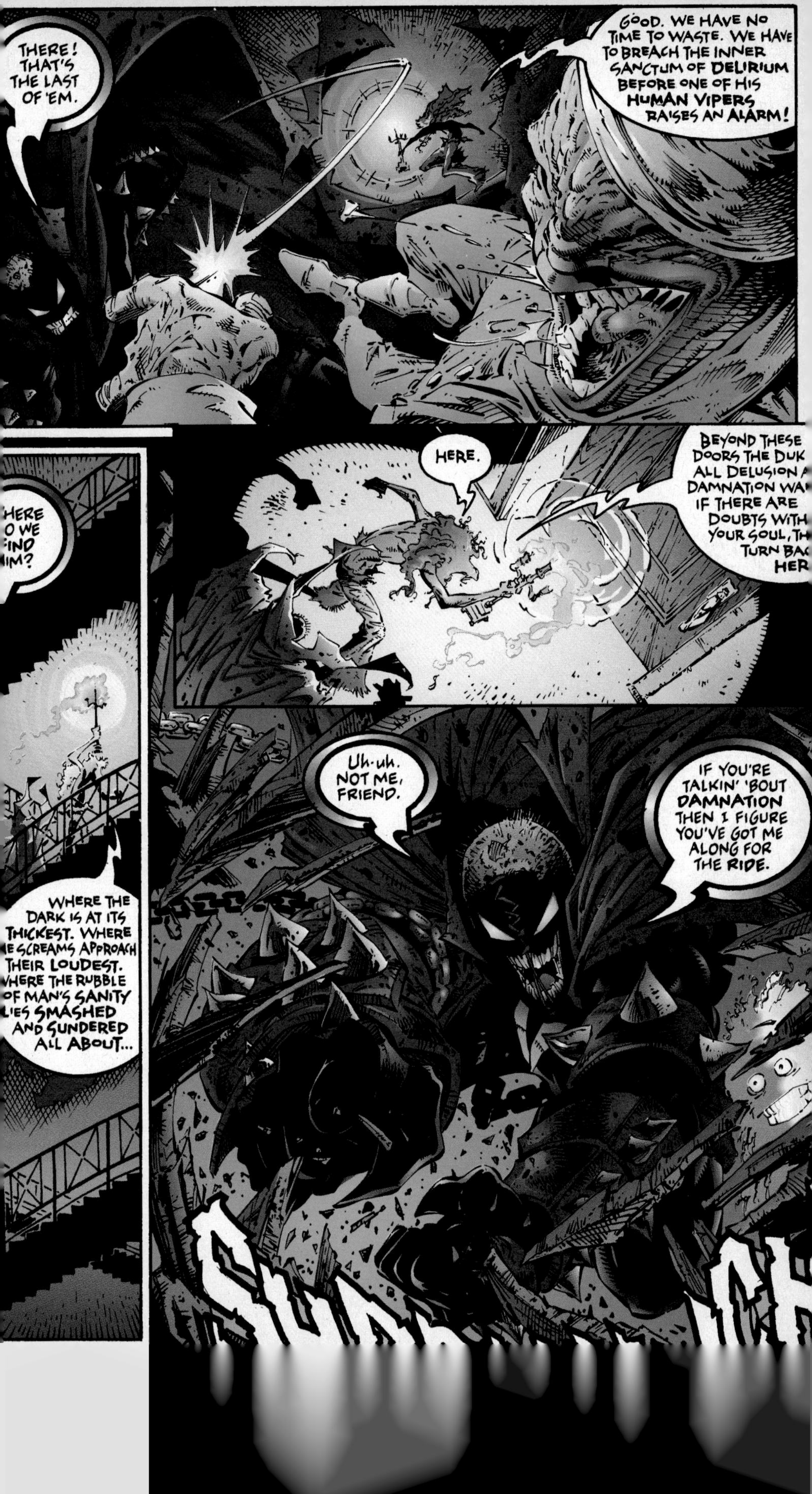

THERE! THAT'S THE LAST OF 'EM.
GOOD. WE HAVE NO TIME TO WASTE. WE HAVE TO BREACH THE INNER SANCTUM OF DELIRIUM BEFORE ONE OF HIS HUMAN VIPERS RAISES AN ALARM!
HERE.
BEYOND THESE DOORS THE DUK ALL DELUSION A DAMNATION WA IF THERE ARE DOUBTS WITH YOUR SOUL, TH TURN BAC HER
HERE O WE FIND IM?
WHERE THE DARK IS AT ITS THICKEST. WHERE E SCREAMS APPROACH THEIR LOUDEST. WHERE THE RUBBLE OF MAN'S SANITY LIES SMASHED AND SUNDERED ALL ABOUT...
Uh-uh. NOT ME, FRIEND.
IF YOU'RE TALKIN' 'BOUT DAMNATION THEN I FIGURE YOU'VE GOT ME ALONG FOR THE RIDE.

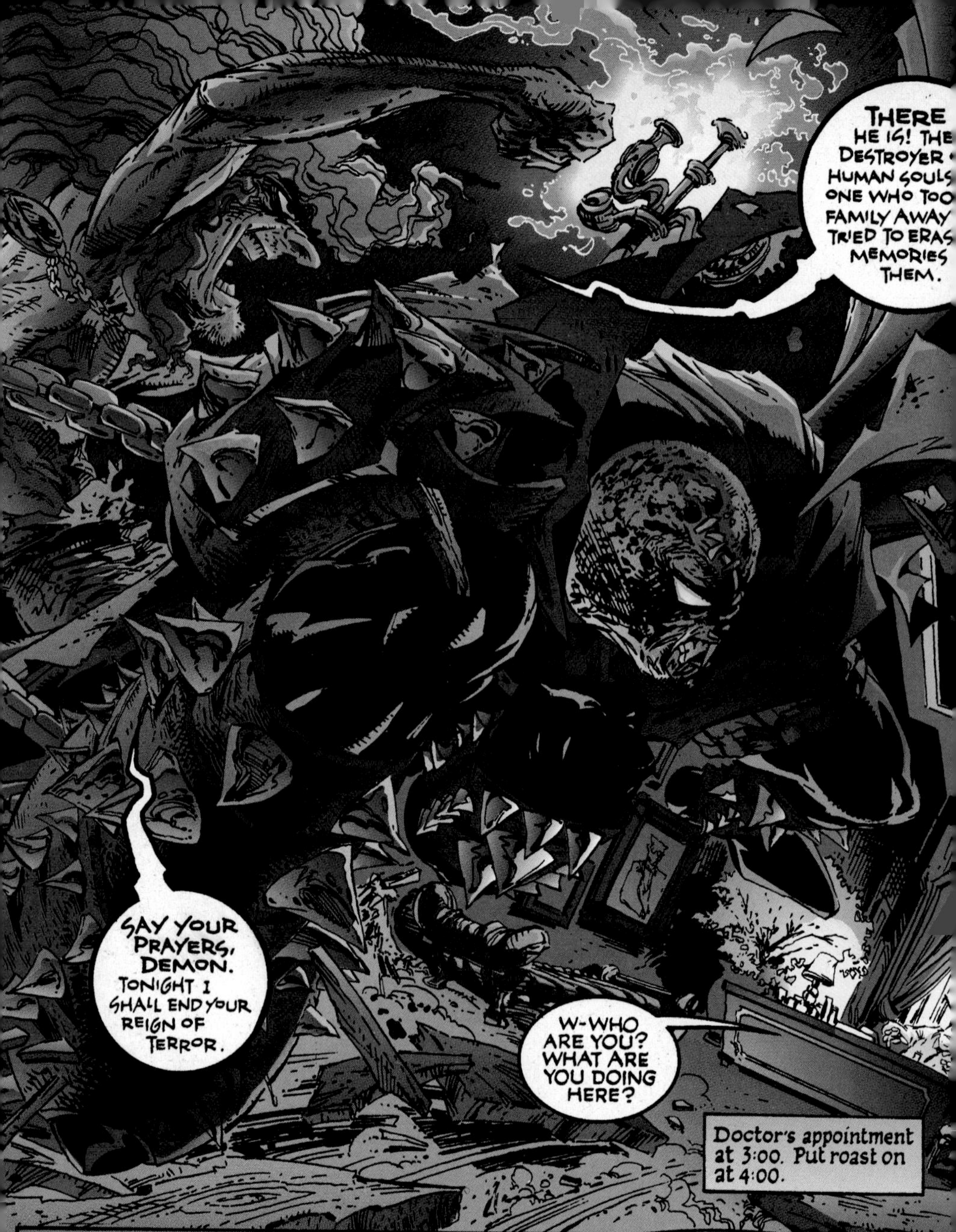
THERE HE IS! THE DESTROYER HUMAN SOULS ONE WHO TOO FAMILY AWAY TRIED TO ERAS MEMORIES THEM.
SAY YOUR PRAYERS, DEMON. TONIGHT I SHALL END YOUR REIGN OF TERROR.
W-WHO ARE YOU? WHAT ARE YOU DOING HERE?
Doctor's appointment at 3:00. Put roast on at 4:00.

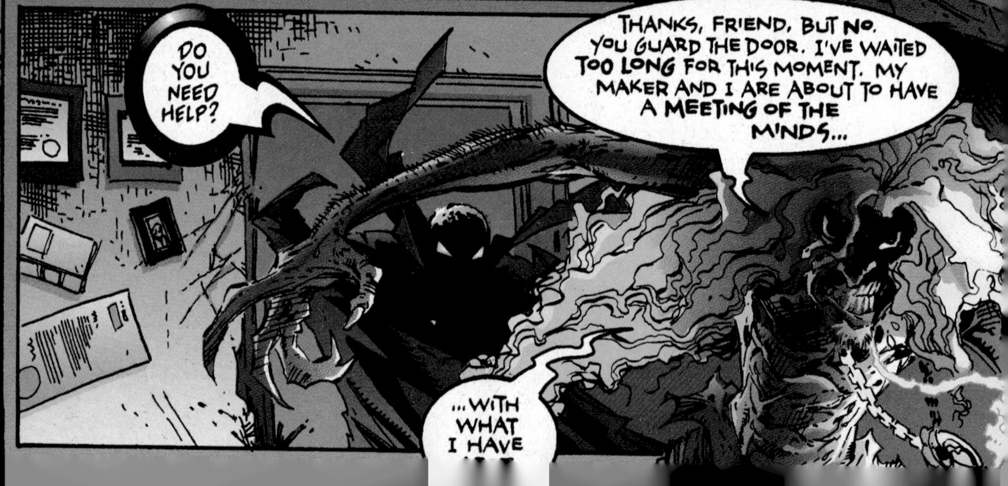
DO YOU NEED HELP?
THANKS, FRIEND, BUT NO. YOU GUARD THE DOOR. I'VE WAITED TOO LONG FOR THIS MOMENT. MY MAKER AND I ARE ABOUT TO HAVE A MEETING OF THE MINDS...
...WITH WHAT I HAVE

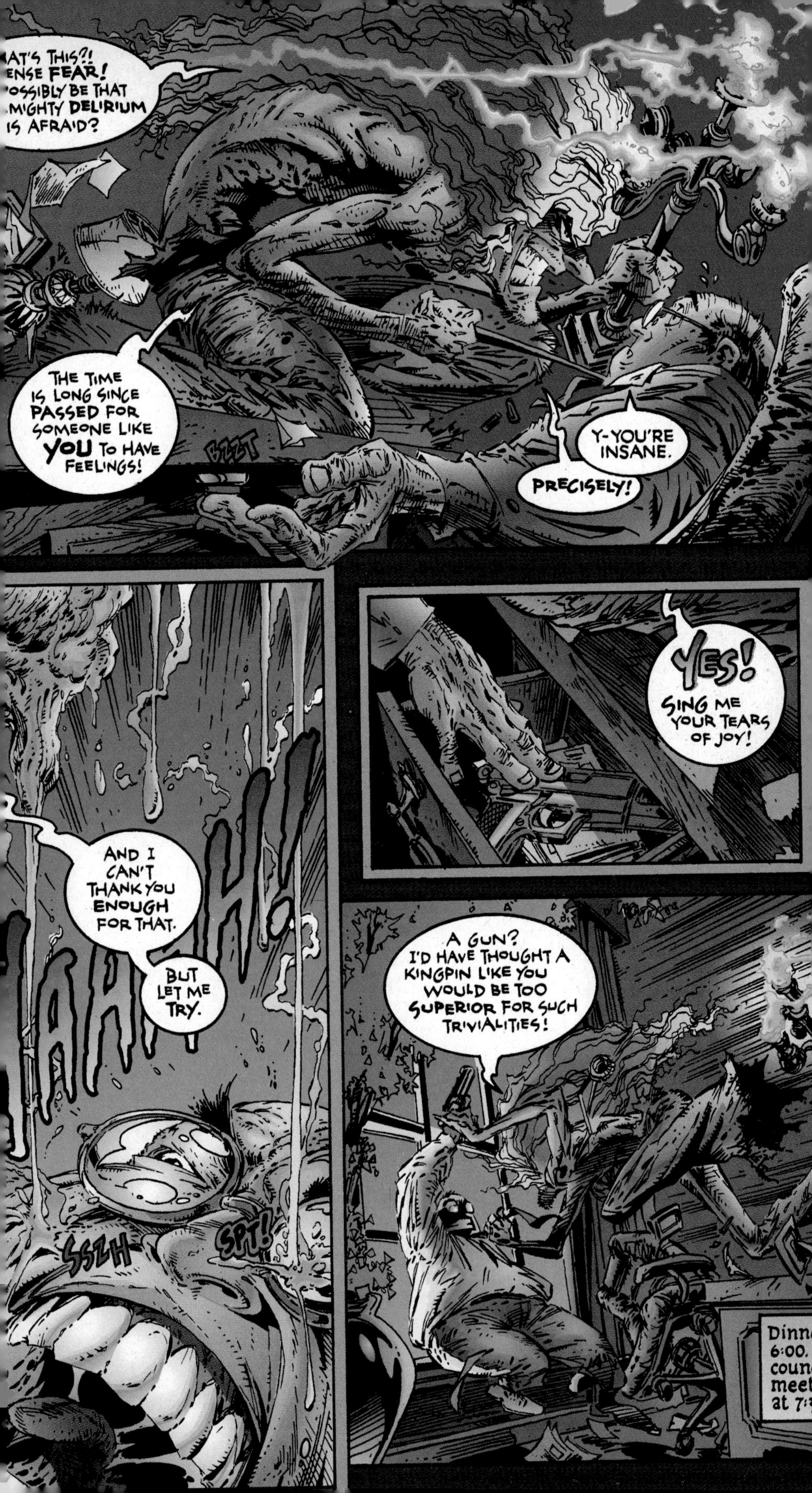
AT'S THIS?! ENSE FEAR! POSSIBLY BE THAT MIGHTY DELIRIUM IS AFRAID?
THE TIME IS LONG SINCE PASSED FOR SOMEONE LIKE YOU TO HAVE FEELINGS!
BZZT
Y-YOU'RE INSANE.
PRECISELY!
AND I CAN'T THANK YOU ENOUGH FOR THAT.
BUT LET ME TRY.
SSZH
SPT!
YES! SING ME YOUR TEARS OF JOY!
A GUN? I'D HAVE THOUGHT A KINGPIN LIKE YOU WOULD BE TOO SUPERIOR FOR SUCH TRIVIALITIES!
Dinne
6:00.
counc
meet
at 7:3

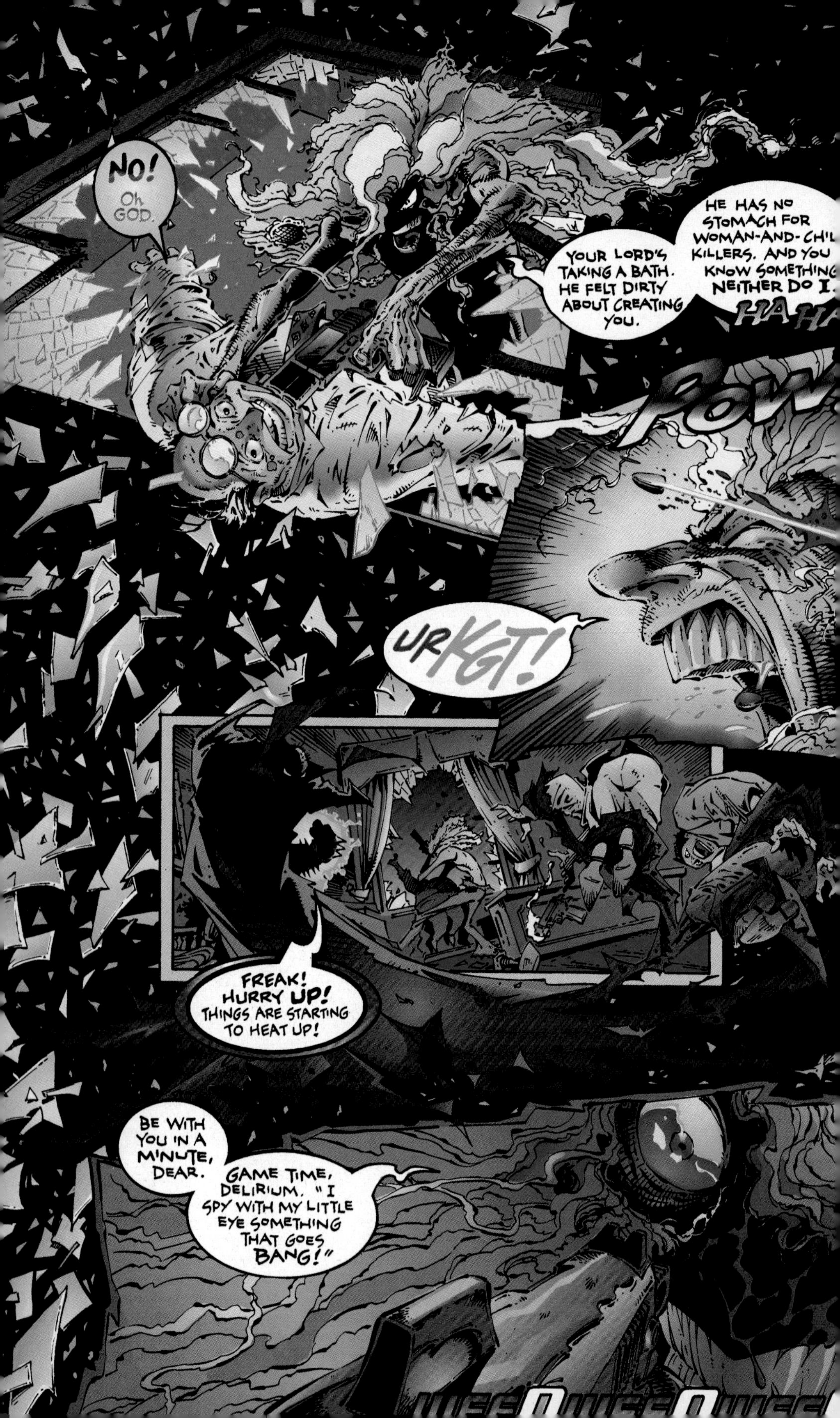
NO! Oh GOD.
YOUR LORD'S TAKING A BATH. HE FELT DIRTY ABOUT CREATING YOU.
HE HAS NO STOMACH FOR WOMAN-AND-CHIL KILLERS. AND YOU KNOW SOMETHING NEITHER DO I.
HAHA
POW
URKGT!
FREAK! HURRY UP! THINGS ARE STARTING TO HEAT UP!
BE WITH YOU IN A MINUTE, DEAR.
GAME TIME, DELIRIUM. "I SPY WITH MY LITTLE EYE SOMETHING THAT GOES BANG!"

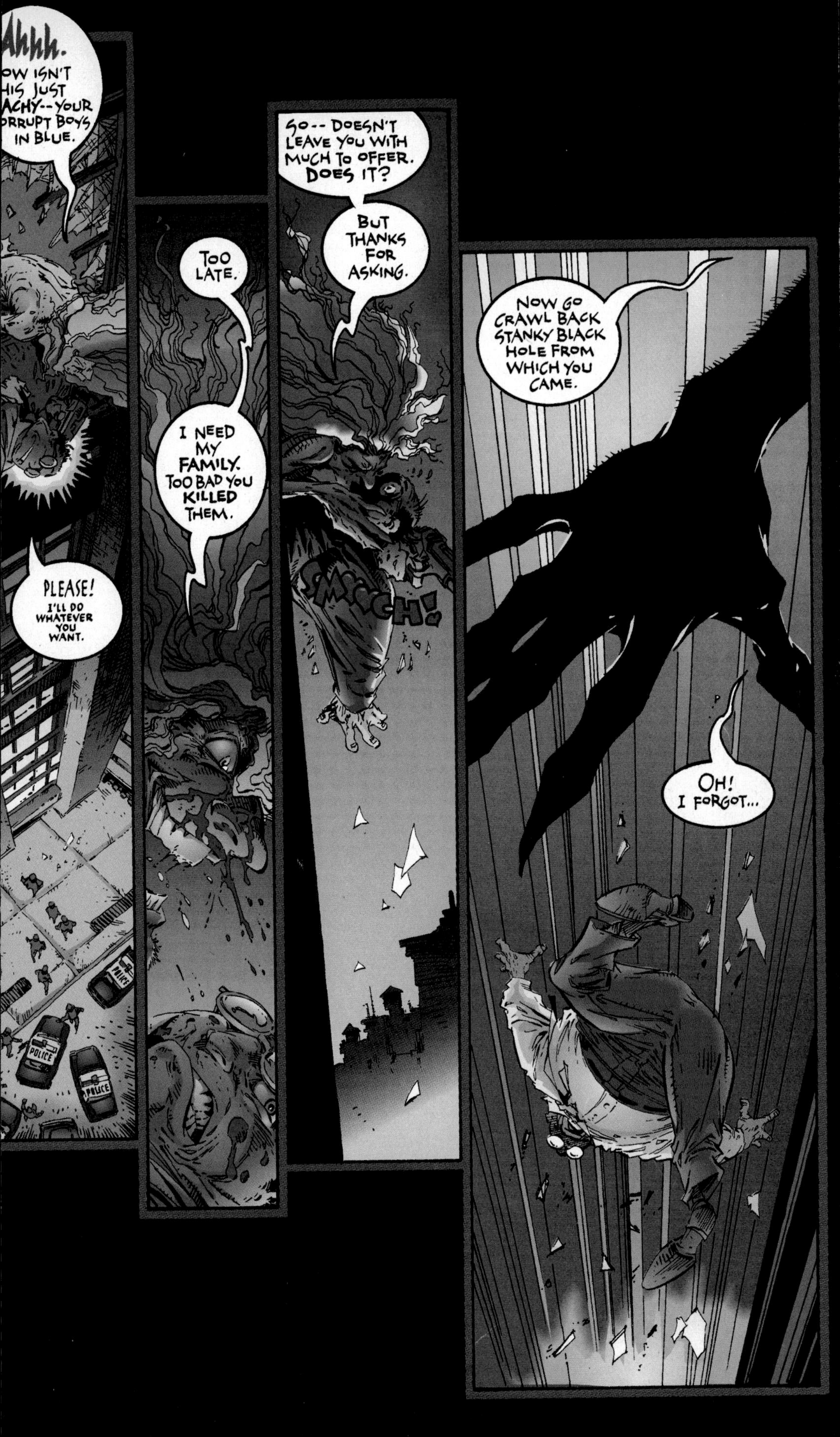

Ahhh.
OW ISN'T HIS JUST ACHY--YOUR ORRUPT BOYS IN BLUE.
PLEASE! I'LL DO WHATEVER YOU WANT.
TOO LATE.
I NEED MY FAMILY. TOO BAD YOU KILLED THEM.
SO-- DOESN'T LEAVE YOU WITH MUCH TO OFFER. DOES IT?
BUT THANKS FOR ASKING.
NOW GO CRAWL BACK STANKY BLACK HOLE FROM WHICH YOU CAME.
OH! I FORGOT...

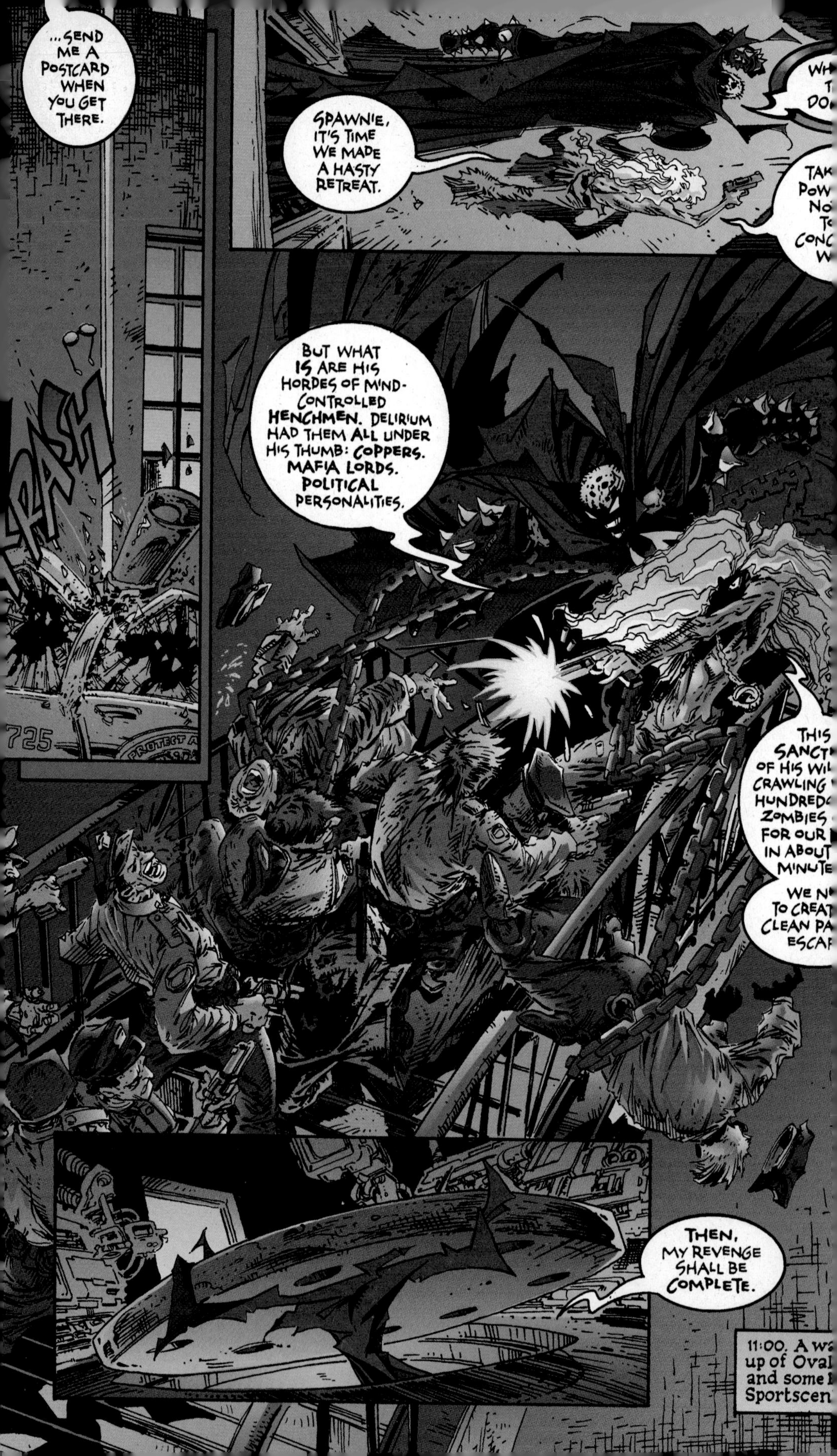
...SEND ME A POSTCARD WHEN YOU GET THERE.
SPAWNIE, IT'S TIME WE MADE A HASTY RETREAT.
BUT WHAT IS ARE HIS HORDES OF MIND-CONTROLLED HENCHMEN. DELIRIUM HAD THEM ALL UNDER HIS THUMB: COPPERS. MAFIA LORDS. POLITICAL PERSONALITIES.
THEN, MY REVENGE SHALL BE COMPLETE.

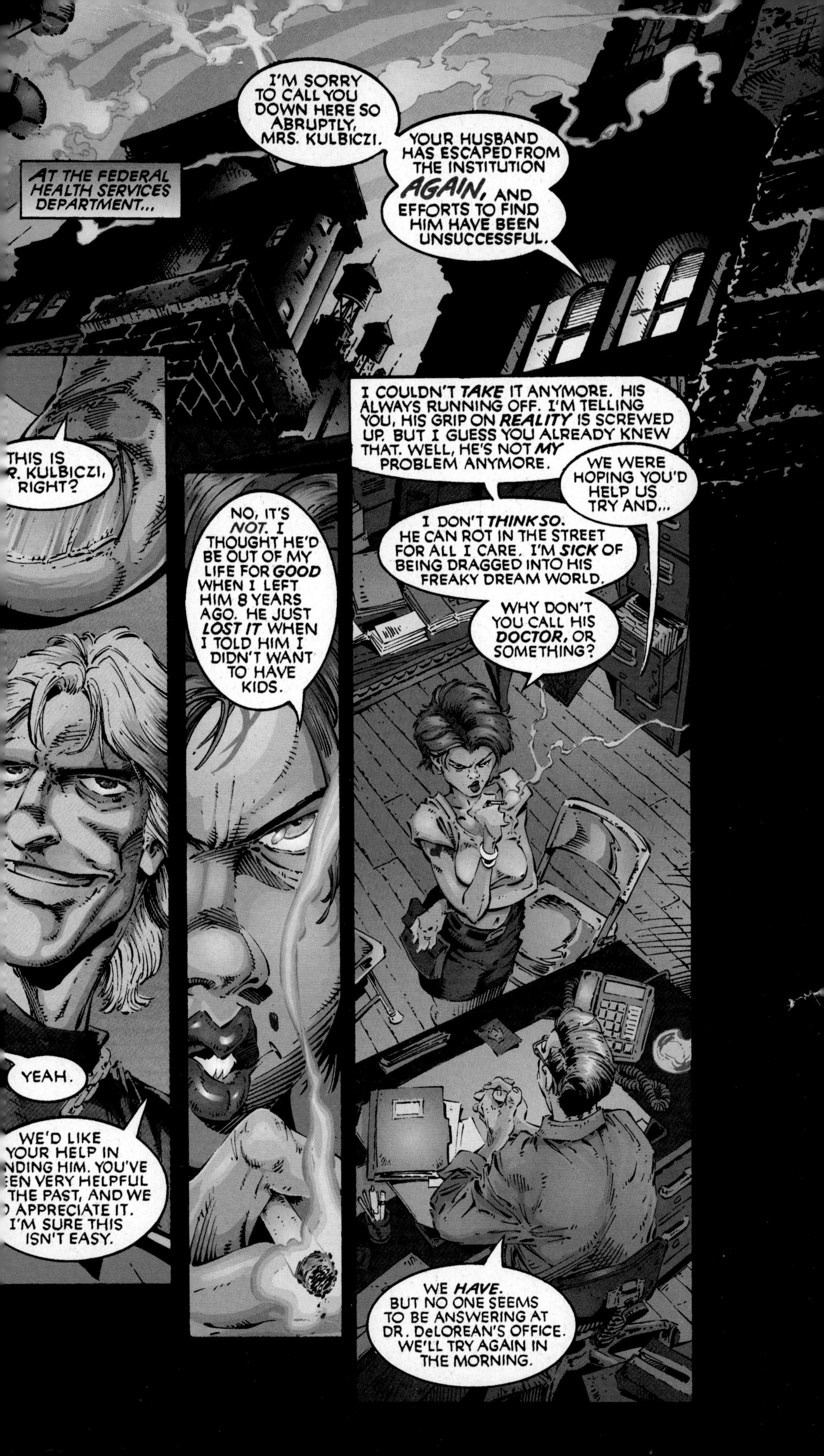
AT THE FEDERAL HEALTH SERVICES DEPARTMENT...
I'M SORRY TO CALL YOU DOWN HERE SO ABRUPTLY, MRS. KULBICZI.
YOUR HUSBAND HAS ESCAPED FROM THE INSTITUTION AGAIN, AND EFFORTS TO FIND HIM HAVE BEEN UNSUCCESSFUL.
THIS IS R. KULBICZI, RIGHT?
YEAH.
WE'D LIKE YOUR HELP IN NDING HIM. YOU'VE EEN VERY HELPFUL THE PAST, AND WE APPRECIATE IT. I'M SURE THIS ISN'T EASY.
NO, IT'S NOT. I THOUGHT HE'D BE OUT OF MY LIFE FOR GOOD WHEN I LEFT HIM 8 YEARS AGO. HE JUST LOST IT WHEN I TOLD HIM I DIDN'T WANT TO HAVE KIDS.
I COULDN'T TAKE IT ANYMORE. HIS ALWAYS RUNNING OFF. I'M TELLING YOU, HIS GRIP ON REALITY IS SCREWED UP. BUT I GUESS YOU ALREADY KNEW THAT. WELL, HE'S NOT MY PROBLEM ANYMORE.
WE WERE HOPING YOU'D HELP US TRY AND...
I DON'T THINK SO. HE CAN ROT IN THE STREET FOR ALL I CARE. I'M SICK OF BEING DRAGGED INTO HIS FREAKY DREAM WORLD.
WHY DON'T YOU CALL HIS DOCTOR, OR SOMETHING?
WE HAVE. BUT NO ONE SEEMS TO BE ANSWERING AT DR. DeLOREAN'S OFFICE. WE'LL TRY AGAIN IN THE MORNING.

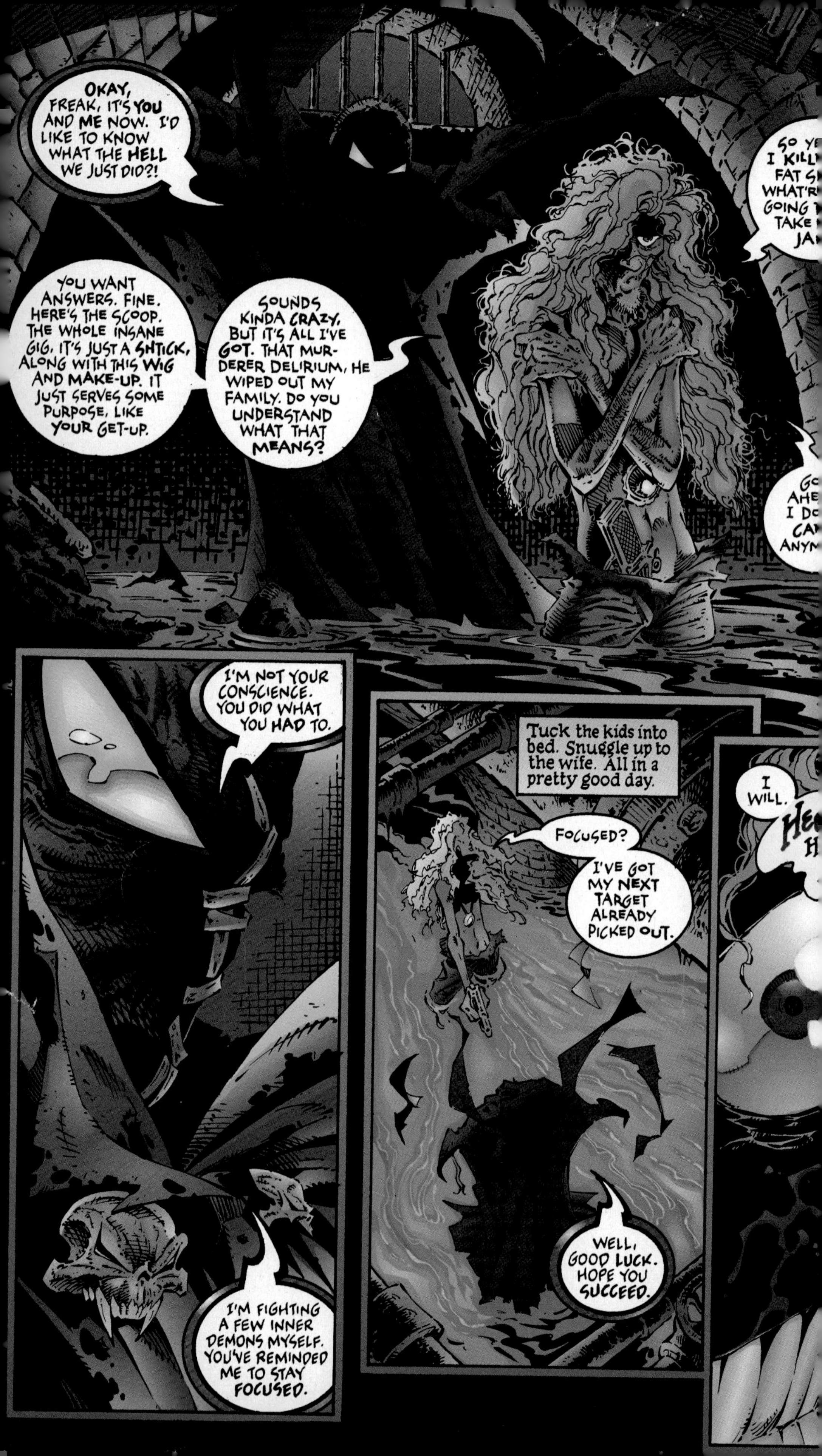
OKAY, FREAK, IT'S YOU AND ME NOW. I'D LIKE TO KNOW WHAT THE HELL WE JUST DID?!
YOU WANT ANSWERS. FINE. HERE'S THE SCOOP. THE WHOLE INSANE GIG, IT'S JUST A SHTICK, ALONG WITH THIS WIG AND MAKE-UP. IT JUST SERVES SOME PURPOSE, LIKE YOUR GET-UP.
SOUNDS KINDA CRAZY, BUT IT'S ALL I'VE GOT. THAT MURDERER DELIRIUM, HE WIPED OUT MY FAMILY. DO YOU UNDERSTAND WHAT THAT MEANS?
I'M NOT YOUR CONSCIENCE. YOU DID WHAT YOU HAD TO.
I'M FIGHTING A FEW INNER DEMONS MYSELF. YOU'VE REMINDED ME TO STAY FOCUSED.
Tuck the kids into bed. Snuggle up to the wife. All in a pretty good day.
FOCUSED?
I'VE GOT MY NEXT TARGET ALREADY PICKED OUT.
WELL, GOOD LUCK. HOPE YOU SUCCEED.
I WILL.

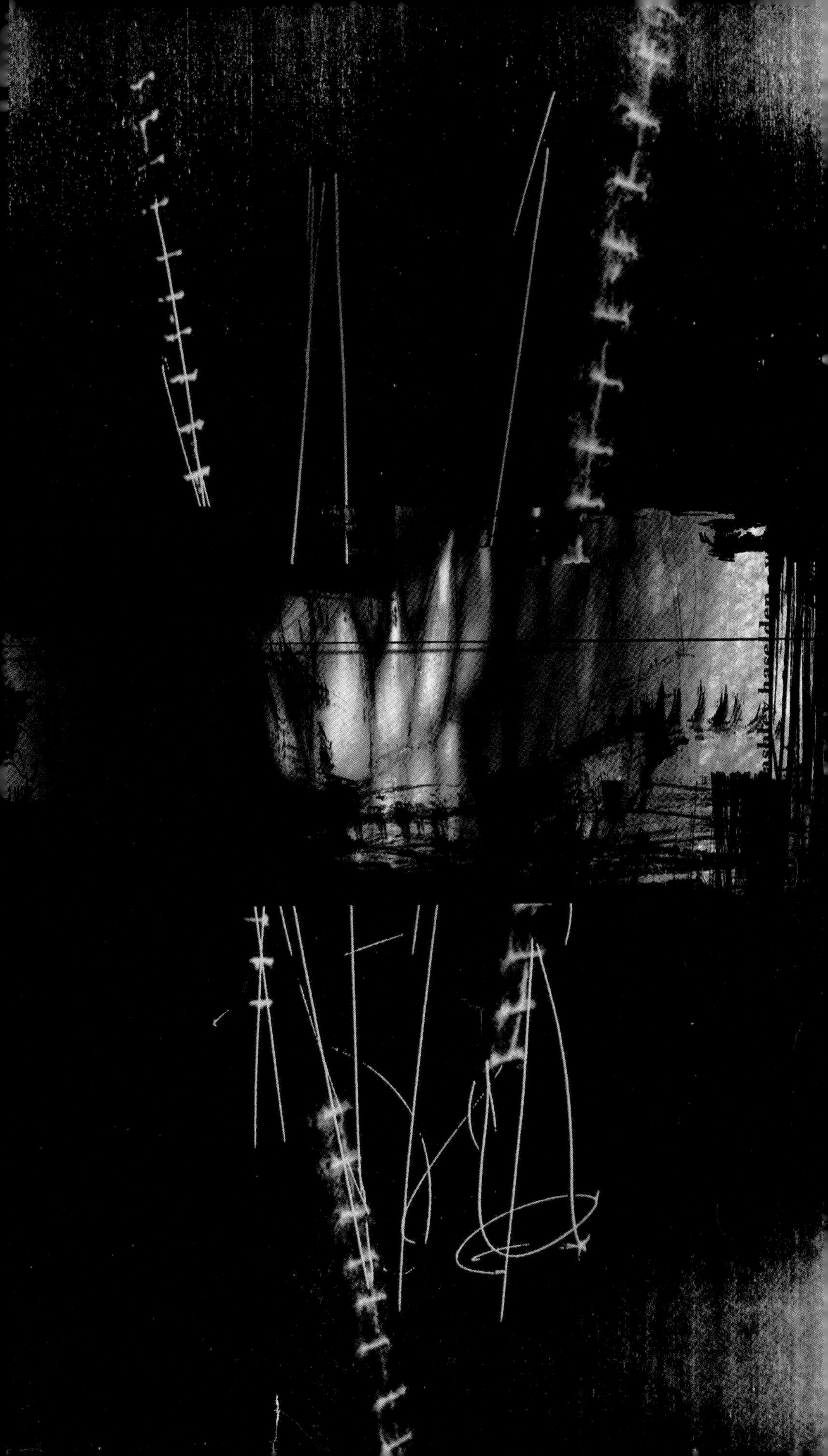
ashley haselden

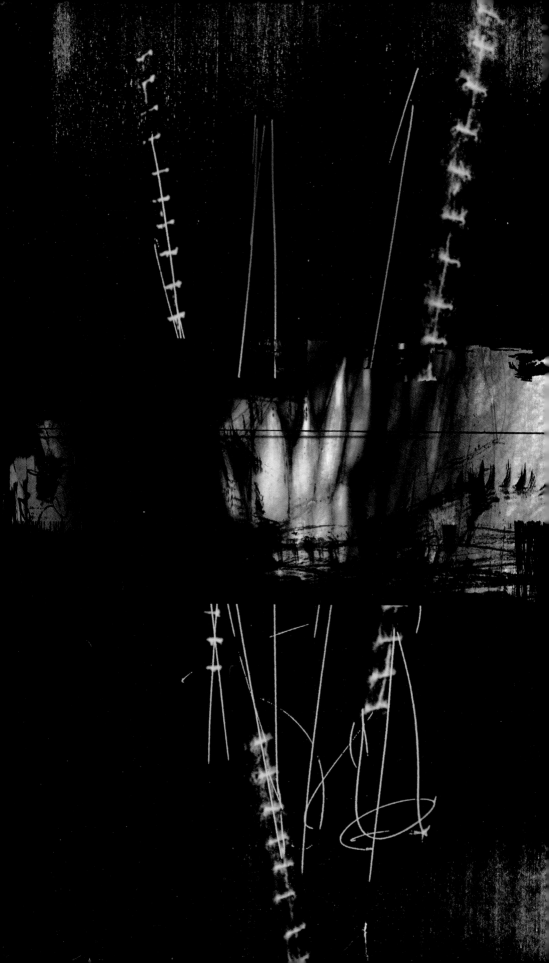

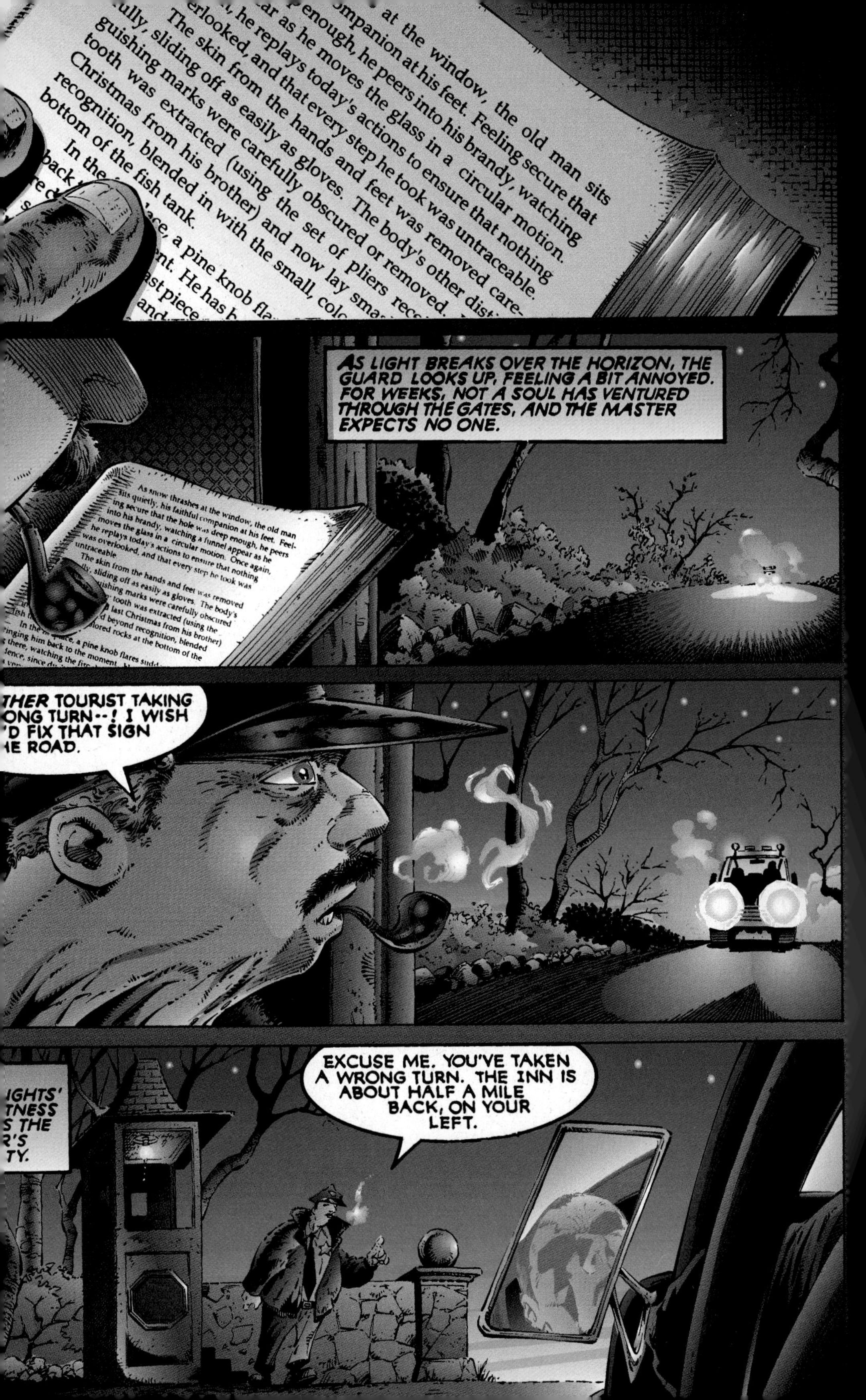

at the window, the old man sits
companion at his feet. Feeling secure that
enough, he peers into his brandy, watching
as he moves the glass in a circular motion.
he replays today's actions to ensure that nothing
erlooked, and that every step he took was untraceable.
The skin from the hands and feet was removed care-
sliding off as easily as gloves. The body's other
guishing marks were carefully obscured or removed.
tooth was extracted (using the set of pliers
Christmas from his brother) and now lay
recognition, blended in with the small,
bottom of the fish tank.
AS LIGHT BREAKS OVER THE HORIZON, THE GUARD LOOKS UP, FEELING A BIT ANNOYED. FOR WEEKS, NOT A SOUL HAS VENTURED THROUGH THE GATES, AND THE MASTER EXPECTS NO ONE.
THER TOURIST TAKING ONG TURN--! I WISH 'D FIX THAT SIGN HE ROAD.
EXCUSE ME. YOU'VE TAKEN A WRONG TURN. THE INN IS ABOUT HALF A MILE BACK, ON YOUR LEFT.

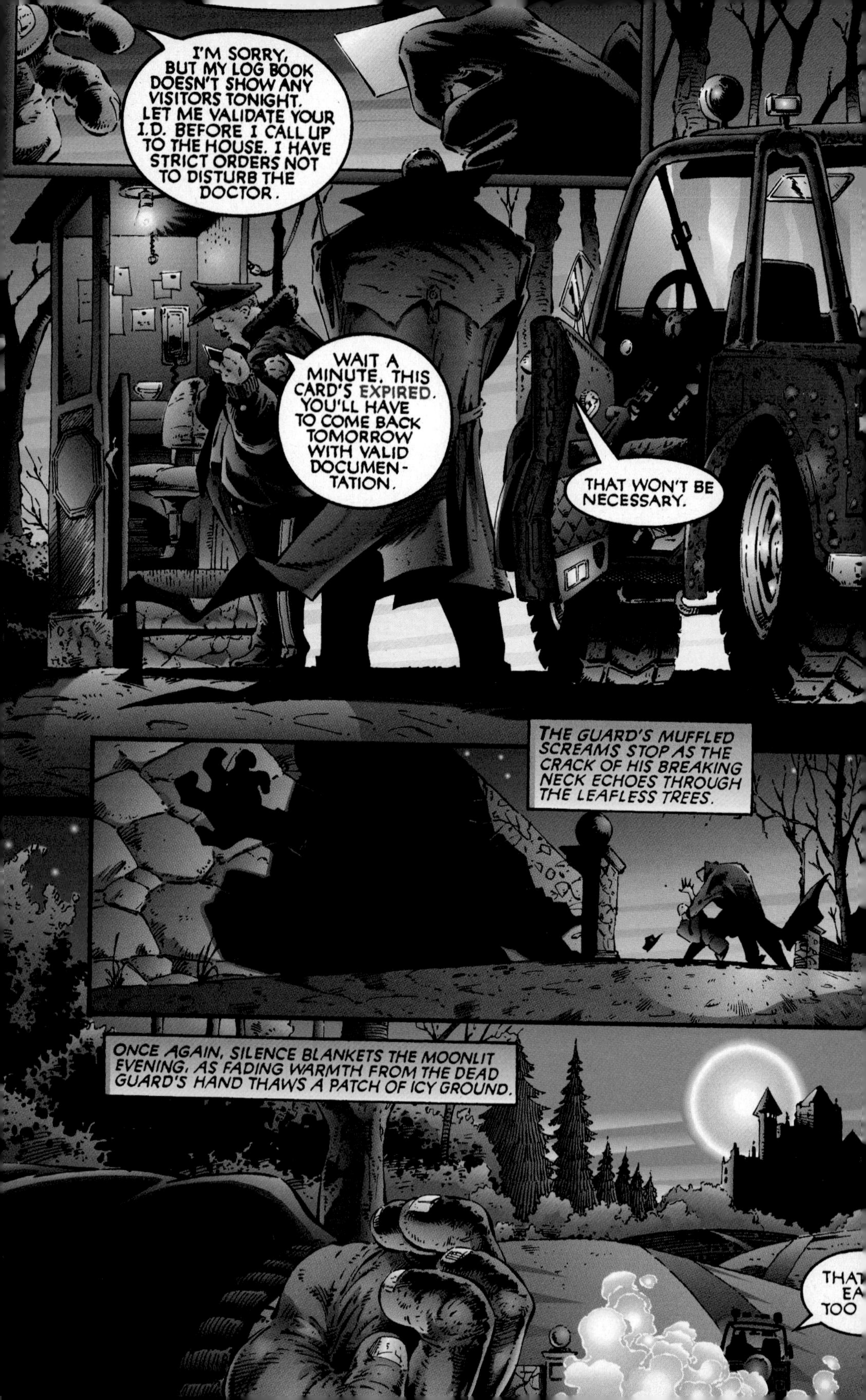
I'M SORRY, BUT MY LOG BOOK DOESN'T SHOW ANY VISITORS TONIGHT. LET ME VALIDATE YOUR I.D. BEFORE I CALL UP TO THE HOUSE. I HAVE STRICT ORDERS NOT TO DISTURB THE DOCTOR.
WAIT A MINUTE. THIS CARD'S EXPIRED. YOU'LL HAVE TO COME BACK TOMORROW WITH VALID DOCUMENTATION.
THAT WON'T BE NECESSARY.
THE GUARD'S MUFFLED SCREAMS STOP AS THE CRACK OF HIS BREAKING NECK ECHOES THROUGH THE LEAFLESS TREES.
ONCE AGAIN, SILENCE BLANKETS THE MOONLIT EVENING, AS FADING WARMTH FROM THE DEAD GUARD'S HAND THAWS A PATCH OF ICY GROUND.

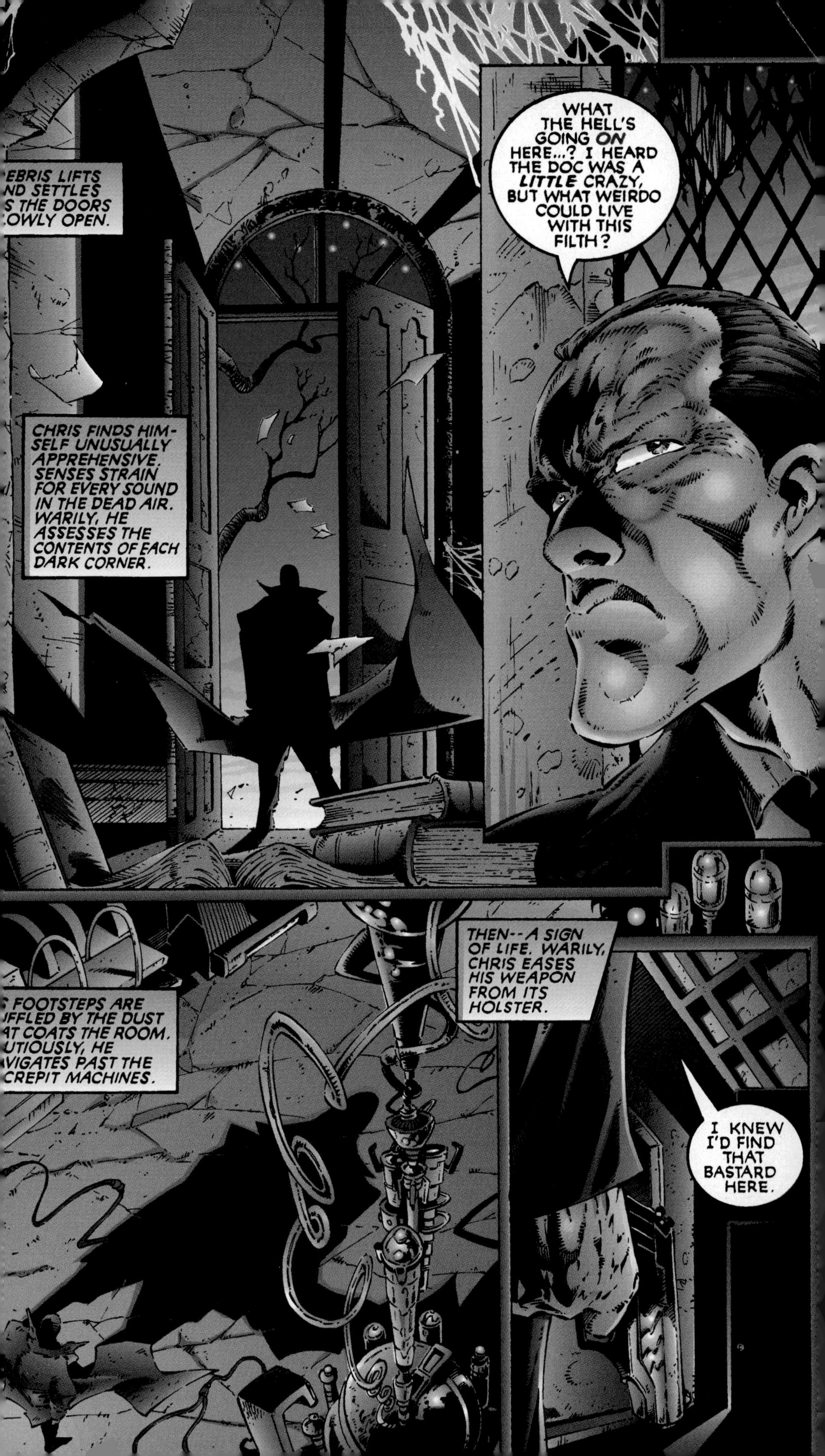

EBRIS LIFTS
ND SETTLES
S THE DOORS
OWLY OPEN.
WHAT THE HELL'S GOING ON HERE...? I HEARD THE DOC WAS A LITTLE CRAZY, BUT WHAT WEIRDO COULD LIVE WITH THIS FILTH?
CHRIS FINDS HIMSELF UNUSUALLY APPREHENSIVE. SENSES STRAIN FOR EVERY SOUND IN THE DEAD AIR. WARILY, HE ASSESSES THE CONTENTS OF EACH DARK CORNER.
FOOTSTEPS ARE
IFFLED BY THE DUST
AT COATS THE ROOM.
UTIOUSLY, HE
VIGATES PAST THE
CREPIT MACHINES.
THEN--A SIGN OF LIFE. WARILY, CHRIS EASES HIS WEAPON FROM ITS HOLSTER.
I KNEW I'D FIND THAT BASTARD HERE.

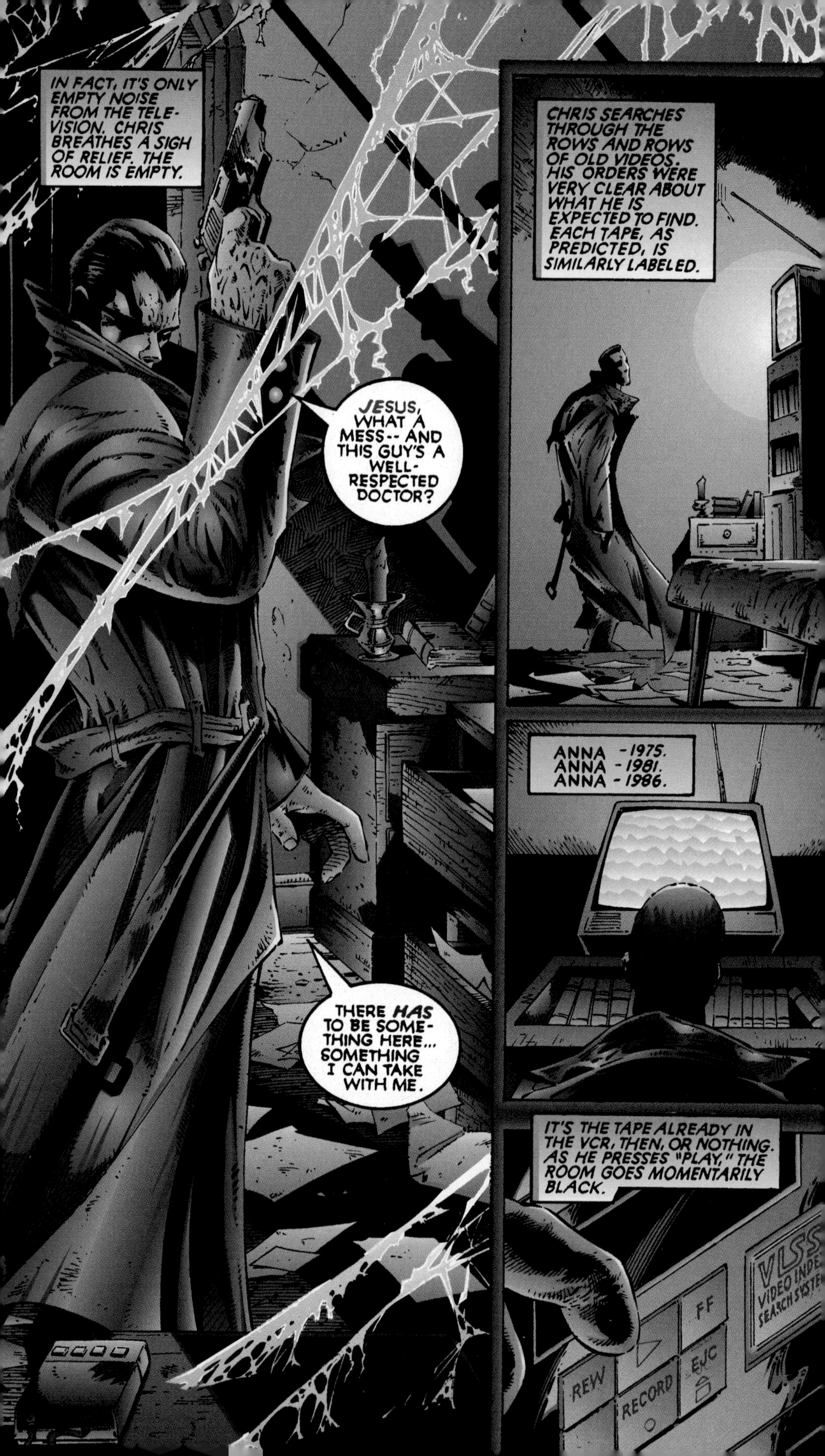
IN FACT, IT'S ONLY EMPTY NOISE FROM THE TELE- VISION. CHRIS BREATHES A SIGH OF RELIEF. THE ROOM IS EMPTY.
JESUS, WHAT A MESS-- AND THIS GUY'S A WELL- RESPECTED DOCTOR?
THERE HAS TO BE SOME- THING HERE... SOMETHING I CAN TAKE WITH ME.
CHRIS SEARCHES THROUGH THE ROWS AND ROWS OF OLD VIDEOS. HIS ORDERS WERE VERY CLEAR ABOUT WHAT HE IS EXPECTED TO FIND. EACH TAPE, AS PREDICTED, IS SIMILARLY LABELED.
ANNA -1975. ANNA -1981. ANNA -1986.
IT'S THE TAPE ALREADY IN THE VCR, THEN, OR NOTHING. AS HE PRESSES "PLAY," THE ROOM GOES MOMENTARILY BLACK.
REW
RECORD
FF
EJC

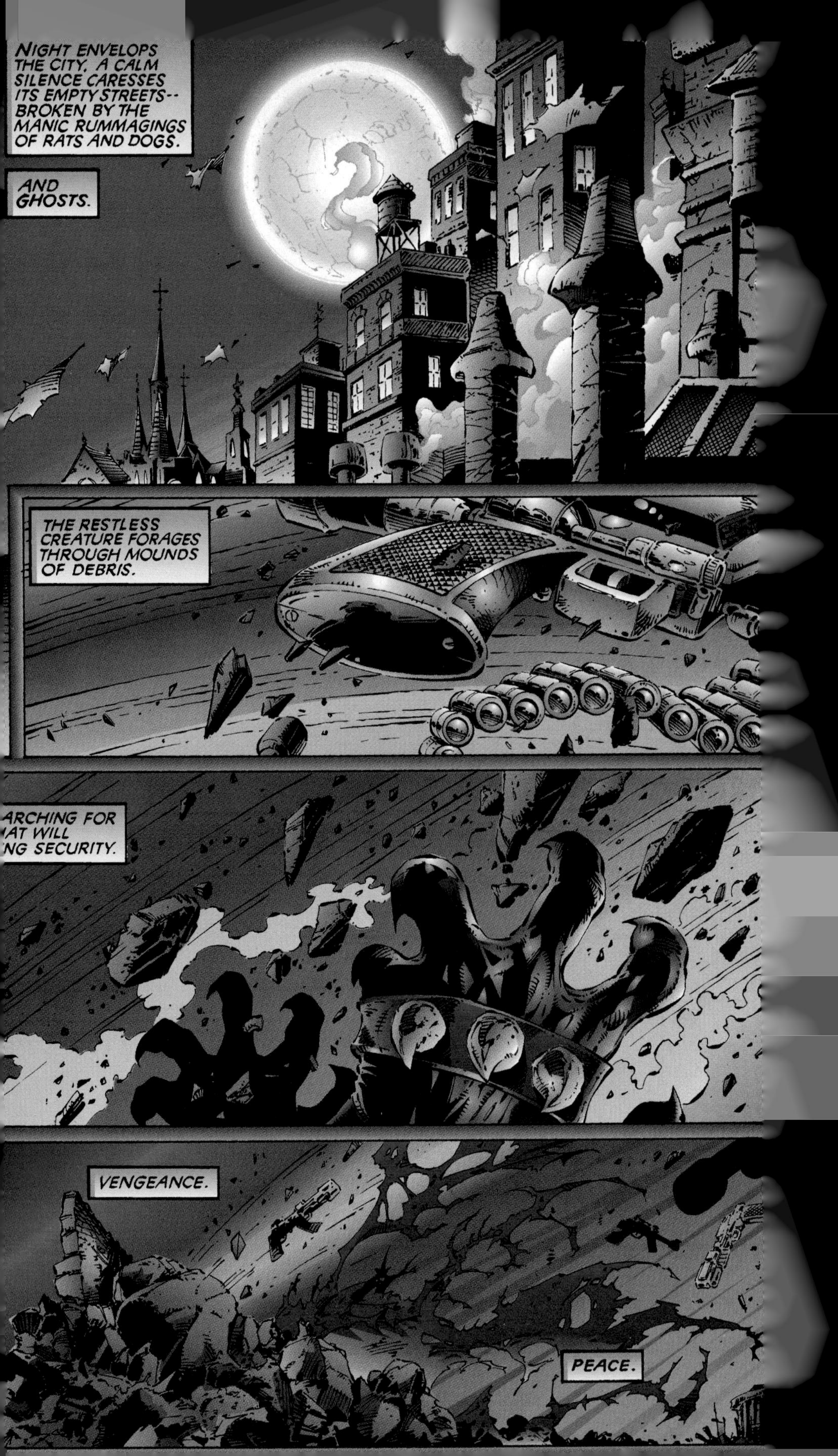
NIGHT ENVELOPS THE CITY. A CALM SILENCE CARESSES ITS EMPTY STREETS-- BROKEN BY THE MANIC RUMMAGINGS OF RATS AND DOGS.
AND GHOSTS.
THE RESTLESS CREATURE FORAGES THROUGH MOUNDS OF DEBRIS.
ARCHING FOR
AT WILL
NG SECURITY.
VENGEANCE.
PEACE.

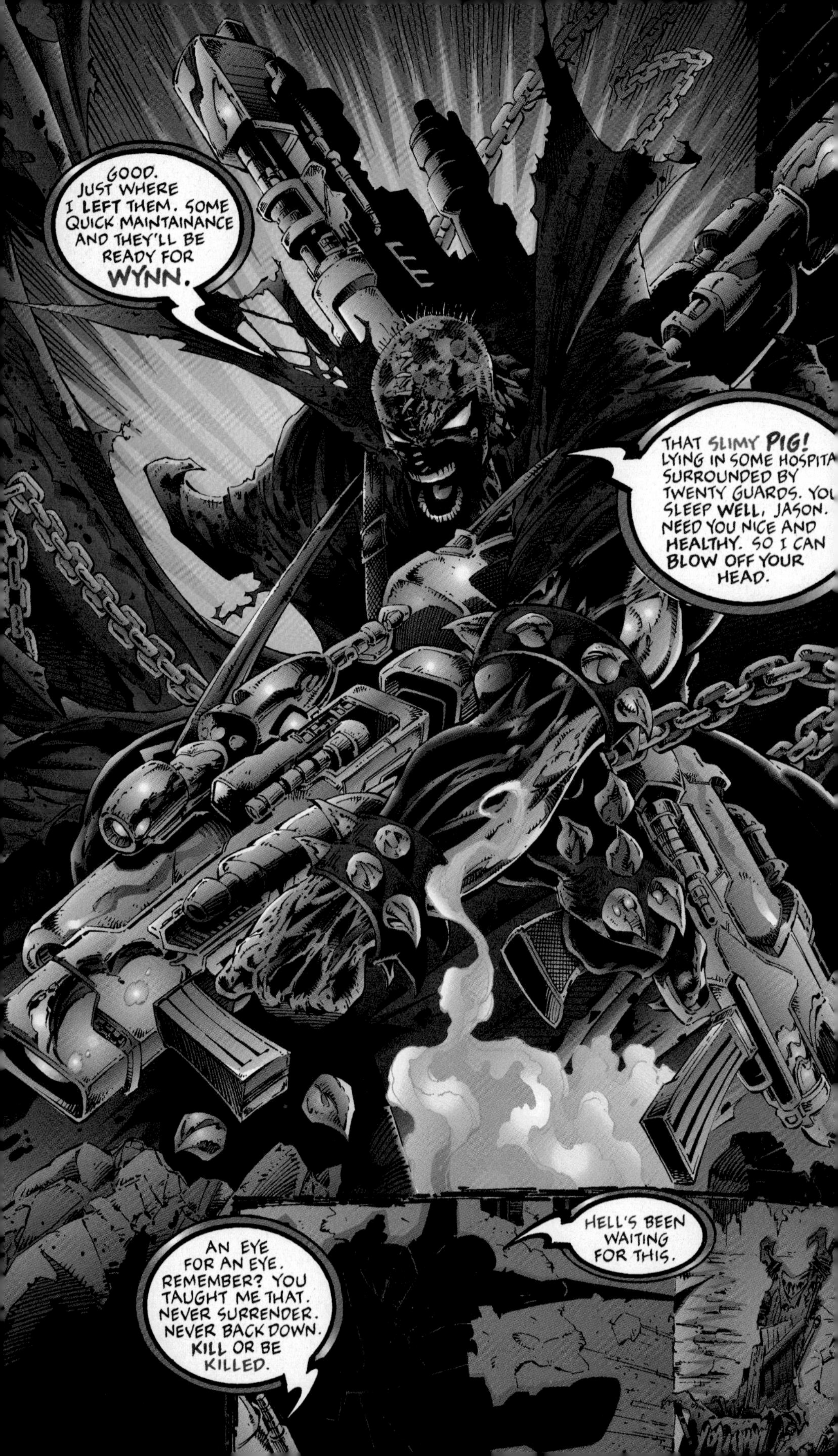
GOOD. JUST WHERE I LEFT THEM. SOME QUICK MAINTAINANCE AND THEY'LL BE READY FOR WYNN.
THAT SLIMY PIG! LYING IN SOME HOSPITA SURROUNDED BY TWENTY GUARDS. YO SLEEP WELL, JASON. NEED YOU NICE AND HEALTHY. SO I CAN BLOW OFF YOUR HEAD.
AN EYE FOR AN EYE. REMEMBER? YOU TAUGHT ME THAT. NEVER SURRENDER. NEVER BACK DOWN. KILL OR BE KILLED.
HELL'S BEEN WAITING FOR THIS.

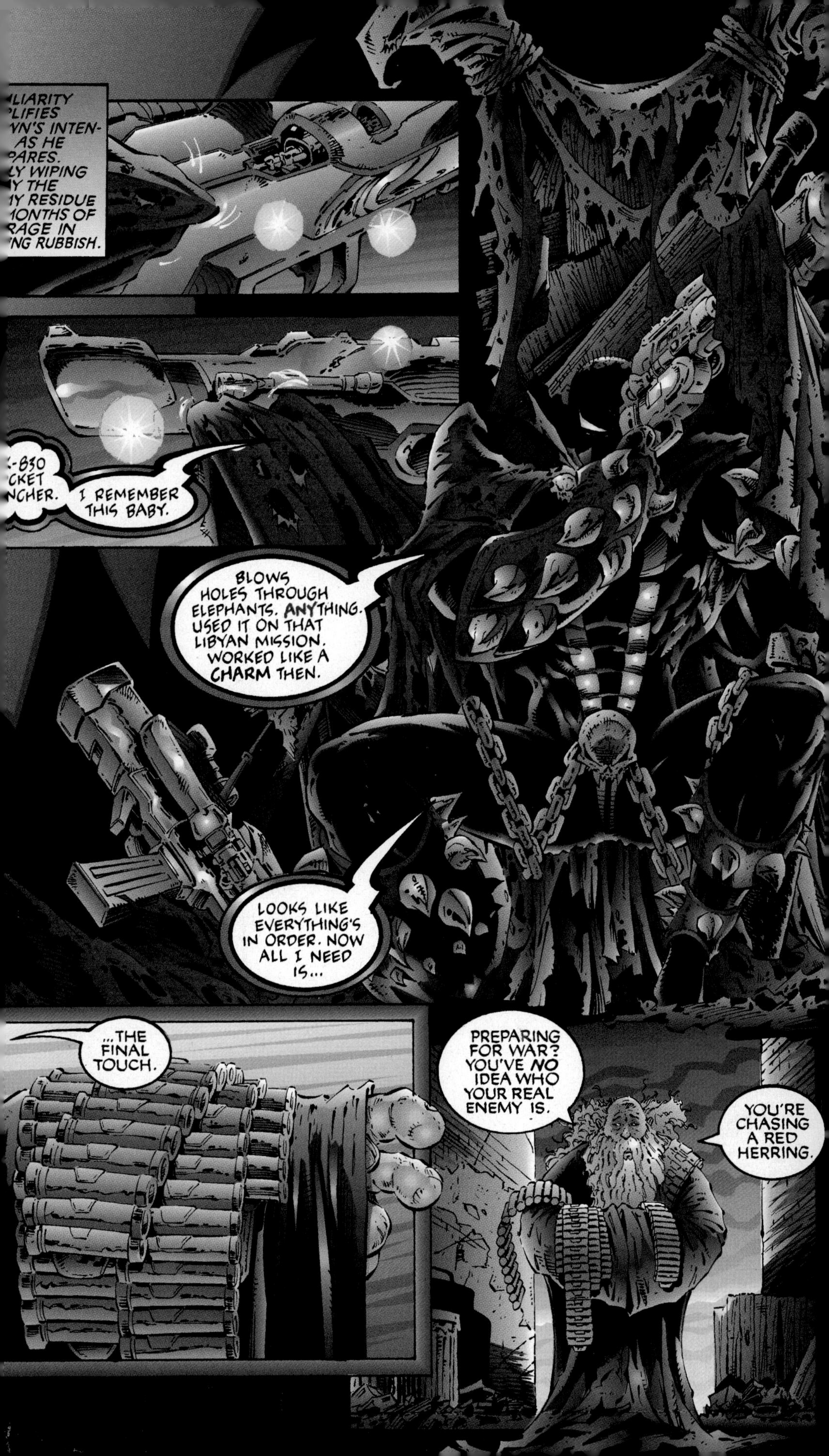

LIARITY
PLIFIES
VN'S INTEN-
AS HE
PARES.
LY WIPING
Y THE
Y RESIDUE
MONTHS OF
RAGE IN
NG RUBBISH.
-830
CKET
NCHER.
I REMEMBER THIS BABY.
BLOWS HOLES THROUGH ELEPHANTS. ANYTHING. USED IT ON THAT LIBYAN MISSION. WORKED LIKE A CHARM THEN.
LOOKS LIKE EVERYTHING'S IN ORDER. NOW ALL I NEED IS...
...THE FINAL TOUCH.
PREPARING FOR WAR? YOU'VE NO IDEA WHO YOUR REAL ENEMY IS.
YOU'RE CHASING A RED HERRING.

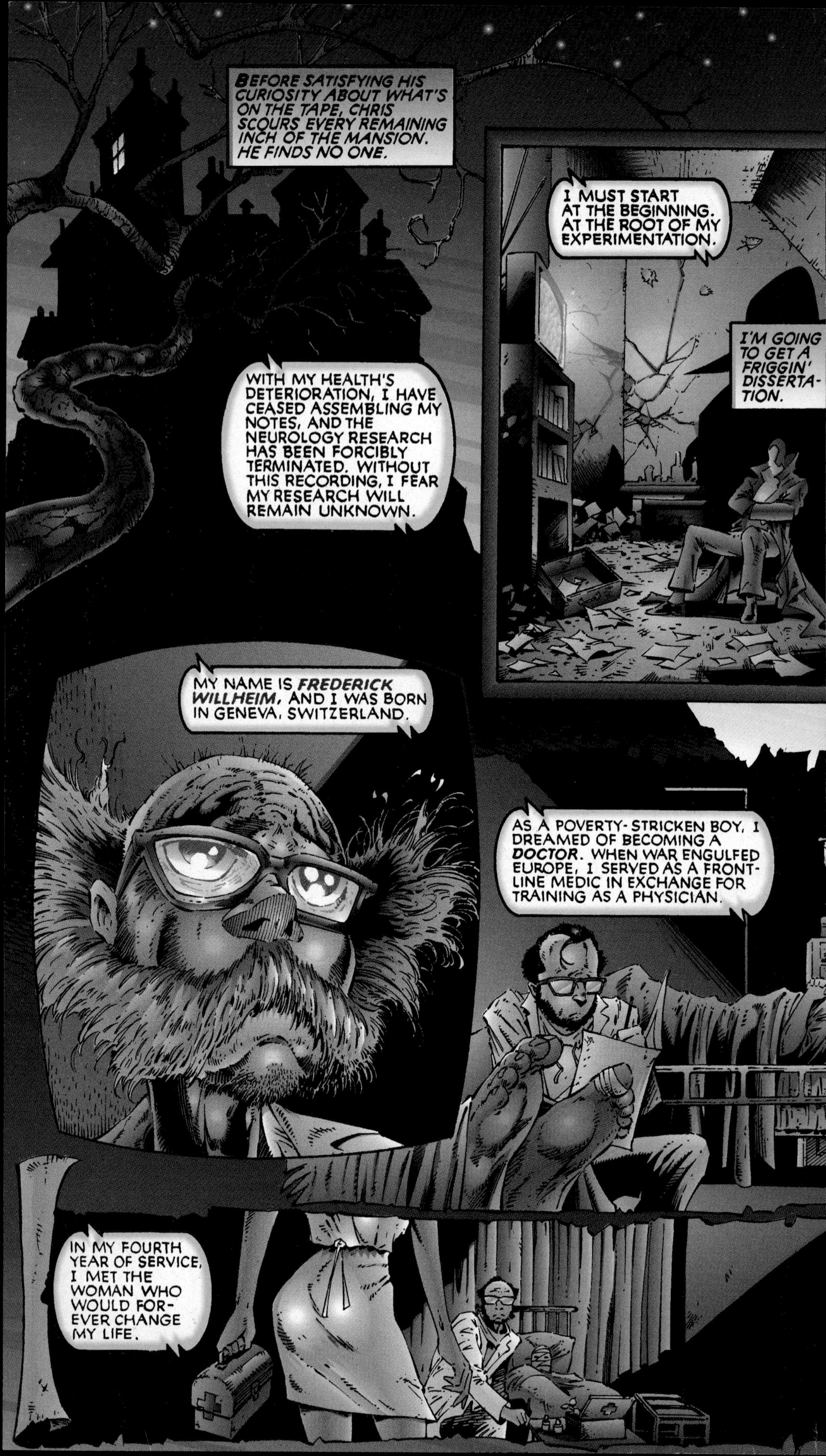
BEFORE SATISFYING HIS CURIOSITY ABOUT WHAT'S ON THE TAPE, CHRIS SCOURS EVERY REMAINING INCH OF THE MANSION. HE FINDS NO ONE.
I MUST START AT THE BEGINNING. AT THE ROOT OF MY EXPERIMENTATION.
I'M GOING TO GET A FRIGGIN' DISSERTATION.
WITH MY HEALTH'S DETERIORATION, I HAVE CEASED ASSEMBLING MY NOTES, AND THE NEUROLOGY RESEARCH HAS BEEN FORCIBLY TERMINATED. WITHOUT THIS RECORDING, I FEAR MY RESEARCH WILL REMAIN UNKNOWN.
MY NAME IS FREDERICK WILLHEIM, AND I WAS BORN IN GENEVA, SWITZERLAND.
AS A POVERTY-STRICKEN BOY, I DREAMED OF BECOMING A DOCTOR. WHEN WAR ENGULFED EUROPE, I SERVED AS A FRONT-LINE MEDIC IN EXCHANGE FOR TRAINING AS A PHYSICIAN.
IN MY FOURTH YEAR OF SERVICE, I MET THE WOMAN WHO WOULD FOREVER CHANGE MY LIFE.

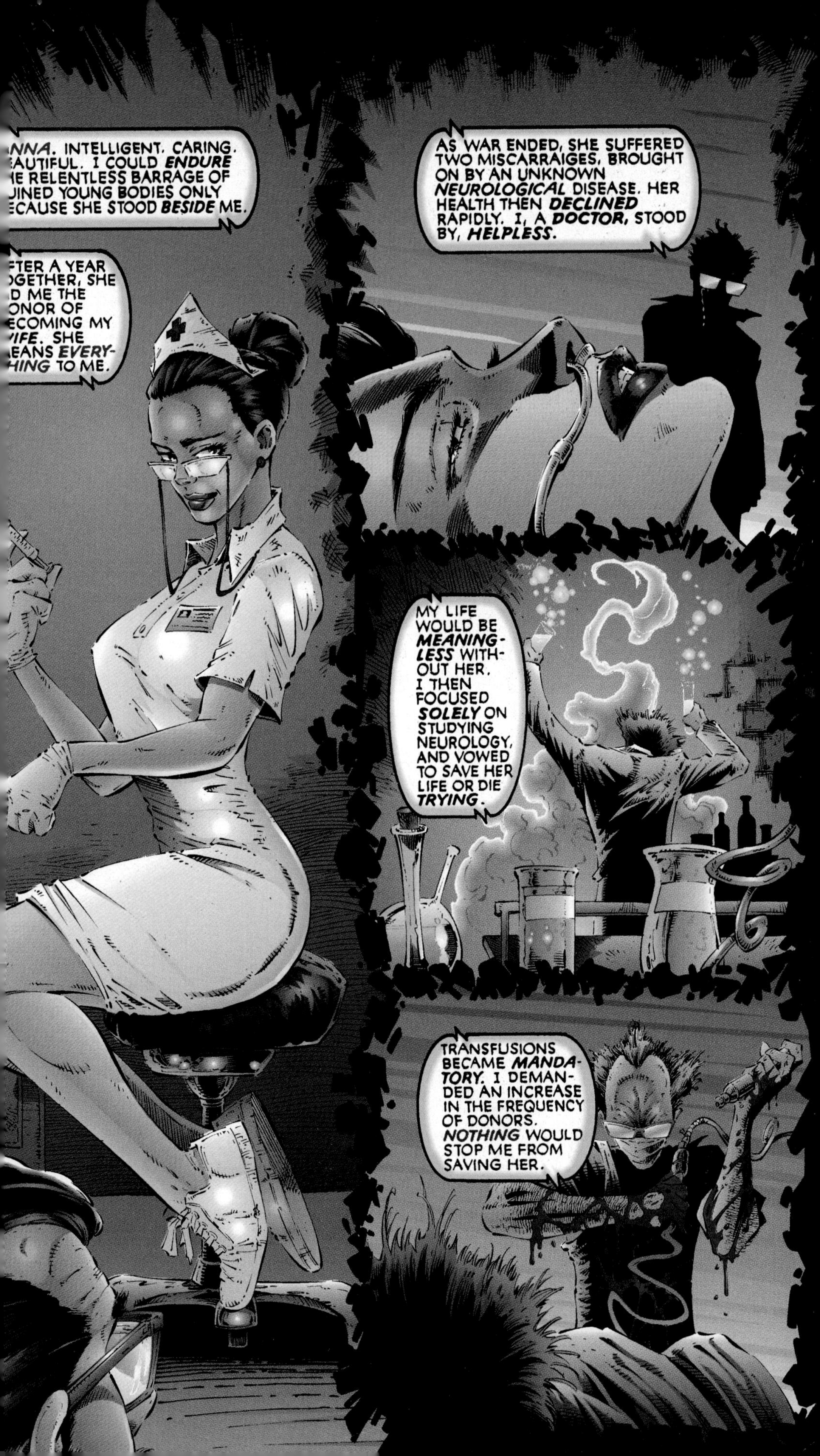
NNA. INTELLIGENT. CARING. EAUTIFUL. I COULD ENDURE HE RELENTLESS BARRAGE OF UINED YOUNG BODIES ONLY ECAUSE SHE STOOD BESIDE ME.
FTER A YEAR OGETHER, SHE D ME THE ONOR OF ECOMING MY VIFE. SHE EANS EVERY-HING TO ME.
AS WAR ENDED, SHE SUFFERED TWO MISCARRAIGES, BROUGHT ON BY AN UNKNOWN NEUROLOGICAL DISEASE. HER HEALTH THEN DECLINED RAPIDLY. I, A DOCTOR, STOOD BY, HELPLESS.
MY LIFE WOULD BE MEANING-LESS WITH-OUT HER. I THEN FOCUSED SOLELY ON STUDYING NEUROLOGY, AND VOWED TO SAVE HER LIFE OR DIE TRYING.
TRANSFUSIONS BECAME MANDA-TORY. I DEMAN-DED AN INCREASE IN THE FREQUENCY OF DONORS. NOTHING WOULD STOP ME FROM SAVING HER.

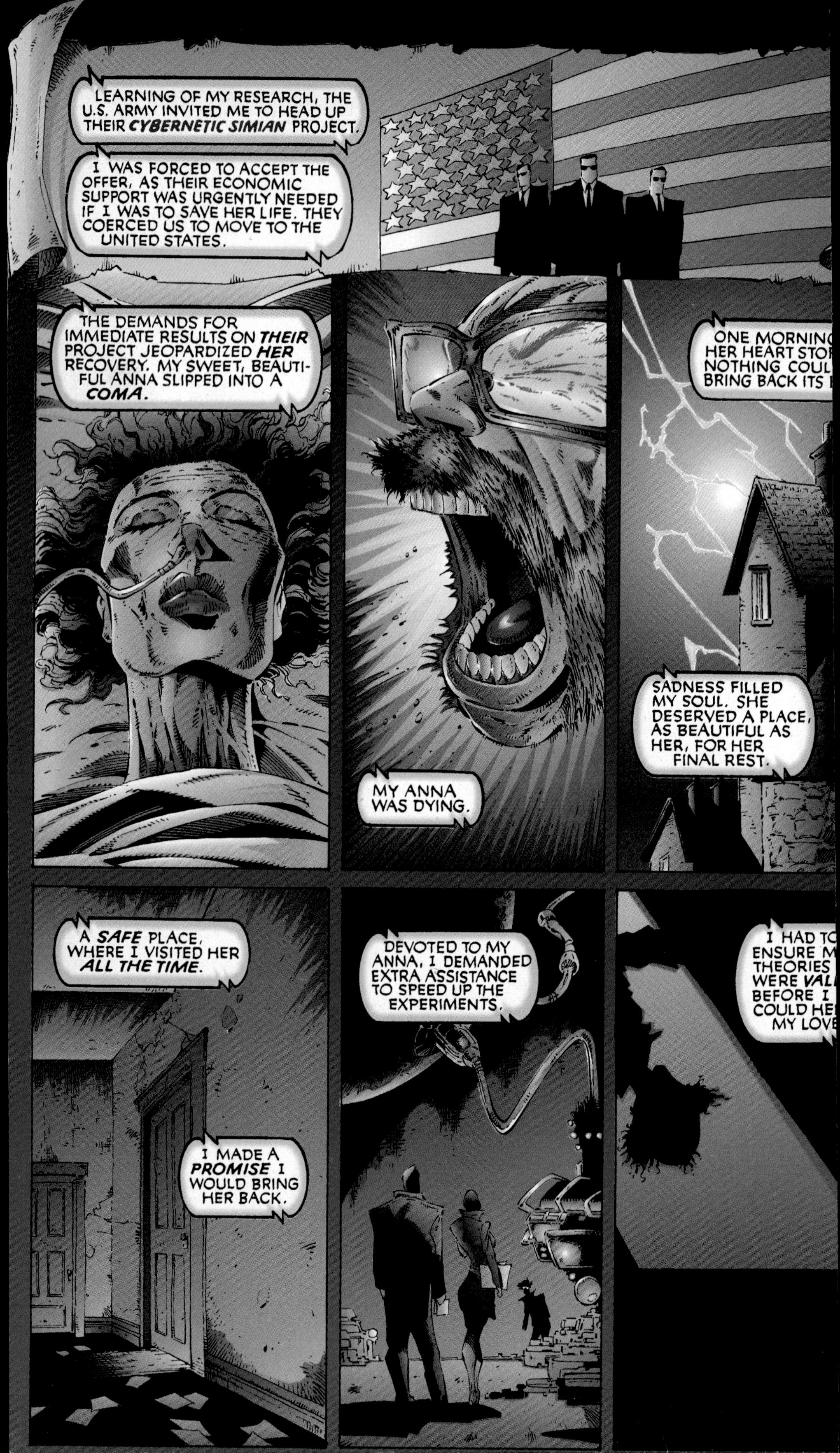
LEARNING OF MY RESEARCH, THE U.S. ARMY INVITED ME TO HEAD UP THEIR *CYBERNETIC SIMIAN* PROJECT.
I WAS FORCED TO ACCEPT THE OFFER, AS THEIR ECONOMIC SUPPORT WAS URGENTLY NEEDED IF I WAS TO SAVE HER LIFE. THEY COERCED US TO MOVE TO THE UNITED STATES.
THE DEMANDS FOR IMMEDIATE RESULTS ON *THEIR* PROJECT JEOPARDIZED *HER* RECOVERY. MY SWEET, BEAUTIFUL ANNA SLIPPED INTO A *COMA*.
MY ANNA WAS DYING.
ONE HER HEART NOTHING BRING BACK ITS
SADNESS FILLED MY SOUL. SHE DESERVED A PLACE, AS BEAUTIFUL AS HER, FOR HER FINAL REST.
A *SAFE* PLACE, WHERE I VISITED HER *ALL THE TIME*.
I MADE A *PROMISE* I WOULD BRING HER BACK.
DEVOTED TO MY ANNA, I DEMANDED EXTRA ASSISTANCE TO SPEED UP THE EXPERIMENTS.
I HAD ENSURE THEORIES WERE BEFORE I COULD MY

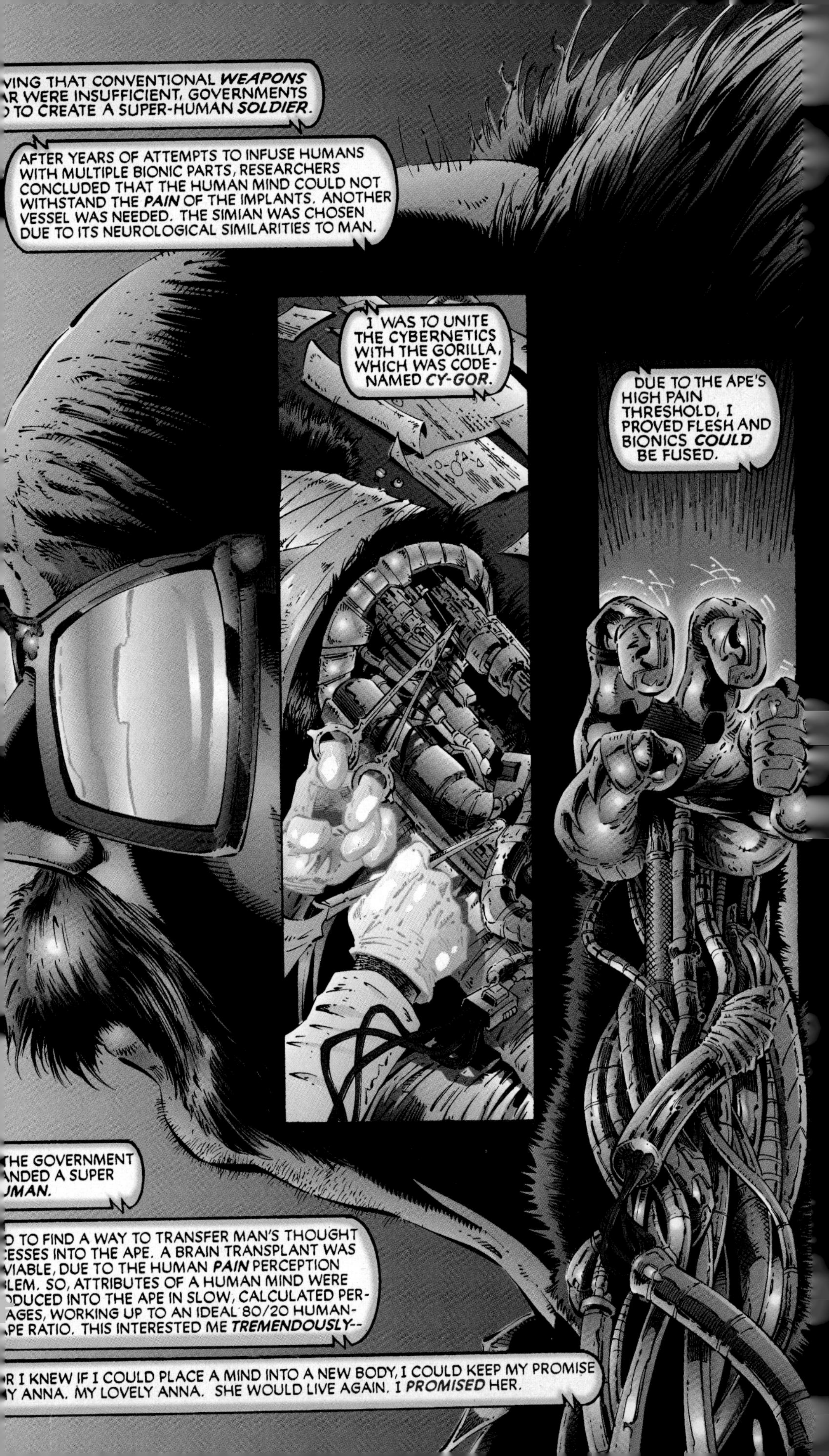
VING THAT CONVENTIONAL WEAPONS
AR WERE INSUFFICIENT, GOVERNMENTS
TO CREATE A SUPER-HUMAN SOLDIER.
AFTER YEARS OF ATTEMPTS TO INFUSE HUMANS WITH MULTIPLE BIONIC PARTS, RESEARCHERS CONCLUDED THAT THE HUMAN MIND COULD NOT WITHSTAND THE PAIN OF THE IMPLANTS. ANOTHER VESSEL WAS NEEDED. THE SIMIAN WAS CHOSEN DUE TO ITS NEUROLOGICAL SIMILARITIES TO MAN.
I WAS TO UNITE THE CYBERNETICS WITH THE GORILLA, WHICH WAS CODE-NAMED CY-GOR.
DUE TO THE APE'S HIGH PAIN THRESHOLD, I PROVED FLESH AND BIONICS COULD BE FUSED.
THE GOVERNMENT
ANDED A SUPER
UMAN.
D TO FIND A WAY TO TRANSFER MAN'S THOUGHT
CESSES INTO THE APE. A BRAIN TRANSPLANT WAS
VIABLE, DUE TO THE HUMAN PAIN PERCEPTION
LEM. SO, ATTRIBUTES OF A HUMAN MIND WERE
DDUCED INTO THE APE IN SLOW, CALCULATED PER-
AGES, WORKING UP TO AN IDEAL 80/20 HUMAN-
PE RATIO. THIS INTERESTED ME TREMENDOUSLY--
R I KNEW IF I COULD PLACE A MIND INTO A NEW BODY, I COULD KEEP MY PROMISE
Y ANNA. MY LOVELY ANNA. SHE WOULD LIVE AGAIN. I PROMISED HER.

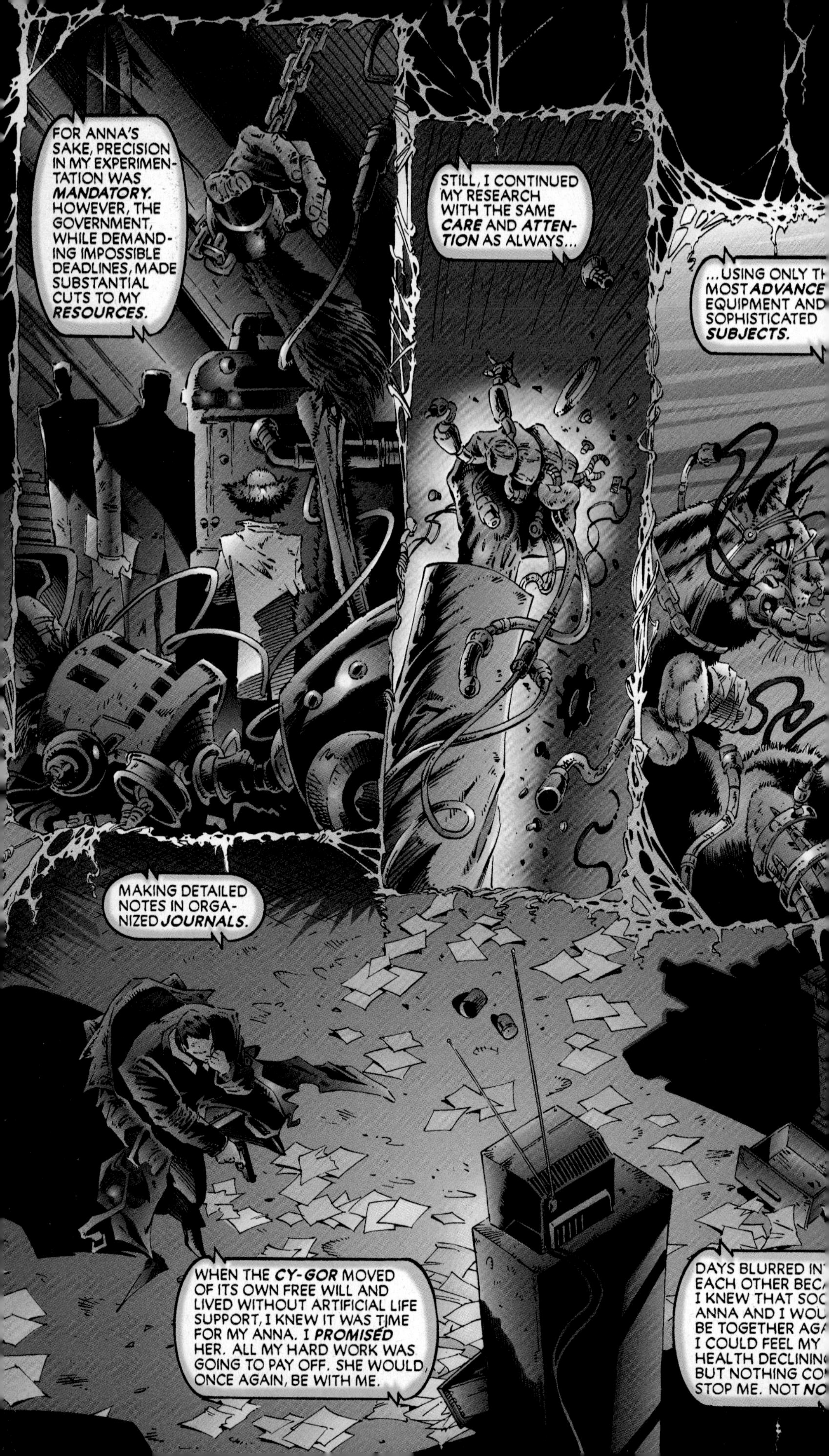
FOR ANNA'S SAKE, PRECISION IN MY EXPERIMENTATION WAS MANDATORY. HOWEVER, THE GOVERNMENT, WHILE DEMANDING IMPOSSIBLE DEADLINES, MADE SUBSTANTIAL CUTS TO MY RESOURCES.
STILL, I CONTINUED MY RESEARCH WITH THE SAME CARE AND ATTENTION AS ALWAYS...
...USING ONLY TH MOST ADVANCE EQUIPMENT AND SOPHISTICATED SUBJECTS.
MAKING DETAILED NOTES IN ORGANIZED JOURNALS.
WHEN THE CY-GOR MOVED OF ITS OWN FREE WILL AND LIVED WITHOUT ARTIFICIAL LIFE SUPPORT, I KNEW IT WAS TIME FOR MY ANNA. I PROMISED HER. ALL MY HARD WORK WAS GOING TO PAY OFF. SHE WOULD ONCE AGAIN, BE WITH ME.
DAYS BLURRED INT EACH OTHER BEC I KNEW THAT SOO ANNA AND I WOU BE TOGETHER AGA I COULD FEEL MY HEALTH DECLININ BUT NOTHING CO STOP ME. NOT NO

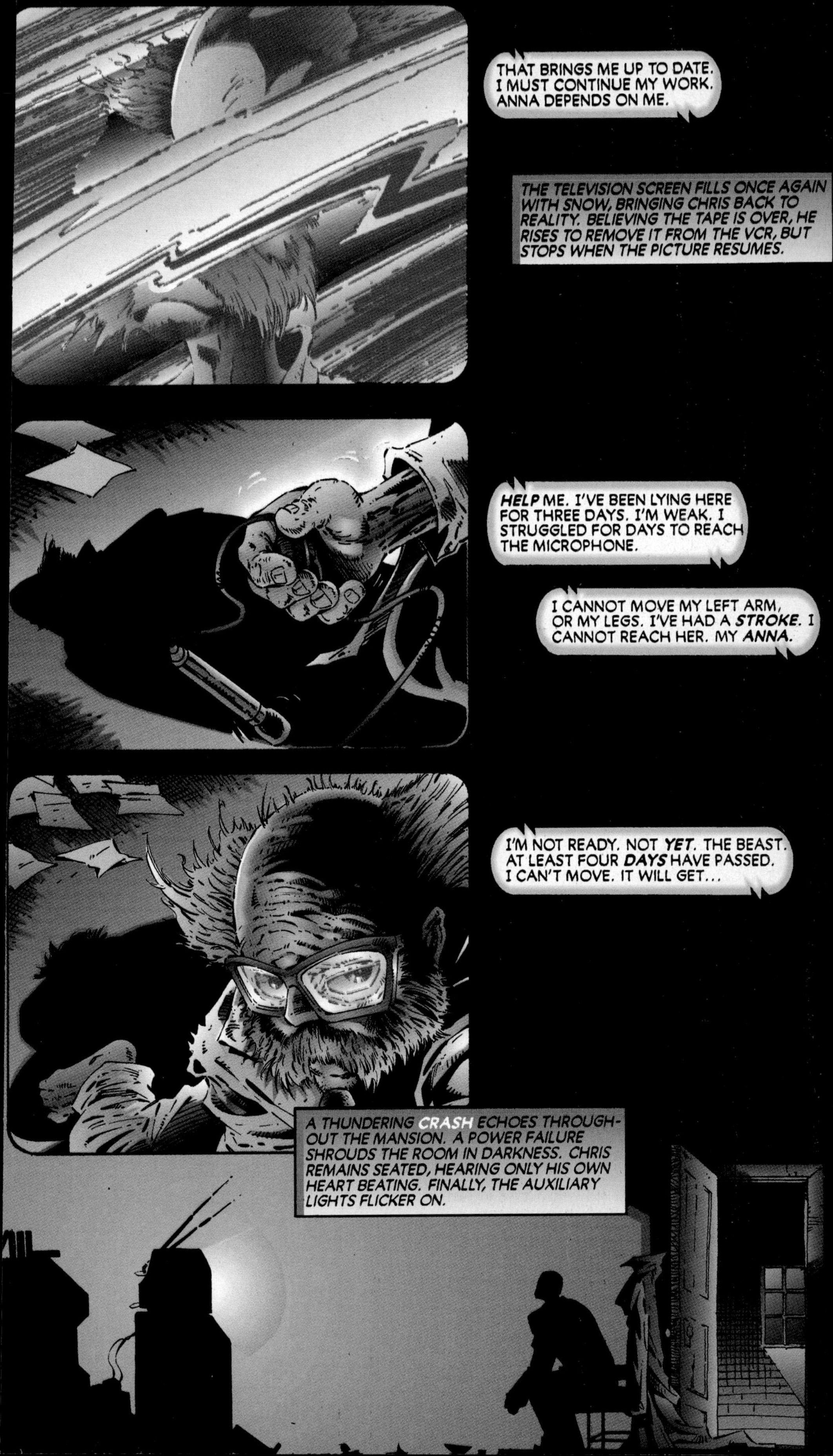

THAT BRINGS ME UP TO DATE. I MUST CONTINUE MY WORK. ANNA DEPENDS ON ME.
THE TELEVISION SCREEN FILLS ONCE AGAIN WITH SNOW, BRINGING CHRIS BACK TO REALITY. BELIEVING THE TAPE IS OVER, HE RISES TO REMOVE IT FROM THE VCR, BUT STOPS WHEN THE PICTURE RESUMES.
HELP ME. I'VE BEEN LYING HERE FOR THREE DAYS. I'M WEAK. I STRUGGLED FOR DAYS TO REACH THE MICROPHONE.
I CANNOT MOVE MY LEFT ARM, OR MY LEGS. I'VE HAD A STROKE. I CANNOT REACH HER. MY ANNA.
I'M NOT READY. NOT YET. THE BEAST. AT LEAST FOUR DAYS HAVE PASSED. I CAN'T MOVE. IT WILL GET...
A THUNDERING CRASH ECHOES THROUGH-OUT THE MANSION. A POWER FAILURE SHROUDS THE ROOM IN DARKNESS. CHRIS REMAINS SEATED, HEARING ONLY HIS OWN HEART BEATING. FINALLY, THE AUXILIARY LIGHTS FLICKER ON.

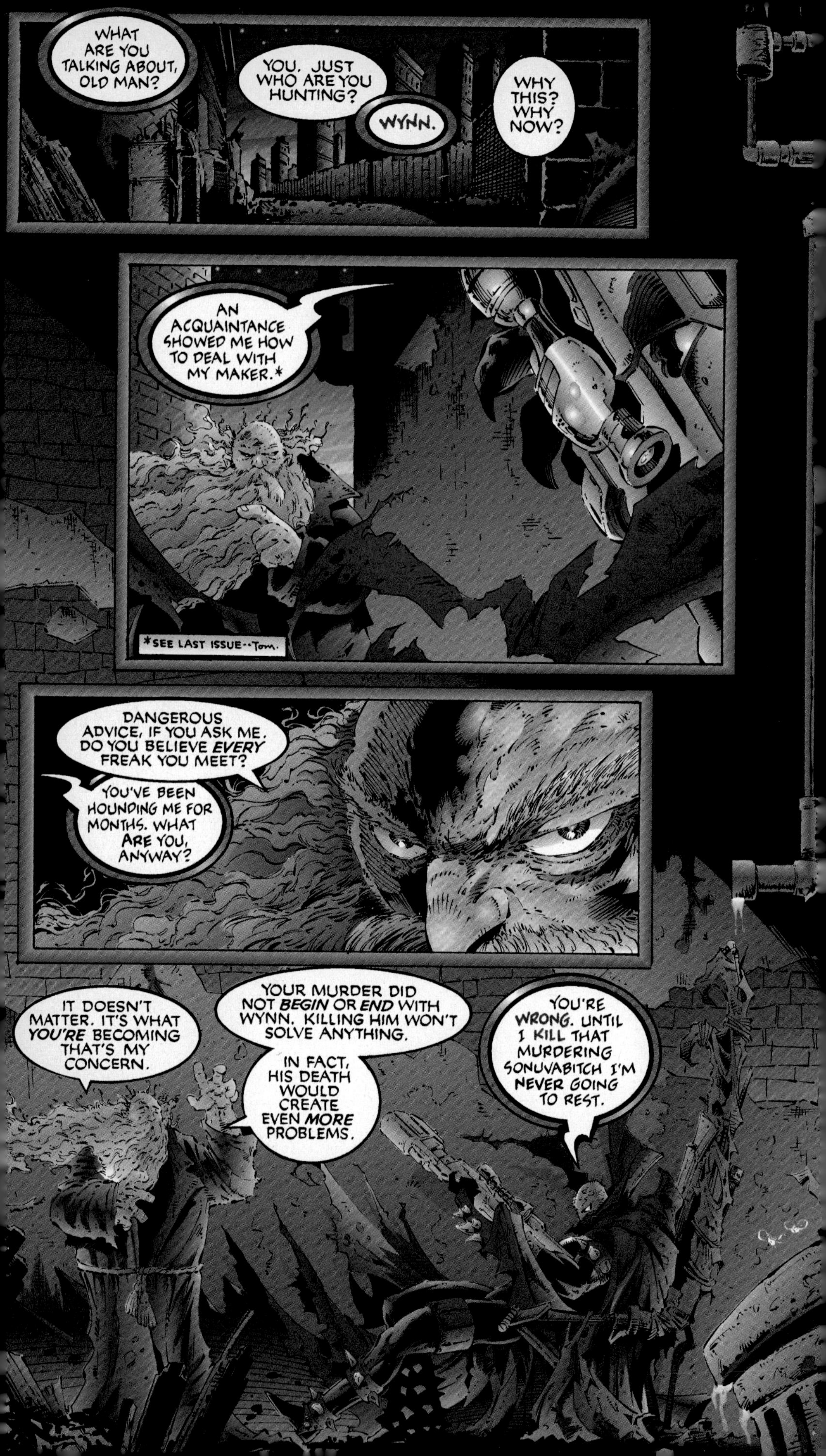
WHAT ARE YOU TALKING ABOUT, OLD MAN?
YOU. JUST WHO ARE YOU HUNTING?
WYNN.
WHY THIS? WHY NOW?
AN ACQUAINTANCE SHOWED ME HOW TO DEAL WITH MY MAKER.*
*SEE LAST ISSUE--Tom.
DANGEROUS ADVICE, IF YOU ASK ME. DO YOU BELIEVE EVERY FREAK YOU MEET?
YOU'VE BEEN HOUNDING ME FOR MONTHS. WHAT ARE YOU, ANYWAY?
IT DOESN'T MATTER. IT'S WHAT YOU'RE BECOMING THAT'S MY CONCERN.
YOUR MURDER DID NOT BEGIN OR END WITH WYNN. KILLING HIM WON'T SOLVE ANYTHING.
IN FACT, HIS DEATH WOULD CREATE EVEN MORE PROBLEMS.
YOU'RE WRONG. UNTIL I KILL THAT MURDERING SONUVABITCH I'M NEVER GOING TO REST.

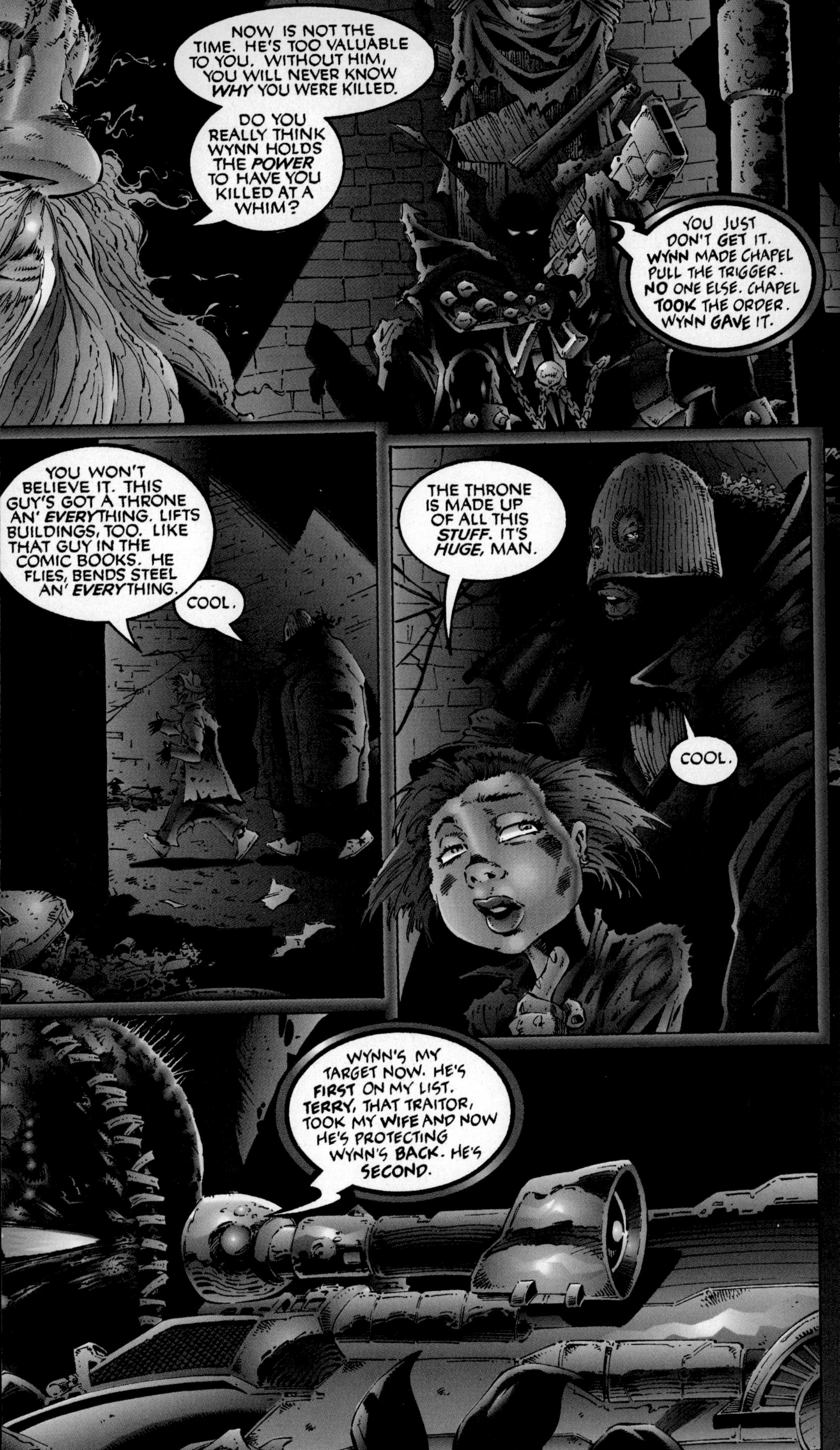
NOW IS NOT THE TIME. HE'S TOO VALUABLE TO YOU. WITHOUT HIM, YOU WILL NEVER KNOW *WHY* YOU WERE KILLED.
DO YOU REALLY THINK WYNN HOLDS THE *POWER* TO HAVE YOU KILLED AT A WHIM?
YOU JUST DON'T GET IT. **WYNN** MADE CHAPEL PULL THE TRIGGER. **NO** ONE ELSE. CHAPEL **TOOK** THE ORDER. WYNN **GAVE** IT.
YOU WON'T BELIEVE IT. THIS GUY'S GOT A THRONE AN' *EVERY*THING. LIFTS BUILDINGS, TOO. LIKE THAT GUY IN THE COMIC BOOKS. HE FLIES, BENDS STEEL AN' *EVERY*THING.
COOL.
THE THRONE IS MADE UP OF ALL THIS *STUFF*. IT'S *HUGE*, MAN.
COOL.
WYNN'S MY TARGET NOW. HE'S **FIRST** ON MY LIST. **TERRY**, THAT TRAITOR, TOOK MY **WIFE** AND NOW HE'S PROTECTING WYNN'S **BACK**. HE'S **SECOND**.

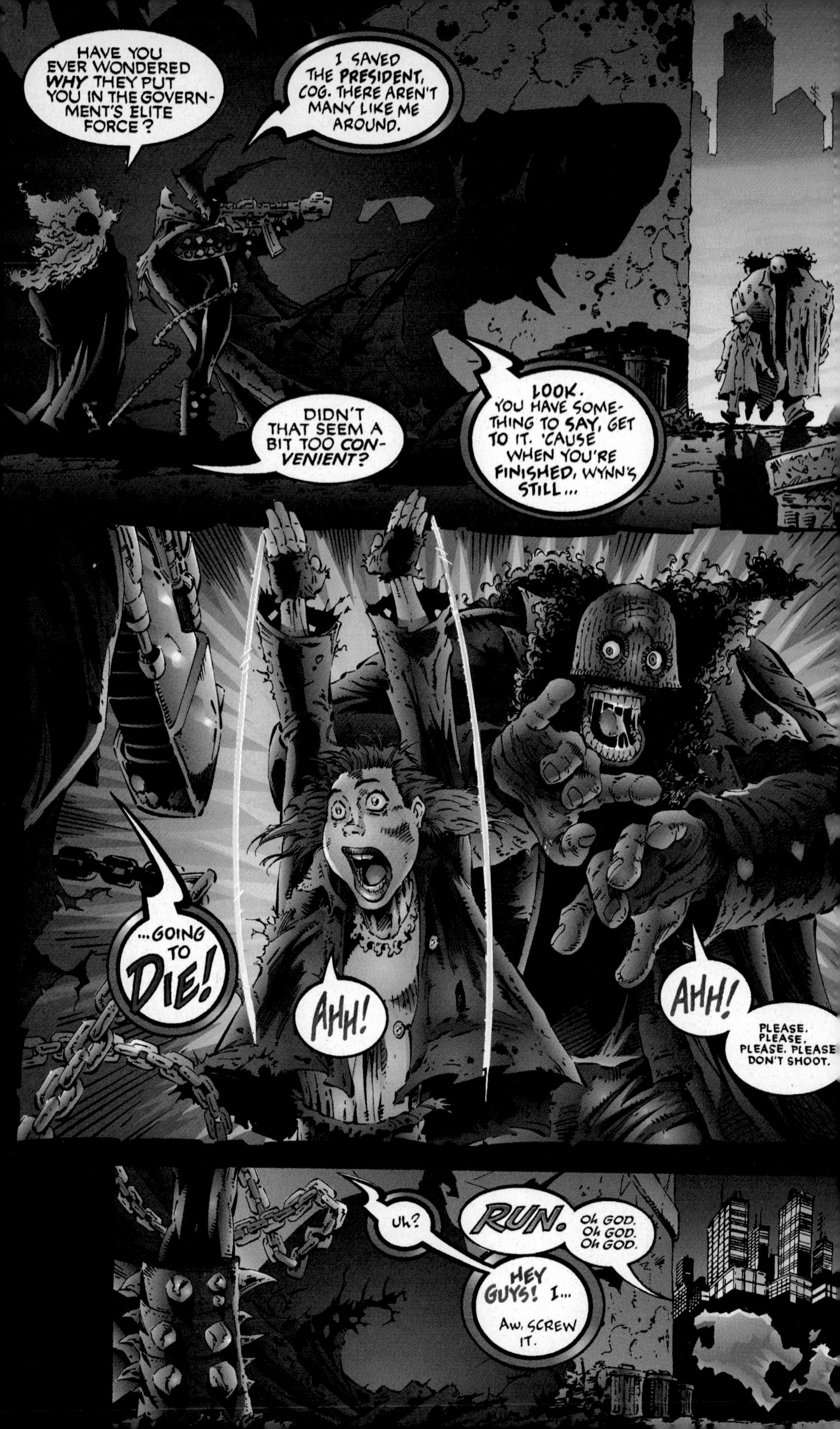
HAVE YOU EVER WONDERED WHY THEY PUT YOU IN THE GOVERN-MENT'S ELITE FORCE?
I SAVED THE PRESIDENT, COG. THERE AREN'T MANY LIKE ME AROUND.
DIDN'T THAT SEEM A BIT TOO CON-VENIENT?
LOOK. YOU HAVE SOME-THING TO SAY, GET TO IT. 'CAUSE WHEN YOU'RE FINISHED, WYNN'S STILL...
...GOING TO DIE!
AHH!
AHH!
PLEASE. PLEASE. PLEASE. PLEASE DON'T SHOOT.
Uh?
RUN.
Oh GOD. Oh GOD. Oh GOD.
HEY GUYS! I...
AW, SCREW IT.

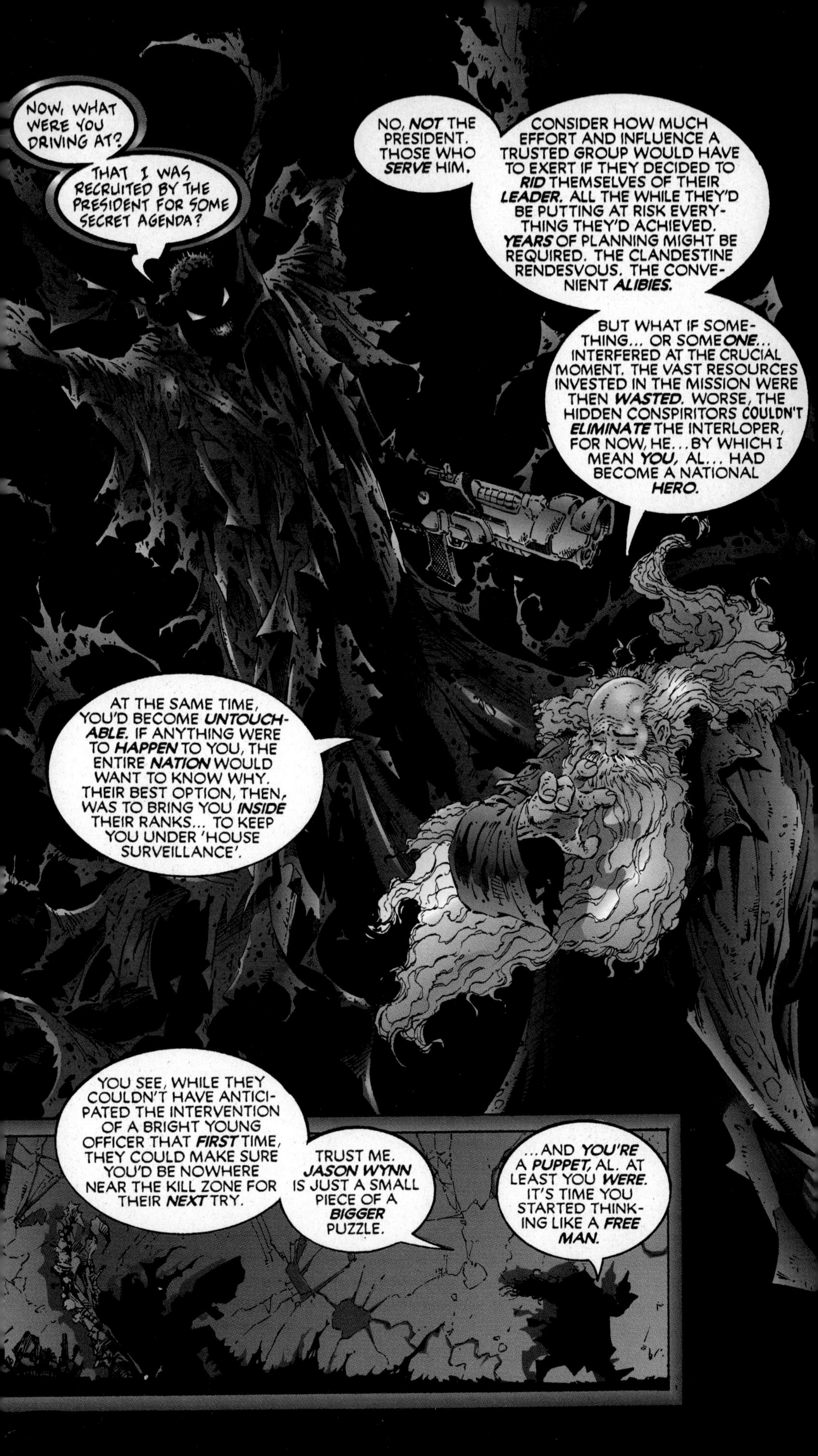
NOW, WHAT WERE YOU DRIVING AT?
THAT I WAS RECRUITED BY THE PRESIDENT FOR SOME SECRET AGENDA?
NO, NOT THE PRESIDENT. THOSE WHO SERVE HIM.
CONSIDER HOW MUCH EFFORT AND INFLUENCE A TRUSTED GROUP WOULD HAVE TO EXERT IF THEY DECIDED TO RID THEMSELVES OF THEIR LEADER. ALL THE WHILE THEY'D BE PUTTING AT RISK EVERYTHING THEY'D ACHIEVED. YEARS OF PLANNING MIGHT BE REQUIRED. THE CLANDESTINE RENDESVOUS. THE CONVENIENT ALIBIES.
BUT WHAT IF SOMETHING... OR SOMEONE... INTERFERED AT THE CRUCIAL MOMENT. THE VAST RESOURCES INVESTED IN THE MISSION WERE THEN WASTED. WORSE, THE HIDDEN CONSPIRITORS COULDN'T ELIMINATE THE INTERLOPER, FOR NOW, HE. . . BY WHICH I MEAN YOU, AL. . . HAD BECOME A NATIONAL HERO.
AT THE SAME TIME, YOU'D BECOME UNTOUCHABLE. IF ANYTHING WERE TO HAPPEN TO YOU, THE ENTIRE NATION WOULD WANT TO KNOW WHY. THEIR BEST OPTION, THEN, WAS TO BRING YOU INSIDE THEIR RANKS... TO KEEP YOU UNDER 'HOUSE SURVEILLANCE'.
YOU SEE, WHILE THEY COULDN'T HAVE ANTICIPATED THE INTERVENTION OF A BRIGHT YOUNG OFFICER THAT FIRST TIME, THEY COULD MAKE SURE YOU'D BE NOWHERE NEAR THE KILL ZONE FOR THEIR NEXT TRY.
TRUST ME. JASON WYNN IS JUST A SMALL PIECE OF A BIGGER PUZZLE.
...AND YOU'RE A PUPPET, AL. AT LEAST YOU WERE. IT'S TIME YOU STARTED THINKING LIKE A FREE MAN.

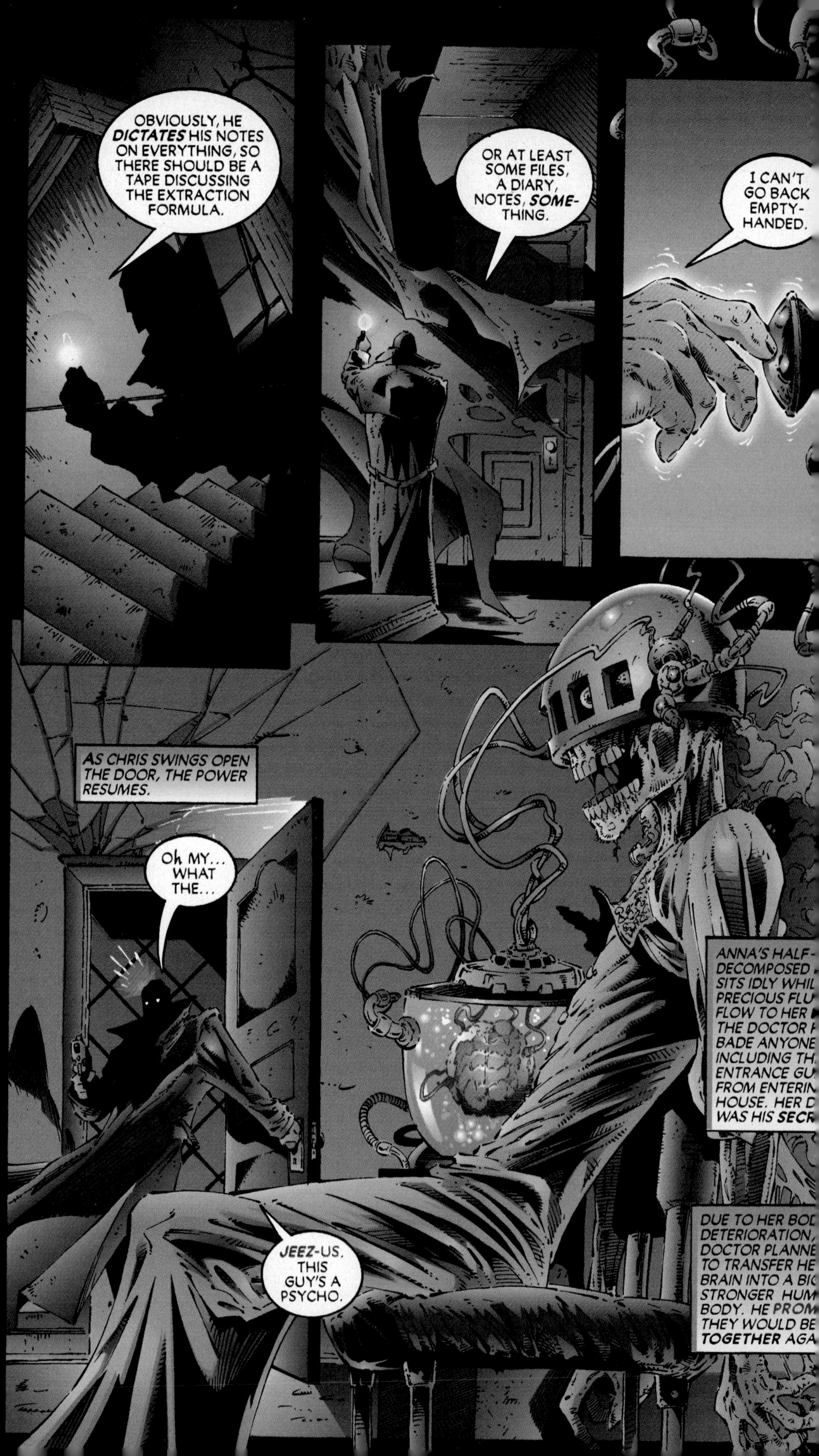
OBVIOUSLY, HE DICTATES HIS NOTES ON EVERYTHING, SO THERE SHOULD BE A TAPE DISCUSSING THE EXTRACTION FORMULA.
OR AT LEAST SOME FILES, A DIARY, NOTES, SOME-THING.
I CAN'T GO BACK EMPTY-HANDED.
AS CHRIS SWINGS OPEN THE DOOR, THE POWER RESUMES.
Oh MY... WHAT THE...
JEEZ-US. THIS GUY'S A PSYCHO.
ANNA'S HALF- DECOMPOSED SITS IDLY WHIL PRECIOUS FLU FLOW TO HER THE DOCTOR BADE ANYONE INCLUDING TH ENTRANCE GU FROM ENTERIN HOUSE. HER D WAS HIS SECR
DUE TO HER BOD DETERIORATION, DOCTOR PLANNE TO TRANSFER HE BRAIN INTO A BIG STRONGER HUM BODY. HE PROM THEY WOULD BE TOGETHER AGA

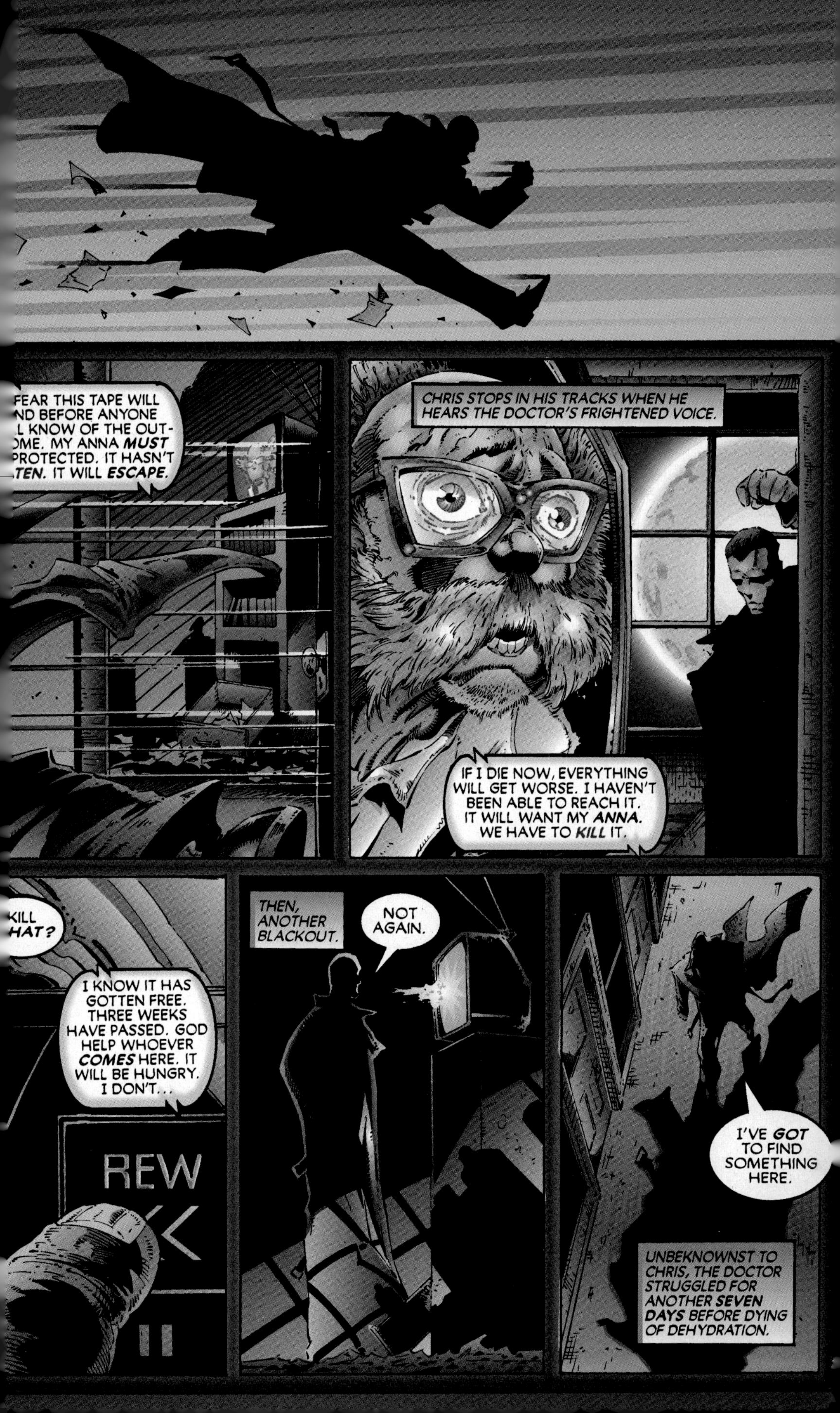

FEAR THIS TAPE WILL ND BEFORE ANYONE L KNOW OF THE OUT- OME. MY ANNA MUST PROTECTED. IT HASN'T TEN. IT WILL ESCAPE.
CHRIS STOPS IN HIS TRACKS WHEN HE HEARS THE DOCTOR'S FRIGHTENED VOICE.
IF I DIE NOW, EVERYTHING WILL GET WORSE. I HAVEN'T BEEN ABLE TO REACH IT. IT WILL WANT MY ANNA. WE HAVE TO KILL IT.
KILL HAT?
I KNOW IT HAS GOTTEN FREE. THREE WEEKS HAVE PASSED. GOD HELP WHOEVER COMES HERE. IT WILL BE HUNGRY. I DON'T...
REW
THEN, ANOTHER BLACKOUT.
NOT AGAIN.
I'VE GOT TO FIND SOMETHING HERE.
UNBEKNOWNST TO CHRIS, THE DOCTOR STRUGGLED FOR ANOTHER SEVEN DAYS BEFORE DYING OF DEHYDRATION.

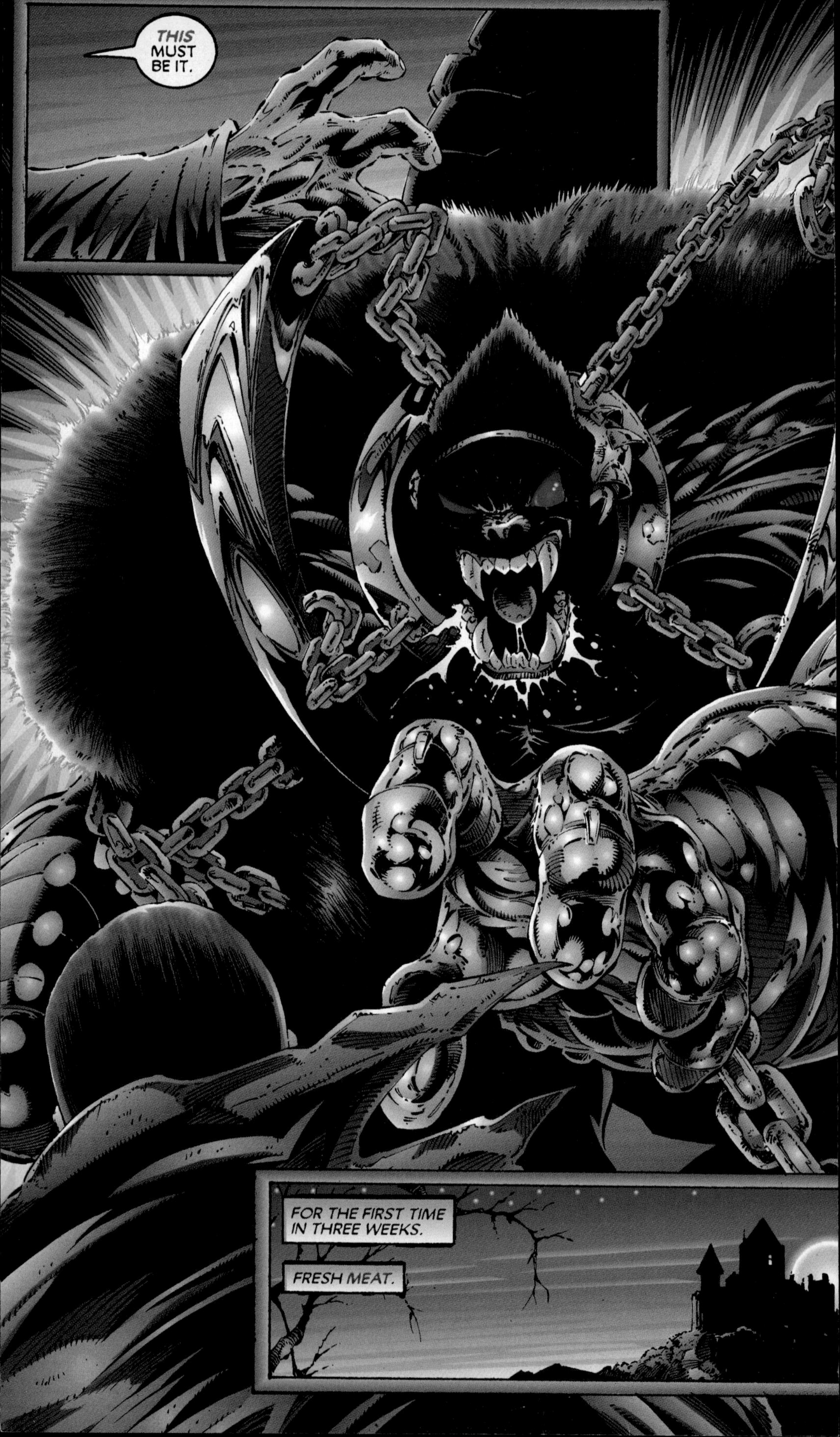
THIS MUST BE IT.
FOR THE FIRST TIME IN THREE WEEKS.
FRESH MEAT.

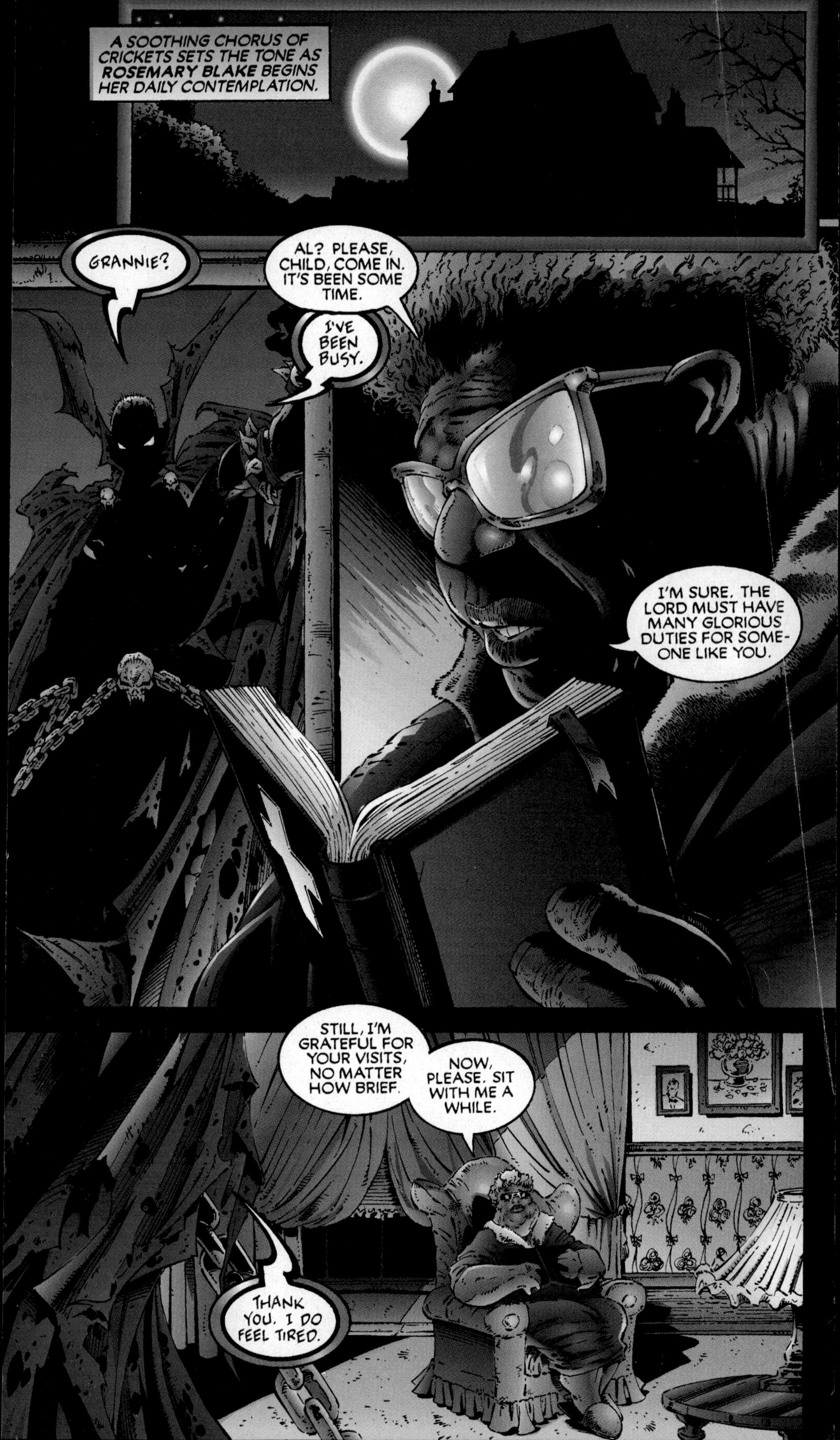

A SOOTHING CHORUS OF CRICKETS SETS THE TONE AS ROSEMARY BLAKE BEGINS HER DAILY CONTEMPLATION.
GRANNIE?
AL? PLEASE, CHILD, COME IN. IT'S BEEN SOME TIME.
I'VE BEEN BUSY.
I'M SURE. THE LORD MUST HAVE MANY GLORIOUS DUTIES FOR SOME-ONE LIKE YOU.
STILL, I'M GRATEFUL FOR YOUR VISITS, NO MATTER HOW BRIEF.
NOW, PLEASE. SIT WITH ME A WHILE.
THANK YOU. I DO FEEL TIRED.

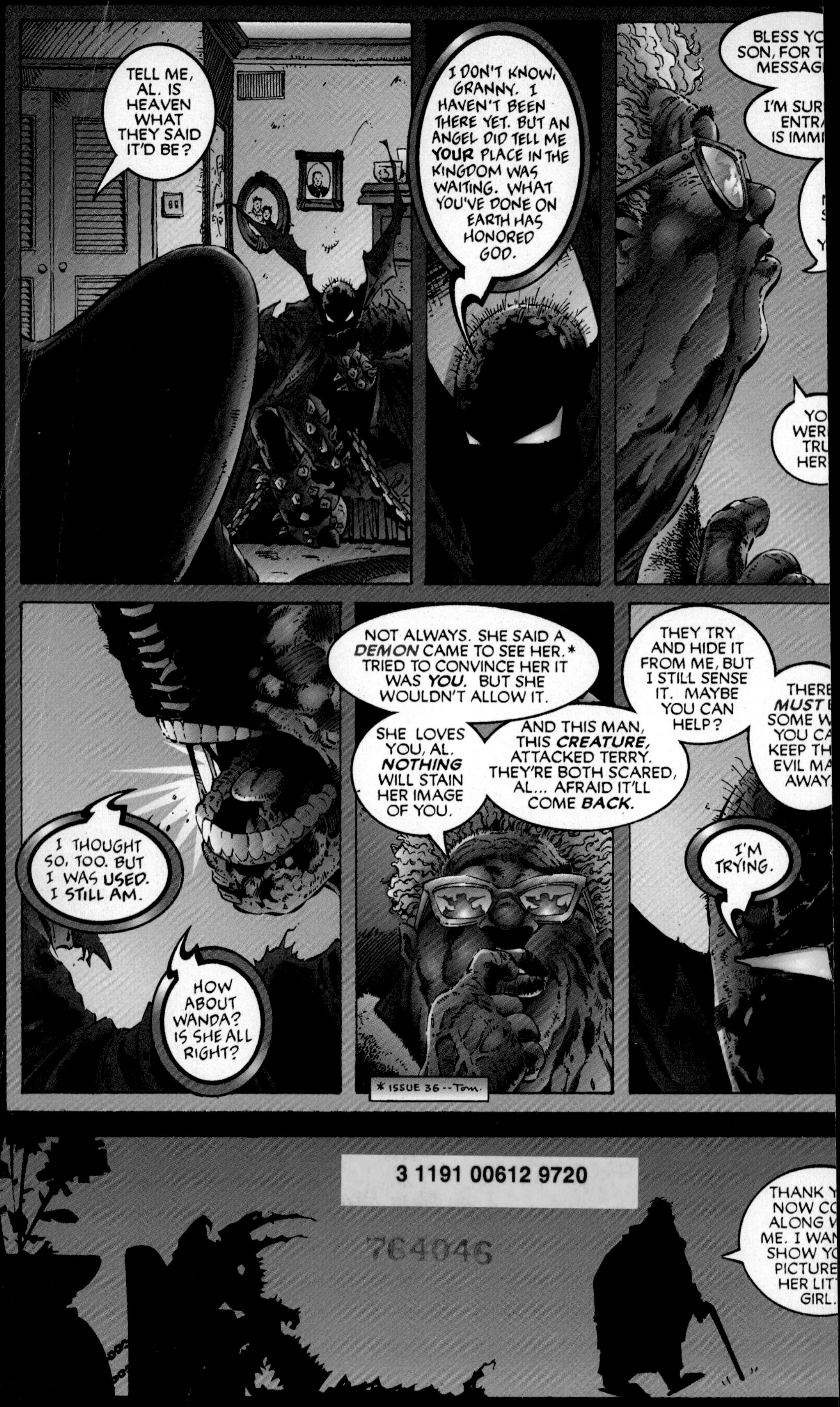
TELL ME, AL. IS HEAVEN WHAT THEY SAID IT'D BE?
I DON'T KNOW, GRANNY. I HAVEN'T BEEN THERE YET. BUT AN ANGEL DID TELL ME YOUR PLACE IN THE KINGDOM WAS WAITING. WHAT YOU'VE DONE ON EARTH HAS HONORED GOD.
BLESS YO SON, FOR T MESSAG
I'M SUR ENTRA IS IMMI
YO WER TRU HER
NOT ALWAYS. SHE SAID A DEMON CAME TO SEE HER.* TRIED TO CONVINCE HER IT WAS YOU. BUT SHE WOULDN'T ALLOW IT.
SHE LOVES YOU, AL. NOTHING WILL STAIN HER IMAGE OF YOU.
I THOUGHT SO, TOO. BUT I WAS USED. I STILL AM.
AND THIS MAN, THIS CREATURE, ATTACKED TERRY. THEY'RE BOTH SCARED, AL... AFRAID IT'LL COME BACK.
HOW ABOUT WANDA? IS SHE ALL RIGHT?
THEY TRY AND HIDE IT FROM ME, BUT I STILL SENSE IT. MAYBE YOU CAN HELP?
I'M TRYING.
THERE MUST SOME W YOU CA KEEP TH EVIL MA AWAY
* ISSUE 36 -- Tom.
THANK Y NOW CO ALONG W ME. I WAN SHOW YO PICTURE HER LIT GIRL.